Perfect Days in...

VANC
THE CANA ...ROCKIES

Travel with **Insider Tips**

Contents

 TOP 10   4

That Vancouver Feeling   6

For chapters: See inside front cover

Not to be missed!
Our TOP 10 hits – from the absolute No. 1 to No. 10 –
help you plan your tour of the most important sights.

ICEFIELDS PARKWAY ➤ 134

Two-dozen glaciers and over twenty peaks make the Icefields Parkway, through the Banff and Jasper National Parks, the most spectacular of all of Canada's scenic roads.

STANLEY PARK ➤ 52

This wonderful park was first a military reserve, which spared the old-growth forest hemlock and Douglas fir, leaving it just as it was before the arrival of European explorers.

INNER HARBOUR, VICTORIA ➤ 90

One of the most beautiful natural harbours on the Pacific coast with the Empress Hotel, a hotel steeped in tradition that opened in 1908, as the starting point for relaxing strolls.

CALGARY TOWER ➤ 167

The prairies to the east and the soaring mountain wall of the Rockies to the west – the observation platform on the 191m (627ft) high tower is the ideal place to get your bearings.

ROYAL TYRRELL MUSEUM ➤ 168

The museum's striking dinosaur exhibits and great location in the arid, otherworldly Alberta Badlands, make the excursion from Calgary very worthwhile.

OKANAGAN ➤ 114

A captivatingly diverse terrain: the lush, verdant Okanagan Valley and its appendix, the semi-arid Osoyoos Desert, are two of the best wine producing areas in North America.

PACIFIC RIM NATIONAL PARK ➤ 92

The old fishing port of Tofino is now a popular starting point for tours to the whales, bears and the other natural wonders of the national park, which is studded with islands.

WELLS GRAY PROVINCIAL PARK ➤ 116

The park's numerous spectacular waterfalls – the most impressive is the high Helmcken Falls – are the main attraction on this excursion.

GLACIER & MT REVELSTOKE NATIONAL PARKS ➤ 118

Canadian nature at its most dramatic: steep mountains with precipitous avalanche chutes, 400 glaciers and Rogers Pass, a scenic mountain pass.

GRANVILLE ISLAND ➤ 58

The heart and soul of trend-setting Vancouver – galleries and indie theatres, organic gardeners, artists and bon vivants, they all come together on Granville Island (➤ left).

THAT
VANCOUVER

Experience western Canada's unique flair and find out what makes it tick – just like the locals themselves.

ROCKING ROBSON

Dynamic, trendy, multi-ethnic **Robson Street** (⊞ 204 C3), which runs from dowtown to the West End, embodies the youthful nature of Vancouver like no other thoroughfare. The more than 100 **boutiques**, **restaurants**, **bars**, and **pavement cafés** are popular meeting places for those who want to people watch or who want spot the latest food and drink fads. This is where trends are born and others – such as a morning jog around the block or a Stanley Park bike ride after work – are celebrated.

AMONG GIANTS

Cathedral Grove is a stand of old growth forest: a damp, steaming still life of toppled cedars, waist-high ferns and towering tree trunks under a leafy canopy. Walk in the undergrowth, take in the earthy the smell of decay, and admire the ancient Douglas firs (some with a circumference of 9m/30ft) in the **MacMillan Provincial Park** near Cameron Lake (⊞ 202 A2) on Vancouver Island; it is the last temperate rainforest in North America (Hwy 4).

GET UP CLOSE TO "WILLY"

No brochure on British Columbia would be complete without a picture of orcas rising out of the sea against a backdrop of the mist shrouded **Coast Mountains**. Seeing these intelligent marine mammals is an absolute must on a trip to western Canada. The small fishing village of **Telegraph Cove** on Vancouver Island is the best place to view the mammals made famous by the *Free Willy* films (Stubbs Island Whale Watching; tel: 250/928-3185; www stubbs-island.com).

TOFINO BEACH WALKS

In winter, the notorious Aleutian Low hurls one storm after the other against Vancouver Island's Pacific coast. The result is sandy beaches that are as hard as cement, especially in the vicinity of Tofino (► 92), which are ideal for long beach walks in the summer. Here you can watch as Pacific swells crash against the rocks and surfers

FEELING

Get up close to the Pacific with a beach walk

That Vancouver Feeling

from around the world ride the breaking waves. Tofino is widely regarded as Canada's surf capital.

THE ROCKIES BY BIKE

Wapitis, coyotes and black bears, dense coniferous forests and, towering above them, the massive peaks of the Canadian Rockies: cycle the 55km (34mi) **Bow Valley Parkway** (➕ 200 C4) from Banff to Lake Louise and experience the scenic Canadian landscape even more closely (rent a bicycle from Soul Ski & Bike, 203A Bear Street; tel: 403/760-1650; www. soulskiandbike.com).

The Kootenay Parkway runs through the eponymous national park

LIFE IS A HIGHWAY

Get into the car, make yourself comfortable behind the steering wheel, and set off on a scenic road trip. There are many spectacular drives to choose from, and a few of the top ones include the **Sea-to-Sky-Highway** from Vancouver to Whistler, the **Kootenay Parkway** through the Kootenay National Park (➤ 153) and **Highways 97 and 20** from Williams Lake via the Chilcotin Plateau to Bella Coola on the Pacific coast.

SPEND A NIGHT IN A TEPEE

As the moon rises, the stars start to glitter in the night sky, and a gentle breeze flaps the canvas… a night spent in one of the traditional conical tents of the tepee village at **Head-Smashed-In** (➤ 156) will be an unforgettable experience. The tepees are usually equipped with mattresses and blankets and, if you are lucky, a storyteller from the Blackfoot tribe might join you around the campfire in the evening.

WILDERNESS TRAIL

Wildflower meadows, mountains, magnificent views, and fiery sunsets: take a break from driving and go on a guided hike through the **Wells Gray Provincial Park** (➤ 116, Wells Gray Adventures, Clearwater; tel: 250/587-6444; www.skihike.com). By the day you will explore the wilderness in the hinterland, by night you will sleep in rustic cabins at the tree line – a truly authentic way to experience Canada.

The Magazine

THIS IS VANCOUVER
City of Light
and the Long View

Vancouver goes from strength to strength. Always among the world's most beautiful and vibrant cities, it continues to grow, its reputation enhanced by the 2010 Winter Olympics and its streets ever more dynamic and cosmopolitan.

The weather in the streets might not always be the best – it rains in Vancouver…and then it rains some more – but the setting is sublime; the environment is clean and safe; the well-integrated multicultural population embraces diversity with enthusiasm; you can ski pretty much year-round; there's swimming and sunbathing on beaches just minutes from city centre downtown; the city's Stanley Park is one of North America's biggest and wildest; and the restaurants are world class.

Vancouver's skyline reflected in the water

Zest for Life

Vancouver gives the lie to Canada's perceived image problem, the notion that this is a country that's worthy but dull, beautiful but boring – nice place, nice people, no fun. With its zest for life, spectacular scenery, excellent nightlife, urban beaches, funky cafés, fashionable bars and wild outdoor activities, Vancouver gloriously rejects the cliché with a flair that rivals West Coast hotspots such as San Francisco and Los Angeles.

Stroll around Canada Place to see how the city celebrates modern architecture and its magnificent port (➤ 60). Look up at the mountains – that's where the locals ski in Olympic standard conditions and facilities; then look out to sea – that's where they sail their boats. Or sit in a café on Granville Island (➤ 58) – that's where they shop, stroll and people-watch.

Pacific Player

Vancouver's location on the Pacific has resulted in a long history of immigration from China and other Asian countries, and today Vancouver's Chinatown is the third-largest in North America, while about half of the 2.5 million inhabitants in the greater Vancouver area are Asian. The Pacific has been a lifeline for British Columbia (BC) since coastal First Nations peoples thrived on its maritime bounty. About three quarters of BC's citizens live on the coast and the Pacific and Asian markets play an increasingly important role in Vancouver's economy and society.

The Magazine

A Dynamic City

Vancouver has boomed – figures from the last census in 2011 show that its population increased 9.3 percent in six years. It continues to grow, and remains Canada's fastest-growing city. On the ground, this dynamism is obvious in the city's neighbourhoods, many of which, while retaining their historic character, are also experiencing dramatic change.

Neighbourhood Watch

Key among them is downtown, Vancouver's commercial heart, built across a peninsula jutting into Burrard Inlet. Traditionally centred on Robson and Burrard streets, it is now spreading south and east, extending the reach of its malls, smart hotels, gleaming condominiums, major galleries and towering office blocks.

Gastown, east of downtown, represents the city's historic heart, where Vancouver was born. Here, too, redevelopment has seen change, from a skid row in the 1970s to a prettified tourist trap and now an increasingly vibrant mixture of galleries, bars and restaurants.

Farther east, Chinatown largely resists change, and is still almost entirely Chinese in character, full of exotic sights and sounds.

At the other extreme, on downtown's western flanks, the West End is a restrained and largely residential area, though even here the quiet, tree-lined streets are increasingly over-shadowed by new high-rise condominiums along the Coal Harbour waterfront.

Farther Afield

On the north shore of the Burrard Inlet are North and West Vancouver (also known as North and West Van), both largely residential. South from downtown, across the waters of False Creek, is South Vancouver, a sprawling and much larger residential and commercial area. Here, too, there are distinctive neighbourhoods, not least Kitsilano (or "Kits"), the

Left: Entrance of the Marine Building Middle: Downtown Right: Canada Place

entre of alternative Vancouver in the 1960s. Now somewhat smarter, it
etains its earlier laid-back feel, especially on its beach and easy-going
ars and restaurants.

Not far from Kits, in False Creek, is the alluring Granville Island, a one-
me semi-industrial wasteland that is now a buzzing mix of markets, cafés,
rewery, small businesses and specialty stores. Trendier still is Yaletown,
n old warehouse district on the south extreme of the downtown peninsula
at has become one of the city's most compelling enclaves.

Insider
Tip

hree Great Period Buildings...

Marine Building 1930

355 Burrard Street Vancouver's only surviving art deco masterpiece –
and early skyscraper – is enriched with period bas-reliefs and boasts
the most beautiful lobby and elevators in the city.

Toronto-Dominion Bank 1920

580 West Hastings Street This Mediterranean-style building is Vancouver
architect Marbury Somervell's finest legacy.

St James Anglican Church 1936

303 East Cordova Street Historic churches are rare here. This is as an
elegant tribute by Adrian Gilbert Scott.

.and Three Great Modern Ones

Vancouver Public Library 1995

350 West Georgia Street Moshe Safdie's stunning building is no less than
a modern-day Roman Colosseum and, with the nearby General Motors
Place, provides a focus for the dynamic eastward spread of the city.

Robson Square 1979

800 Robson Street Arthur Erickson pulled together a modern plaza and
the city's old law courts and government buildings.

MacMillan Bloedel Building 1969

1075 West Georgia Street Arthur Erickson also designed this neoclassical masterpiece for the giant forestry company MacMillan Bloedel.

Creative
VANCOUVER
Something in the air...

There's so much creativity in Vancouver that there really must be something in the air that flows from the mountains and sea that surround this vibrant and stylish city.

Vancouver on Film

Vancouver's creative cutting edge is found in movie-making – the city has emerged as the largest film and TV production centre in North America after Los Angeles and New York. This is not so much because of home-grown stars – though Michael J. Fox, Pamela Anderson, Ryan Reynolds and James Doohan (Scotty in *Star Trek*), among others, hail from the city – but because of low costs and a wide range of urban and outdoor locations.

Hitting the High Notes

The city also nurtures an outstanding rollcall of painters, photographers, poets, writers (notably Douglas Coupland, author of *Generation X*), actors and musicians. High-profile rock star Bryan Adams lived his early years in Vancouver. Diana Krall was born on Vancouver Island. Singer-songwriter Nelly Furtado comes from Victoria. Vancouver rings the changes, from romantic balladeer Sarah McLachlan to the unique sound of folk band the Be Good Tanyas. The city also boasts some classical music institutions, including the Vancouver Symphony Orchestra and the Vancouver Chamber Choir. Making up a triumphant triumvirate of magnificent music is the acclaimed Vancouver Opera (▶84 for info on all 3).

RUDYARD'S VANCOUVER YARD

Rudyard Kipling made several visits to Vancouver and liked the city so much that he bought several plots of land, including two on the corner of what are now Fraser and East Eleventh Streets. Kipling owned them for more than 30 years but sold them at an eventual loss.

Above: Vancouver Art Gallery
Left: Ornately carved totem pole,
Stanley Park
Below left: Nelly Furtado

Art at the Edge

Vancouver has always had a strong arts culture, thanks in part to the work of First Nations artists such as the masterly Bill Reid (1928–98), a craftsman of First Nations Haida descent. Reid's life and work is immortalized in the Bill Reid Gallery open since 2008 (► 65). A still towering presence in British Columbia art is Emily Carr, whose work can be seen in the Vancouver Art Gallery (► 63). Today Vancouver buzzes with artistic talent. There are hundreds of small private galleries covering every level of art, with the South Granville area and Granville Island being rich browsing grounds, while West Georgia Street's Buschlen Mowatt Gallery is the top private venue for contemporary art, including the First Nations genre.

From **HAIDA** to **HIGH-RISE**

Few cities can claim to have their roots in a mixture of native village and hard-drinking saloon bar. And not many have gone from forest clearing to major metropolis in less than a century. Even fewer take their name from a man who honoured the city with his presence for less than a day.

British Columbia – and the patch of land that became Vancouver – were the domain of sophisticated First Nations peoples, such as the Haida, for at least 10,000 years. The first European landing was probably made by Captain Cook in 1778. And one member of Cook's crew was a midshipman by the name of George Vancouver.

George Vancouver

By 1791 young George had become a captain and was employed in mapping parts of the Pacific coast for Britain. A year later, he discovered the estuary of the Fraser River just south of Vancouver and sailed around a forested headland and into a magnificent natural inlet, the future site of the great city. Captain George named the place Burrard after one of his crew. He traded with the indigenous Squamish on the headland, now the present day Stanley Park, then sailed on after spending less than a day in their company. Vancouver's name wasn't given to the nascent city until 1886.

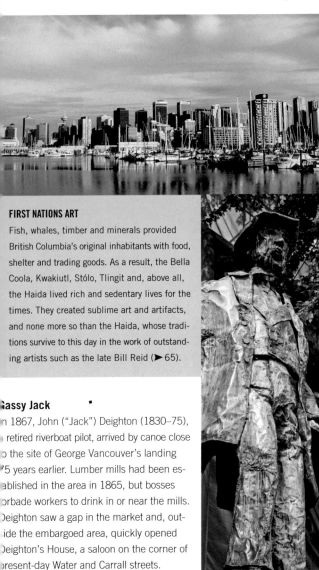

FIRST NATIONS ART

Fish, whales, timber and minerals provided British Columbia's original inhabitants with food, shelter and trading goods. As a result, the Bella Coola, Kwakiutl, Stólo, Tlingit and, above all, the Haida lived rich and sedentary lives for the times. They created sublime art and artifacts, and none more so than the Haida, whose traditions survive to this day in the work of outstanding artists such as the late Bill Reid (▶65).

Gassy Jack

In 1867, John ("Jack") Deighton (1830–75), a retired riverboat pilot, arrived by canoe close to the site of George Vancouver's landing 75 years earlier. Lumber mills had been established in the area in 1865, but bosses forbade workers to drink in or near the mills. Deighton saw a gap in the market and, outside the embargoed area, quickly opened Deighton's House, a saloon on the corner of present-day Water and Carrall streets. Business was brisk and Jack soon opened a second bar, where his bragging monologues earned him the nickname "Gassy." In time, a ramshackle settlement, "Gassy's Town," sprang up around the saloons and today a life-size statue of Gassy Jack stands in Maple Tree Square, the heart of Gastown (▶72).

Top left: Captain Vancouver's expedition ships
Top: The harbour today
Above: Gassy Jack statue

CALL OF THE WILD
The wilderness on your doorstep

Walk the streets of Banff and there's a good chance you'll find yourself face-to-antler with a verge-nibbling elk. Climb aboard many a Vancouver bus and you'll find pine needles on the floor, tramped there by commuters from the forested slopes above the city.

Beware the Bear

Bears are always big news; they fascinate most visitors and there are plenty of them in Western Canada. Their range extends across most of the Rockies and British Columbia, but you're more likely to spot them by the roadside than on popular trails.

There are two kinds of big bear: grizzly and black. The grizzly is definitely bigger and has a slightly scooped face and a distinctive hump behind its head. The other one is the black bear, which is smaller and nowhere near as cuddly as it looks. Both types of bear are potentially very dangerous. They are not slow and bumbling: they can outrun a racehorse. Never run away from a bear; draw away slowly. Another misconception is that bears can't climb trees. They certainly can, and very well – so don't put it to the test.

Watching for Whales

In Western Canada the whale matches the bear for the wow factor. There are several companies taking visitors whale-watching even in Vancouver, but most are in Victoria

Top: A grizzly bear; Left: Tail of a grey whale

A signpost at Takakkaw Falls in Yoho National Park

and Tofino (➤92) on Vancouver Island. Here, the offshore waters are on
the major migration routes for gray, orca and other whales.
The whales are mostly en route between their breeding and calving
grounds in Baja California and their summer feeding grounds in the
Bering and Chukchi seas off Siberia, an 8,000km (5,000mi) journey,
the longest migration of any mammal. Most whales are northbound past
Vancouver Island between March and April and southbound during late
September and early October.

Best Foot Forward

When it comes to the real call of the wild, you should head for the spectacular mountains, forests and remote coasts of Western Canada. In such
wild country there are outstanding opportunities for horseback riding and
mountain biking as well as watersports such as canoeing and whitewater
rafting. There's even fun to be had in mid-air with paragliding or, zip-lining, a
wild ride down an inclined cable. Yet, the simplest – and cheapest – escape
of all is on your own two feet. Be properly equipped for these longer treks,
however, and check details with the park authorities before setting off.

Superb Scenery

If all you want is a casual stroll, but in stunning surroundings, you can follow low-level, surfaced walkways of only a kilometre or two at venues such as Johnston Canyon (➤ 140), or crank up the mileage on the uphill trek to the Lake Agnes Teahouse (➤ 188).

For outstanding longer hikes, stride on from Lake Agnes, *après* tea, to the Plain of Six Glaciers (➤ 190); or head for Yoho National Park (➤ 150) and the superb 20km (12.5mi) Iceline Trail that follows steep zigzags to the edge of several glaciers above the Takakkaw Falls; or head along the splendid West Coast Trail in the Pacific Rim National Park (➤ 93).

Left: Boardwalk, Pacific Rim National Park; Below: A black bear; Right: Columbia Icefield

BEAR NECESSITIES

Roadside bear encounters often produce the Rockies' infamous "bear jams," caused when people spot a roadside bear and abandon their cars with cameras. A bear subjected to repeated bear jams may become desensitized to traffic. This can lead to vehicle–bear collisions that are potentially fatal to all. Difficult though it may be, you should resist adding to a bear jam and simply drive slowly by.

ROCKY
MOUNTAINS

The Canadian Rockies have had two makeovers. Once when they formed as the result of geological ructions millions of years ago, and a second time when they were made, in the economic sense, by the coming of the transcontinental Canadian Pacific Railway at the end of the 19th century.

Genesis of the Landscape

The Rockies began with the Canadian Shield, a huge granite mass that covered much of North America around a billion years ago. Throughout millions of years, eroded sediments from the Shield were washed westward across the continent and were deposited in what is now the Pacific Ocean.

During the millennia that followed, these sediments, boosted by the accumulation of lime-rich algae and other sea creatures, grew to a thickness of some 19.5km (12mi).

All of this colossal weight steadily compressed mud to shale, sand to sandstone, and marine detritus to limestone, and all survive in the geometric bands of multicolored rock that you now see in the mountains of Banff (▶ 139).

LADY ON THE LINE

When the Canadian Pacific Railway breached the Rockies in 1886, Lady Agnes MacDonald, wife of the Canadian prime minister, rode the line for 998km (620mi) on a specially adapted external chair fitted to a cow-catcher on the front of a locomotive. The trip was part of a special symbolic journey to mark the opening of the line. Her most exhilarating moments came as the train careered down the so-called Big Hill, a terrifyingly steep gradient in Yoho National Park. The descent, she remarked, presented "a delightful opportunity for a new sensation." Her husband couldn't match his redoubtable partner; he managed just 40km (25mi) on the cow-catcher before retreating under cover.

Making Mountains

In those far distant times the future building blocks of the Rockies were still underwater. But enormous collisions between landmasses about 175 million years ago bulldozed the mass of sediments into the vast corrugations of the Rockies' present-day western ranges. Just when the dust began to settle – about 100 million years ago – a second cataclysm raised new mountains that became the Rockies' main eastern ranges. Wind, rain and glaciers then carved, scoured and eroded at the rate of around 1m (3ft) every 17,000

years. Most reshaping has taken place during the three main ice ages of the last 240,000 years – a mere moment, geologically speaking, in the Rockies' billion-year history.

Made by Rail

For much of this "mere moment" the Rockies remained almost unsullied wilderness, visited, if at all, by First Nations trappers, fur traders and the occasional European explorer. All this changed dramatically with the coming of the Canadian Pacific Railway (CPR). A bid to start the line began in 1871. Lack of funds and various political scandals delayed work until 1881, but once under way, progress across Ontario and the Prairies was swift. Winnipeg and then Calgary were soon reached.

West of Calgary the line inched toward Banff and the Rockies. When it reached them it transformed the mountains – almost at a stroke – in terms of their accessibility and the way in which they were perceived. A simple event, such as the discovery of hot springs in 1885 by three railways workers, gave birth to the mighty Banff National Park (► 139). Soon, the building of grand railway hotels such as the Banff Springs (► 157) and Chateau Lake Louise (► 142) began to encourage visitors to the area.

The first trans-Canadian train pulled into Vancouver in 1887. The railway was the making of the city and of many tiny settlements along the way that are now the likes of Calgary and Winnipeg. It was also the making of the once empty prairies – between 1896 and 1913, some 13 million settlers headed west in search of a new life along the line.

The view from The Lookout above Peyto Lake in Alberta

How the
West was Won

The Canadian frontier, unlike its US counterpart, was more mild than wild west. There were just three recorded gun fights in the 19th century – and pretty inept ones at that. Not that it was all plain sailing. The Canadian west still had to be won, and the men who won it were the Mounties.

Today, the Mounties form the national police service of Canada, and are officially known as the Royal Canadian Mounted Police (RCMP). But their roots are in the North-West Mounted Police (NWMP), founded in 1873 for service in the Canadian west.

Much of the force's early organization and traditions survive, including the uniform, which was a direct result of the force's shaky beginnings – at the time, the only uniforms available were old British army tunics, hence the famous red serge jackets.

> "Much of the force's early organization and traditions survive"

Trouble at Cypress Hills

One reason for the force's half-baked origins was the urgency of its formation. Alarmed by news of a massacre at Cypress Hills on the Albertan border, the Ottawa government quickly raised a 299-strong troop, organized it like a British cavalry detachment, and then dispatched it on what would become known as the "March West".

Drink, and whiskey in particular, was at the root of the problem. American adventurers had begun to drift across the unpoliced Canadian border, bartering illegal (and often dubiously adulterated) whiskey with the aboriginal population. Such was the drunken lawlessness that ensued that the area became known as "Whoop-up Country". The facts of the massacre were

The RCMP have toured Canada performing a Musical Ride every year since 1901

never fully established, but it seems five indigenous women were raped and 21 men killed, probably by drunken white hunters. Nonetheless, the Mounties' even-handedness in dealing with the episode helped contribute to their long-standing reputation for probity and fairness. NWMP detachments were established at Fort Macleod in 1874, the force's first western post. Fort Edmonton followed in 1875, Fort Calgary about a year later.

The success of the March West and of the early forts altered the course of North American history. Had the border country – then still only nominally Canadian – remained lawless, the Canadian Pacific Railway (➤ 23) might have had to take a more northerly route, Canada's western plains might have remained unsettled, and US expansionists might have made a play for the agriculturally rich heartlands of present-day Alberta and Saskatchewan.

The Mounties Become a National Force

The force further distinguished itself in Alberta, BC and beyond during the wild days of the Yukon's Klondike Gold Rush after 1895, keeping order, saving lives and collecting duty on the vast quantities of gold that were found. In time, this and other service, saw the NWMP recognized as a national force, and a symbol of the reach and authority of the Canadian federation. This role was acknowledged in 1920, when the force was renamed the Royal Canadian Mounted Police – or Mounties for short.

GREEN PIECE

Environment Matters

Bombs gave birth to the most famous environmental action group of all time – the renowned and sometimes reviled pressure group Greenpeace. The organization was born in Vancouver's English Bay in 1971 when a group of activists set off on board a converted fishing boat to protest against the United States testing nuclear devices in Alaska.

Environmental Protests

The protest boat, the *Phyllis Cormack*, was renamed *Green Peace 1* and the name was later revised to Greenpeace. By 1974 the organization had turned its sights against whaling. The rest is history and Greenpeace now has a world-wide presence wherever perceived threats to the environment are identified.

Canada's commercial and political record on environmentalism is not pristine. Today there is fierce debate over the oil shale industry that has made Calgary, especially, a longstanding boom town, but that raises questions over the industry's perceived threat to sustainability. Government involvement in the granting of logging licenses has long been contentious also.

National Parks

It is probably in the mighty national parks where environmentalism has the most powerful resonance. The sheer scale of such mountain wildernesses makes them seem impregnable, but threats do exist to the parks' often fragile eco systems. We could easily love them to death, such is the growing pressure of tourism. Perhaps the greatest threat is the hidden devastation of global warming and pollution, the inevitable counterpoints to our consumer society and the ironic bedfellows of the delight and admiration we feel for the wilderness. Solutions to these universal threats rest with all of us.

Ambitious Goals

Vancouver is at the leading edge of environmental initiatives while maintaining its image as a hip and sophisticated metropolis. The 2010 Winter Olympics designation has boosted a "Green Vancouver" ethos with a commitment that all new venues for the 2010 Olympics are designed to minimize waste, emissions, energy consumption and water use.

Vancouver has more than 400km (250mi) of cycle lanes and the city is set to introduce a fleet of hydrogen buses to its already environmentally conscious transit system. In 2005 a car-free day was launched in Vancouver that has seen an increasing number of the city's main streets empty of cars each June 15. In addition, Vancouver has implemented the Greenest City 2020 initiative, a strategy to deal with the city's environmental challenges and to guide it toward becoming the greenest city in the world by 2020.

Left: Drift logs in the Pacific Rim National Park; Right: Maligne River, Jasper National Park, Alberta

THE WORLD
AT YOUR TABLE

Vancouver has one of North America's most ethnically diverse populations. And where a population leads, the recipes and restaurants are never far behind. The city has more than 3,000 restaurants and its inhabitants eat out more than do those of any other Canadian city.

Outside dining on Granville Island

Influences and Ingredients

China is one of the most obvious culinary influences. Cheap restaurants and noodle houses proliferate in Chinatown, with more expensive and refined Chinese restaurants found across the city. Catching up fast are other Asian cuisines, especially Japanese and Vietnamese, closely followed by Thai, Korean and Cambodian. European immigration has also spawned many Italian, Greek and other European influences.

With all of these go the more familiar local staples – fish and seafood are generally outstanding – and the sophisticated fusion cuisine that combines

British Columbia's superb natural ingredients such as salmon, seafood, game, beef, fresh fruit and vegetables with the culinary styles and ingredients of Italian, Mexican, French and world cuisine generally. Outstanding examples of fusion can be enjoyed at such restaurants as Vancouver's Le Crocodile (►79) or Victoria's Canoe Brewpub (►105) and L'Ecole (►106).

OCEAN WISE

Vancouver has adopted a sustainable fish industry initiative called Ocean Wise (www.oceanwise.ca). The scheme is fronted by the Vancouver Aquarium and numbers more than 50 restaurants in Vancouver, Calgary and beyond, including 900 West (►81) and CinCin (►79).

No Laughing Matter

With western Canada's superb food you might be tempted to try Canadian wine, two words that some years ago would have raised sceptical eyebrows among the world's wine cognoscenti.

Traditionally, beer and whiskey were the thirst quenchers of Canadian life and today domestic beers such as Labatt Blue and Molson Canadian dominate, although regional favourites such as Kokanee lager from British Columbia's Kootenay region are hugely popular, while micro-breweries produce some lip-smacking beverages.

Canadian wine is not yet a world leader and the main producers are in Ontario, but British Columbia's Okanagan Valley (►114) is building a solid reputation in viniculture with a rack of fruity, deep-tasting vintages. Most Canadian wines are white, although there is an increasing number of light red wines. Canada's celebrated "ice wine," made from frozen grapes, and noted for the intensity of its flavour and texture, has some world leaders in Okanagan vintages.

WINE WISE

If you want the true Canadian wine experience, a careful check of labels is advised. Blending of domestic product with imported basic wines still takes place in producing some cheaper wines.

For a closer wine experience, contact visitor centres in the Okanagan (►114) for details of local vineyards and estates, many of which are open to the public.

The Magazine

SNOWSTORMING!

It's always snow time in Western Canada, where world-class ski resorts are of such high quality that Calgary hosted the 1988 Winter Olympics and Vancouver the 2010 Games.

Vancouver itself rarely gets snow that lasts, but within sight of the city are the neighbouring winter sports centres of Mount Seymour (www.mountseymour.com), Cypress Mountain (www.cypressmountain.com) and Grouse Mountain (www.grousemountain.com), while 90 minutes north of the city are the world-famous slopes of Whistler Blackcomb (www.whistlerblackcomb.com).

Powder Option

The Rockies have always been winter wonderlands; not just for all levels but for serious off-piste runs and challenging powder chutes. If your pockets are as deep as snowdrifts, you can always indulge in heli-skiing by reaching exclusive areas by helicopter. Or try snowcat skiing, in which you're whisked away to virgin powder on board a big snowcat.

Banff's mainstream ski resorts are Lake Louise, Sunshine Village and Mount Norquay (check them out on www.skibig3.com), while Jasper's

Left and far right: Canada offers plenty of opportunities to ski or snowboard
Middle left: Athabasca Glacier in Jasper National Park Middle right: Whistler

ICING ON THE CAKE

Skating is the basis of Canada's favourite spectator sport, ice hockey. Vancouver has many indoor and seasonal outdoor rinks where you can glide the light fantastic; but for a winter wonderland experience head for Grouse Mountain, where the mountain-top rink has a fairy-tale ambience at night. In the Rockies there are maintained outdoor lake venues at Lake Louise (► 142), Pyramid Lake (► 147) and Emerald Lake (► 152).

best is the long-established Marmot Basin (www.skimarmot.com) just 19km (12mi) south of Jasper. At the same time, smaller but high-quality resorts are emerging elsewhere in the Rockies and interior BC. Among these are Kicking Horse (www.kickinghorseresort.com), Fernie (www. skifernie.com) and Panorama (www.panoramaresort.com).

Boarding It

Snowboarding first developed in North America. You might not be up to the "big air" tricks of somersaulting off a launch pad, but there are plenty of opportunities for simple freecarve runs at such mainstream resorts as Cypress Mountain and Lake Louise. And bobsleigh enthusiasts can now enjoy snow tubing at Cypress Mountain and Mount Seymour.

Cross Country

For the experienced, cross-country skiing is a terrific way of enjoying the snowy wilderness. At Cypress, north of Vancouver, there are 19km (12mi) of cross-country trails and some backcountry trails are kept clear in winter in the Lake Louise, Jasper and Banff areas.

Festival FEVER

Calgary is not alone in hosting spectacular events. Brace yourself for festival fever in Vancouver, too.

Left: Chinese New Year Celebration; Middle: Fireworks; Right: St. Patrick's Day Parade

January: Chinese New Year Festival and Parade (www.vancouver-chinatown.com)

February: Vancouver International Dance Festival (www.vidf.ca)

March: Celtic Fest Vancouver (www.celticfestivalvancouver.com)

May: Vancouver International Children's Festival (www.childrensfestival.ca)

June, July: Vancouver International Jazz Festival (www.coastaljazz.ca)

June–September: Bard on the Beach Shakespeare Festival (www.bardonthebeach.org), Vanier Park

July: Pride Week (www.vancouverpride.ca), including flamboyant parade

August: Celebration of Light (www.hondacelebrationoflight.com), international firework display competition

September, October: Vancouver International Film Festival (www.viff.org), including firework displays

December: Light displays and events all over town (www.ticketstonight.org)

MAGAZINES & WEBSITES

For what's on in Vancouver check out:

- *Vancouver Magazine* (www.vanmag.com)
- *Where Vancouver* (www.where.ca/Vancouver)
- *Visitor's Choice* (www.visitorschoice.com)
- *The Georgia Straight* free newspaper (www.straight.com)

Finding Your Feet

First Two Hours

Transportation within the cities is provided by bus, light rail, Skytrain or taxi, and airport shuttle services. Inter-centre transportation includes airplane, long-haul buses, ferry, seaplane and helicopter, or train.

Ground Transportation Fees (excluding tip)
$ under CDN$6 $$ CDN$6–$12 $$$ CDN$12–$16 $$$$ over CDN$16

Arriving: Vancouver

■ International flights land at the main terminal of **Vancouver International Airport** (tel: 604/207-7077; www.yvr.ca), 13km (8mi) south of the city centre. There are information and foreign-exchange desks immediately as you exit customs and immigration. Car rental desks are on Level One beyond the parking area.

■ The best way into the city is on TransLink, using the Canada Line (www.translink.ca). Services run every 8–20 minutes and journey time to Waterfront station, for SeaBus and Sky Train connections, is 26 minutes. Services operate from 5:10am–12:57am. The line has two other downtown stations at Yaletown – Roundhouse and Vancouver City Centre. The airport station is between the international and domestic terminals. Ticket ($) incur a CDN$5 "Canada Line YVR AddFare" unless you are using a prepaid ticket such as a DayPass (➤37).

■ **TransLink bus** 424 runs between the airport and the Airport Bus Station (for downtown public transit bus connections) every seven minutes (www.translink.ca).

■ **Taxis** ($$$$ to downtown) or only slightly more expensive **limousines** leave from adjoining bays outside the arrivals terminal.

■ Arriving in the city by **bus** or **train** leaves you 2km (1.2mi) southeast of the city centre at the main rail and bus terminal at VIA Rail Pacific Central Station, 1150 Station Street (tel: 604/640-3700 or 1-888/842-7245; www.viarail.ca). From here you can take a taxi to downtown ($$$$).

■ For **public transportation** links walk 150m from the station (with your back to the station bear left across the grass) to the Science World–Main Street **SkyTrain** station (➤37) and take a "Waterfront" train to downtown ($). Tickets are dispensed by automated platform machines.

■ Vancouver's main downtown area occupies a large peninsula. The main east–west street is **Robson Street**, the main north–south artery is **Granville Street**. The principal downtown area concentrates in the grid of streets at the intersection of these two thoroughfares, in particular the area between Robson Street and the waterfront to the north.

City Centre Tourist Office

■ The main visitor centre is the **Vancouver TouristInfo Centre**, Waterfront Centre, Suite 210, 200 Burrard Street at the corner of Canada Place Way; tel: 604/683-2000 or 1-800/663 6000; www.tourismvancouver.com. Open: daily 8:30–6. The centre provides **free maps and brochures**. It also offers a reservation service for tours and entertainments, as well as help reserving accommodations, and has an excellent selection of bed-and-breakfast options. The centre carries public transportation timetables.

Arriving: Victoria

■ **Victoria International Airport** (tel: 250/953-7500; www.victoriaairport. com) is 19km (12mi) north of the city centre. To reach the centre use the **YYJ Airport Shuttle** (tel: 778/351-4995 or 1-888/351-4995; https:// yyjairportshuttle.com; $$$$).

■ Visitors on the integrated bus-ferry connections from Vancouver (➤ 39) arrive at the city **bus terminal** near the Royal British Columbia Museum (➤ 96) at 700 Douglas and Belleville streets (tel: 250/382-6161).

Victoria is a small city, and **orientation** is easy. The downtown area centres on the waterfront, known as the Inner Harbour, and two parallel north–south streets: Douglas and Government. It's a short walk from the harbour to most hotels and all main sights and landmarks – notably the Empress Hotel (➤ 104), Parliament Buildings (➤ 90), and Royal BC Museum (➤ 96). South of downtown stretches a large city park, Beacon Hill Park (➤ 102).

Insider Tip

City Centre Tourist Office

■ Victoria's main **Visitor Centre** is on the waterfront close to the Empress Hotel, 812 Wharf Street; tel: 250/953-2033. Accommodations reservations; tel: 250/953-2033; www.tourismvictoria.com; open: May–Sep daily 8:30–6:30, Oct–Apr 9–5.

Arriving: Calgary

■ **Calgary International Airport** (tel: 403/735-1449 or 1-877/254-7427; www.yyc.com) lies 9.5km (6mi) northeast of the city centre. There is a small tourist information desk on the first level.

The best way into the city is the **Allied Downtown shuttle bus** (tel: 403/299-9555; www.airportshuttlecalgary.ca), which runs about every 30 minutes from 8am–midnight ($$$). It stops outside eleven downtown hotels. Purchase tickets from the bus ticket desk in Arrivals near Gate C or buy online. Buses depart from Bus Bay No 8 immediately outside the terminal.

Calgary Transit Rte 57 (tel: 403/262-1000; www.calgarytransit.com; $) serves the airport, running regularly from the Arrivals level between about 6am and midnight. Journey time is an hour. You need the exact fare. If your destination needs a further bus ride, ask the driver for a transfer. **Taxis** depart from outside Arrivals ($$$$).

Insider Tip

■ **Greyhound** buses from BC, the Rockies and Vancouver arrive at the Greyhound Bus Terminal, 877 Greyhound Way SW (tel: 403/260-0877; www.greyhound.ca). The Downtown Shuttle, Rte 31, picks up nearby at the 16th Street intersection, circling main central locations and the **C-Train station** at 7th Avenue SW and 10th Street. Taxis are moderately priced ($$) to most downtown destinations.

Insider Tip

For Calgary **transportation**, ➤ 38; Calgary Airport to Banff, ➤ 40.

Calgary is a large city with an unfocused downtown area. The key reference points are the Calgary Tower (➤ 167) and nearby Glenbow Museum (➤ 170) in the southeast, and the Bow River in the north. Between these lie most of downtown's major malls and buildings, especially on 7th and 8th avenues SW.

The city is divided into quadrants (NW, NE, SW and SE), so it's essential to pay attention when reading **addresses**: 1438-4th Avenue SW is a long way from 1438-4th Avenue NE. To read addresses, note that the first digit (or digits) refers to the street number, the last digits (or digit) to the building number. Thus 1438-4th Avenue SW is in the southwest quadrant on 14th Street at number 38 close to the intersection with 4th Avenue.

Finding Your Feet

City Centre Tourist Office

■ The **Tourism Calgary** main office is at 200, 238–11 Avenue SE; tel: 403/
263-8510 and 1-800/661-1678; www.visitcalgary.com; daily 8am–5pm).

Intercity Connections to the National Parks

■ Buses ($$$$) link **to Banff and Lake Louise** from Calgary and Calgary
Airport.

■ The only public transportation **from Banff to Jasper** along the Icefields
Parkway is operated by Brewster (tel: 403/762 6767 or 1-800/760-
6943; www.brewster.ca; open: May to mid-Oct only; $$$$).

■ Greyhound runs several services daily **between Vancouver and Calgary**
($$$–$$$$) with drop-offs in Yoho and Banff national parks at Field,
Lake Louise and Banff town (see above).

■ Greyhound services from **Calgary to Vancouver**, as the southern BC
route via Highway 3, run through Kootenay National Park.

Getting Around

**Public transit across the region is good, especially in Vancouver,
where you will probably need to use bus and ferry services,
especially if you wish to visit the attractions of North Vancouver.
Greyhound buses, BC Ferries and internal flights connect larger
centres. Roads, while of good quality, often pass through remote
or wild country.**

Vancouver

Vancouver has an **integrated public transportation system** comprising
buses, light rail (SkyTrain) and ferry (SeaBus). Operated by **TransLink**
(tel: 604/953-3333; www.translink.ca), timetables are available from
public libraries, city and municipal halls, tourist offices and TransLink
offices and terminals.

Tickets

■ **TransLink tickets** ($) are valid across the transportation system.

■ The tickets are available from **ticket machines** at the SeaBus terminal
and on SkyTrain stations, from 7-Eleven stores and all other **stores**
displaying a TransLink Faredealer sticker.

■ You can buy tickets **directly from bus drivers**, but you must have the
right money – place cash in a box on entering: no change is given.

■ **Flat-rate tickets** ($) apply in Zone 1, which covers most of central
Vancouver. Tickets cost more for journeys into zones 2 and 3 (except

---

City Transportation and Transfer Fees

$ under CDN$5	$$ CDN$5–$10
$$$ CDN$10–$20	$$$$ over CDN$20

Inter-Centre Transfer Fees

$ CDN$30–$50	$$ CDN$50–$75
$$$ CDN$75–$100	$$$$ over CDN$100

---

at weekends and after 6:30 week days, when the zone-1 fare applies
for all zones, and for travel on the SeaBus at peak rush-hour periods
from Monday to Friday.

■ Tickets are valid for **90 minutes** of travel across the system.

Transfer tickets are necessary if you plan to use more than one bus
during the 90-minute validity of your ticket. Bus drivers on your first
journey usually – but not always – give you a ticket showing the time
you boarded the bus. If they don't, ask for a **transfer ticket** and retain
the ticket to show on subsequent journeys.

■ **Concession fares** offering a third off regular fares are available for
children aged between 5 and 13, and seniors aged 65 or over with
proof of age.

¹asses

◄ **Day passes** (CDN$9.75) are useful if you make three or more journeys
a day.

Passes are **valid** after 9:30am Monday to Friday and all day on Saturday
and Sunday.

Scratch & Ride are available from the same sources as tickets (➤ 36) –
you buy the pass and keep it until you want to use it, when you "scratch
off" the day and month, thus validating the pass.

³uses

Vancouver buses are **clean, quick and efficient**.

Buy tickets beforehand (see above, ➤ 36), or on board by putting the
right money into the box by the driver.

Night buses run between 2 and 4am on key routes.

You'll also see blue **West Van** buses, which run from downtown to the
suburbs of North and West Vancouver: TransLink tickets are also valid
on these services. For information; tel: 604/985-7777.

■ The useful **Transit Route Map and Guide** ($) lists all routes and has full
details of the system and how it works. It is available from the TouristInfo
Centre (➤ 34) and most stores with TransLink stickers. The TouristInfo
Centre also provides free timetables and the *Metro Vancouver on Transit*
pamphlet (free).

kyTrain

■ SkyTrain is a fully automated **light-rail system** that runs above and below
ground on the Expo, Canada and Millennium lines from the Waterfront
station in downtown to the airport and suburbs, such as Richmond and
Surrey in the south and southeast of the city.

■ Most **visitors** are only likely to use the first four stations of the 20-station
line – Waterfront, Burrard, Granville and Stadium.

SkyTrain services run every **two to eight minutes**.

■ The rapid transit line, Canada Line (www.canadaline.ca; ➤ 34) links
with SkyTrain connections through the Waterfront Station.

eaBus

The **400-seat** SeaBus catamarans operate between the Waterfront
SkyTrain station at the foot of Granville Street and Lonsdale Quay across
the harbour in North Vancouver.

The **12-minute** trip across Burrard Inlet to North Vancouver offers sensational views.

Departures are every 15 or 30 minutes depending on the time of day.

Finding Your Feet

Ferries

■ Tiny ferries run by private companies (Aquabus and False Creek Ferries) provide quick and enjoyable ways of traveling. Services operate between downtown (departures from the foot of Hornby Street) and **Granville Island** (►58), from Granville Island to Vanier Park, and around False Creek.

■ Tickets (CDN$3.50– CDN$5.50) are bought **on board** the boats.

■ For **information** tel: 604/689-5858; www.theaquabus.com or 604/684-7781; www.granvilleislandferries.bc.ca

Lost Property

■ **Lost property and found items** are taken to the TransLink Lost Property office at the SkyTrain Stadium station (590 Beatty Street; tel: 604/953-3334; www.translink.ca/en/Customer-Service/Lost-and-Found.aspx), which is open Mon–Fri 8:30–5. For items left on West Vancouver blue buses; tel: 604/985-7777.

Taxis

■ Vancouver taxis are efficient and moderately priced. Either hail them on the street, or call one of the following: **Black Top** (tel: 604/731-1111), **Vancouver Taxi** (tel: 604/871-1111) or **Yellow Cab** (tel: 604/681-1111).

Victoria

Most sights in Victoria lie within walking distance of the centre, so you're unlikely to need public transportation. The one notable exception is visiting the Butchart Gardens (►99). The city's transit system is similar to Vancouver, but note that Vancouver transit tickets are not valid here.

■ **Buses** run on 50 routes in and around the city. They are operated by Victoria Regional Transit and buses run from around 6am to midnight.

■ **Tickets** ($) are issued for two zones. Tickets can be obtained on board buses (correct money is required as drivers carry no change) or from the Visitor Centre (►35), 7-Eleven stores or other marked stores.

■ **Day passes** ($$) are available in advance from normal ticket outlets.

■ **Information** on bus services is available by telephone (tel: 250/382-6161 www.bctransit.com); from the *Victoria Rider's Guide* ($) pamphlet carried on buses; from the Visitor Centre; and from the *Explore! Victoria by Bus* brochure, available from the Visitor Centre and many other outlets.

Calgary

Like Victoria, Calgary's main sights are within walking distance of one another. Its **public transportation** system is an integrated network of **buses** and light-rail system known as the **C-Train**. The latter is free along its main downtown stretch along 7th Avenue between 10th Street SW and 3rd Street SE

■ **Tickets** ($) and **day passes** ($$) are valid on buses and C-Train, and are available from C-Train stations (coin-only machines), stores with a Calgary Transit sticker, or on board buses if you have the exact fare.

■ **Transit information**: tel: 403/262-1000; www.calgarytransit.com

Intercity Connections

Vancouver to Victoria

■ Getting to Victoria from Vancouver is easy by **air or ferry**.

■ The most exciting and expensive way is to **fly**, either by helicopter ($$$) or by the floatplanes that take off from and land on water ($$$). These depart from Vancouver's Coal Harbour direct to Victoria's Inner Harbour.

West Coast Air flies floatplanes from a marina west of Canada Place; tel: 604/274-1277; toll free 1-800/655-0212; www.harbourair.com.

Harbour Air flies from the same marina to Victoria's Inner Harbour; tel: 604/274-1277 or 1-800/655-0212; www.harbourair.com.

■ **Helijet International Incorporated** flies from the helipad to the east of Canada Place or from the airport; tel: 604/273-4688; toll free 1-800/665-4354; www.helijet.com.

Air Canada flies between the cities' main airports ($$$$); tel: 604/688-5515 or 1-888/247-2262; www.aircanada.com.

■ Most independent travellers use the combined **bus-ferry** connection operated by **Pacific Coach Lines** (tel: 604/662-7575 or 250/385-4411; toll free 1-800/661-1725; www.pacificcoach.com) and **BC Ferries Connector** (reservations tel: 1-888/788-8840, 604/428-9474 outside North America; www.bcferries.com). Buy the through ticket (CDN$48) from the PCL desk at Vancouver or Victoria bus terminals: in Vancouver tickets are bought from an office in the main rail-bus station building. The inclusive ticket takes you on the bus to the ferry terminals at Tsawwassen (on the Vancouver mainland) or Swartz Bay (Victoria) and onto the ferry with the bus. You then rejoin the same bus for the onward leg after crossing the Georgia Strait, the beautiful stretch of sea between the two cities. Buses leave hourly in the summer and every two hours in the winter: point-to-point journey time is 3 hours 30 minutes; 90 minutes of this is on the ferry.

Vancouver to Calgary

■ Visitors flying into Calgary and out of Vancouver, or vice versa, can combine the best of what the region has to offer. Whether you start your trip in Calgary or Vancouver, you have a **variety of options** as to how to cover the ground between the two cities.

The quickest option is to **fly** ($$$$) – journey time is one hour. International and long-haul travellers with major carriers can usually make ticketing arrangements that include this internal leg with their inbound and outbound flights. Departures with **Air Canada** (tel: 604/688-5515 or 1-888/247-2262; www.aircanada.com) or smaller regional and charter firms leave roughly hourly between the two cities.

■ Many people **drive**, however, taking in the Rockies and the scenery of British Columbia. The quickest route is along Highway 1, better known as the Trans-Canada Highway (970km/600mi). Alternatively, take the attractive Highway 3 route, which runs parallel close to the US border. The best option of all from a scenic point of view is a route incorporating Banff, Jasper, Mount Robson, Highway 5, Kamloops and the Fraser Canyon.

■ **Public transportation** offers similar options. Around six **Greyhound** bus services daily run between Calgary and Vancouver on the Trans-Canada ($$$$). Other Greyhound services ply slower routes on Highway 3. Note that even if you do not reserve a seat, you are always assured of a place on **Greyhound** buses. If one bus becomes full, another bus is always added to the service.

Greyhound services are all **no smoking**. Services make only scheduled stops at Greyhound depots (bus stations). On long-distance services buses stop every few hours for snack breaks of around 20 minutes.

Greyhound information; tel: 403/263-1234 in Calgary, 604/683-8133 in Vancouver or toll free in Canada and the US 1-800/661-8747; www.greyhound.ca.

Finding Your Feet

- Public **train** connections with **VIA Rail** (tel: 604/669-3050 or toll free 1-888/VIA-RAIL throughout North America; www.viarail.ca) can be made between Vancouver and Kamloops (8 hours 20 minutes), where there are Greyhound connections to Calgary, or to Jasper (16 hours 30 minutes) for Brewster Transportation bus connections to Banff.
- **Sleeper accommodations** are available as double berths (large seats that become curtained bunks) or private single, double or triple bedrooms (spacious cabins with fold-down beds, table, toilet and closet). Meals are included in the sleeper ticket price.
- The VIA Rail **Canrailpass** is a flexible ticket that allows you to travel on any route between two cities and is valid for 60 consecutive days (economy class prices in 2016: CDN$699 for 7 one-way tickets; CDN$899 for 10 one-way tickets; CDN$1299 for unlimited travel).

Calgary to Banff

- Reaching Banff (➤ 136) is easy. The town lies 127km (79mi) west of Calgary.
- Banff is about 90 minutes' **drive** on the Trans-Canada Highway.
- Visitors arriving at **Calgary International Airport** can take advantage of several direct **bus shuttle** links from the airport to Banff, removing the need to travel into Calgary. There are several operators, including Brewster (tel: 403/762-6700; toll free 1-866/606-6700; www.brewster. ca). Most operators run two to four services daily: some services continue to Lake Louise (➤ 142), 40 minutes beyond Banff.
- Visitors spending time in Calgary should take Greyhound services to Banff and Lake Louise (six daily) from the **city's bus terminal** (➤ 35).
- Note that there is **no scheduled rail service** between Calgary and Banff. The private Rocky Mountaineer Company (tel: 604/606-7245; www. rockymountaineer.com) runs regular high-priced private services in summer and occasional additional services in winter. You must book.

Long-distance Buses

- Long-distance buses offer a comfortable, safe, reliable and **inexpensive** way of traveling around much of the Rockies and BC.
- The largest operator is **Greyhound** (➤ 35), whose services include links between Calgary, Banff, Lake Louise, Vancouver and points between.
- **Brewster Transportation** (➤ 162) runs bus services between Calgary, Banff, Lake Louise and Jasper.
- Most towns have a Greyhound **bus station**, known as a bus depot. Smaller towns may have just an office, often at a filling station or by a central café or restaurant. Buy **tickets** from these offices, not on the bus.
- You can **reserve** and select seats in advance for a small fee for most Greyhound services, but you can always turn up and be sure of finding a seat – if one bus is full, then another is automatically run.

Insider Tip
- Greyhound (www.greyhound.ca; tel: 1-800/661-8747) offer big savings with **discounts of up to 50 percent** on bus tickets purchased at least one week in advance.

Driving

- Drivers in Canada must be **over 21. Full national driving licenses** from the US, UK and other countries are valid. An International Driving Licence is also valid, but should be accompanied by a national license. **Spot-fines** can be levied for failure to carry your license while driving.

■ **Roads** are generally excellent. Fast four-lane roads are known as "expressways"; "highways" (two- or four-lane) link major towns; "secondary highways" are usually undivided roads between smaller towns; "tertiary" roads are minor paved roads; and "gravel" highways are unpaved or bitumen-topped roads often used for logging. They can be very dusty in dry weather and very muddy during rain. All roads are numbered, and most are well signposted. **Distances** are measured in kilometres.

Rules of the Road

■ Drive on the **right**. On multilane roads outside built-up areas it is permissible to overtake on the left or right.
■ At **crossroads** without traffic lights in built-up areas the first car to arrive has priority; if two arrive at the same time, the right-hand car has priority.
■ It is permissible to **turn right at a red light** if there is no traffic from the left. You must first come to a full stop at the intersection.
■ **Flashing yellow lights** are a sign to slow down, and often indicate an accident black spot.
■ The use of **approved infant seats**, for children under 18kg (39.5lb), and front and passenger **seat belts** is compulsory.
■ The uniform **speed limit** on expressways is 100kph (62mph); 90kph (56mph) on the Trans-Canada and Yellowhead highways; 80kph (50mph) on most rural roads; and between 40kph (25mph) and 60kph (37mph) in urban areas. Limits are enforced, with spot-fines for violations.
■ It is illegal to pass yellow/orange **school buses** (from either direction) that are stationary with their warning lights flashing.
■ Driving under the influence of **alcohol** is a serious offense: Alcohol in a car must be carried unopened in the trunk.
■ **Parking** is forbidden on sidewalks, near traffic lights, within 5m (16ft) of a fire hydrant, and within 13m (50ft) of grade crossings.
■ In BC and Alberta drivers must keep **vehicle headlights on** day and night while driving.

Car Breakdowns

If you break down, raise the car hood and tie a white cloth to the driver's side to indicate that help is required. Emergency phones are found at the side of most major roads.
■ Canada's main recovery agency is the **Canadian Automobile Association** CAA tel: 1-800/222-4357; www.caa.ca; www.bcaa.com (for BC); www.ama.ab.ca (for Alberta), with offices in most major towns and cities. The CAA is integrated with the AAA and provides service to its members.

Car Rental

■ Cars can be rented on presentation of a **full driving license**.
■ The **best deals** are often those reserved in advance with firms in your home country, or as part of a fly-drive package. When renting in Canada look out for hidden charges, notably federal **Goods and Services Tax** (GST) and **provincial taxes** (➤ 45). A **"drop-off" charge**, often equivalent to a week's rental, is levied if you pick up the car in one town and leave it in another.
Collision or "**Loss Damage Waiver**," an insurance against accident or damage, is worth considering, but adds to the daily rental rate.

Finding Your Feet

- Check to see whether the rental charge covers **unlimited mileage**, or whether an additional charge cuts in after a **set daily mileage**.
- Many car rental companies now offer **mobile phones** and **GPS devices** for rent.
- Note that many firms will not rent out cars for use on **gravel roads**.
- All companies require either a large **cash deposit** or a **credit card number** before renting out a vehicle.

Accommodation

Accommodations possibilities in Vancouver, Victoria, Calgary and the Rockies are extremely varied, with a choice of everything from hostels and homey bed and breakfasts to immense luxury hotels. It's worth noting that accommodations across the region in all price categories are busy in summer, so reservations are essential.

Accommodations Prices
Expect to pay per double room per night excluding breakfast and taxes:
$ under CDN$100 $$ CDN$100–$200
$$$ CDN$200–$300 $$$$ over CDN$300

Hotels

- Canadian hotels divide into three types. The **most basic and cheap** are invariably cheerless hotels found above bars in towns and city centres. Although centrally located, rooms are usually rundown, and may be above a strip joint or a bar with pounding live music.
- **Mid-range chain hotels** are easy to book online and mean you know the type of accommodations available in advance. Reliable chains include Best Western, Holiday Inn, Ramada Hotels, Sandman, Travelodge and Westin Hotels although a downtown version of a chain may not be as smart as its out-of-town or airport area equivalent.
- At the other extreme is a range of **top-class city and resort hotels**, especially in Vancouver, Banff and Lake Louise, where standards are the equal of any in the United States or Europe.

Motels

Motels may be called **travel lodges, motor lodges, inns or resorts**. Whatever their name they all provide **reliable and mid-priced** accommodations, usually on highways outside towns and cities. Standards are generally high, and you can expect a good bed, private bathroom, television and telephone in most rooms. Some also have family rooms, kitchenettes, saunas and swimming pools. Few, however, provide much in the way of food or drink.

Bed & Breakfast

Bed and breakfast (B&B) or **guest house** accommodations are found in towns, cities and rural backwaters across British Columbia and Alberta. Many cities have central reservation agencies, though visitor centres usually carry extensive listings. Rooms do not always have private bathrooms, and the quality of breakfasts varies enormously.

Hostels

Western Canada has hostels affiliated to **Hostelling International** (HI; www.hihostels.ca), and there are many more independent establishments. Hostels are usually modern, with cafeterias, credit card reservations and long opening hours. Many offer private rooms as well as single-sex dormitories.

Reservations

- It's **vital to reserve** accommodations in Vancouver, Victoria, Banff, Lake Louise and Jasper during July and August. At other times of the year, it's a good idea to call a few days in advance to secure a room. To make a reservation simply give a credit card number over the phone, though if you change your mind be sure to cancel in good time – hotels can charge a night's fee against your card.
- **Confirm check-in times**, as rooms in some hotels may not be available until mid- or late afternoon. It is best if you inform the desk if you'll be arriving late, as many hotels – especially in busy areas – hold reservations only until 4 or 6pm.
- **AAA and CAA Travel Agencies** provide full reservations service for any travel need. These services are available to AAA/CAA members and to the general public, although AAA/CAA members enjoy valuable discounts.
- Banff and Jasper in the Rockies have reservation agencies (contacted via the visitor information centre at each destination ➤ 138, 149) that will find accommodations for a small fee. **Bed-and-breakfast agencies** are common, though most visitor centres help find accommodations free of charge.
- Note that many hotels advertise toll-free telephone reservation numbers. Often these are only toll-free in Canada or the US. Normal international rates will usually be charged if you call from outside those areas.

Costs

- European visitors will be pleasantly surprised by the value for money offered by rural hotels and motels, although **room rates** in Vancouver and the Rockies are relatively high. Bed-and-breakfast rates are usually about the same as mid-range hotels.
- **Prices and accommodations** listings can be obtained in advance from Alberta and BC provincial tourist offices and Canadian travel centres in your home country, though remember that listed prices don't usually include federal and provincial taxes.
- **Room tax** in BC is 5.5%, and 4% in Alberta. An additional tourism tax is also sometimes levied: 2% in BC and 4% in Alberta. Federal Goods and **Services Tax** (GST) is levied at 5% in both provinces.
- If you're traveling with **children**, inquire about a hotel and motel's "**Family Plan**," where children stay free if they share their parents' room. Most places will also introduce a third single bed into a double room for between $5 and $20.
- Hotels and motels also offer numerous **off-season or mid-week deals**, or give special **discounts for extended stays**. Vancouver and Victoria hotels aimed primarily at business travellers may offer weekend rates, and most places offer substantial winter reductions.

Food and Drink

Eating in Vancouver, Calgary and Victoria can be a great pleasure, especially in Vancouver, where the multicultural population has fostered a large range of cuisines. Quality is also high in BC and Alberta, although here the range of eating places is more restricted. Restaurants run the gamut, from small-town diners and fast-food joints to high-class establishments in Vancouver.

- Prices are generally reasonable, but if your budget's tight there's a **huge choice** of cafés, diners, food malls and fast-food outlets across the region.
- North Americans are generally fairly informal, but the **dress code** for the best restaurants is smart-casual – jacket and tie for men are rarely required.
- **Tipping** is far more prevalent in North America than Europe. All serving staff should be tipped unless service has been poor, even in the cheapest cafés and diners. Tip 15–20 percent of the bill (or check) based on the total cost of the meal before taxes (see below).
- Tip staff in **bars** where drinks are brought to your table.
- **A Goods and Services Tax** (GST) of 5% is added to all bills, plus 7% PST in British Columbia.
- **Smoking** is banned in all public spaces, even in their outdoor areas.
- **Licensing laws** are strict in much of western Canada. In many bars you must buy food in order to have a drink, and public drinking in parks, beaches and elsewhere is often prohibited.
- The **minimum age for buying alcohol** is 18 in Alberta and 19 in British Columbia.
- Many restaurants start serving **lunch** from noon. Canadians generally eat **dinner** from around 6 or 7pm – though the more sophisticated city restaurants usually stay open until 11pm or later. Diners and small-town restaurants often close around 9pm or earlier.

Saving Money

- Some of the best-value food is found in **food malls**, where a variety of small food outlets serve a wide range of sandwiches, snacks and ethnic and fast food. Most are found on the lower or uppermost floors of shopping malls, and virtually all have a large communal eating area.
- **Fixed-price menus** are common at lunch, particularly in Japanese and Chinese restaurants.
- Some city bars have a "**Happy Hour**" between 5 and 7pm when drinks are cheaper than normal.

Restaurant Prices

Expect to pay for a three-course meal for two, excluding wine and service:

$ under CDN$50 **$$** CDN$50–$100 **$$$** over CDN$100

Shopping

Vancouver ranks as a major North American shopping destination, with a number of large, modern malls, plenty of designer and specialist stores, and unique retail enclaves such as Yaletown and Granville Island. Victoria and Calgary also have their share of specialist stores, while major mountain centres such as Banff are excellent for purchasing outdoor equipment.

Vancouver's excellent downtown shopping is dominated by Hudson's Bay (➤ 83) – a department store of long-standing fame – and malls such as the prestigious Pacific Centre. It also has smaller malls such as the Sinclair Centre (➤ 83), a converted historic building with fashion and more interesting specialty shops, and the Oakridge Centre, where 150 or so stores focus on fashion. Similar stores can be found in two market-cantered enclaves – **Lonsdale Quay** (➤ 82) and **Granville Island** (➤ 58) – and in hip districts such as Yaletown and the more bohemian **Kitsilano** district on 4th Avenue between Burrard Street and Alma Street. The main downtown shopping street is **Robson**, once described by fashion designer Gianni Versace, as "one of the 10 streets in the world where you have to have a store." The Gastown district has more and more galleries and shops devoted to Inuit and other aboriginal art and artifacts. Chinatown is full of Asian shops and markets. Around Vancouver, **Burnaby**, on the SkyTrain network, is home to BC's biggest mall, **Metropolis at Metrotown** (www.metropolisatmetrotown.com), which has 470 stores and the largest food court in western Canada. In **Richmond**, the **Aberdeen Centre** (www.aberdeencentre.com) is the spearhead of Asian retail.

Victoria is much smaller than Vancouver, but its main shopping streets – on and around Government Street and Douglas Street – are full of shops. The city's nearest equivalent to Vancouver's Granville Island is **Market Square** (www.marketsquare.ca, ➤ 94), a Victorian complex of cafés, restaurants, galleries, craft and small art and design stores. Best buys are chocolates, maple syrup, tea and coffee; books (there are two excellent bookstores), and craft products. The main mall here is the Mayfair Shopping Centre, with 120 stores and services.

Calgary's major shopping is mostly on and around Stephen Avenue Walk, the heart of downtown. The historic Inglewood neighbourhood, on 9th Avenue SE between 10th and 14th streets, has some interesting art galleries, antiques shops, boutiques and eating places, and in Marda Loop, at 33rd Avenue SW and 19th Street SW, there is an eclectic mix of stores. The Chinook Centre, at Macleod Trail and Glenmore Trail SW, is the biggest mall.

In the Rockies, only **Banff** has a significant number of stores, notably for fashion and outdoor clothes.

- Ordinary stores usually **open** Mon–Sat 10–6 (often with later opening on Fri, Sat). **Malls** generally open longer all week, from around 7:30 to 9.
- Most cities and towns have **24-hour pharmacies and convenience stores** such as Mac's and 7-Eleven.
- **Sunday opening** times across much of Canada have long been restricted by the so-called "blue laws," but these are increasingly being relaxed to allow limited opening, typically from noon to 5pm.
- Federal **Goods and Services Tax** (GST) at five percent is charged on most goods. Beware, as often the tax is not included in the displayed price. Additional **provincial taxes** of 7% is also be levied in BC.

Entertainment

Vancouver and the Rockies offer a wide range of outdoor activities, but the region also hosts numerous cultural events. Vancouver is a world-class centre for nightlife and the performing arts, but smaller towns and cities such as Banff and Calgary also offer plenty in the way of bars, clubs and live music.

Festivals and Events

Among the best are the Calgary Stampede, the Banff Festival of the Arts (➤ 161) and the Victoria International Festival. Vancouver has a huge program of world-class festivals, including jazz, folk and classical music; film, comedy and sports, and the New Year Festival in Chinatow (➤ 73).

Art and Culture

Vancouver has a wide range of classical and other **music concerts** – including those of the respected Vancouver Symphony Orchestra – and myriad mainstream and alternative **dance and theatre** companies. Victoria and Calgary also have a thriving cultural scene.

Nightlife

Nightlife in Calgary and Vancouver is lively, with plenty of **bars**, **clubs** and **pubs**. **Comedy clubs** are also popular, as is **live music**. Victoria has some clubs and several great pubs and bars but is more sedate.

Outdoor Activities

■ Western Canada offers some of the world's best opportunities for outdoor activities. **Hiking** is very popular in the Rockies. **Mountain bicycling**, **climbing**, **whitewater rafting**, horseback **riding** and **canoeing** are also excellent, as are facilities for **golf** and **fishing**. **Sailing** and **boating** are also popular.

■ **Winter sports** are exceptional, especially at Whistler (➤ 75), a venue for the 2010 Winter Olympics, but also at Banff and Lake Louise in the Rockies. Just about every other winter activity imaginable is available, from **skating** and **tobogganing** to **ice fishing** and **dogsledding**.

Sport

Ice hockey is virtually Canada's national sport. The Calgary Flames and Vancouver Canucks are both in the main North American National Hockey League (NHL). The season runs from October to May. Tickets must generally be bought in advance. Contact visitor centres for details.

Information

■ Canadian visitor centres and provincial tourist offices provide plenty of information on activities and entertainment. Also check out **weekly entertainment listings** in newspapers and magazines.

■ During your trip, call at **visitor centres** (also known as infocentres or similar), which, as well as providing brochures and current information, can often reserve you directly onto tours or sell tickets for shows, concerts and other events. Tickets can also be purchased in cities through central reservation agencies such as **Ticketmaster** (www.ticketmaster.ca/).

■ Virtually all centres have staff who can advise on outdoor activities locally, something that is particularly true of national and other park centres, where expert staff can recommend suitable hikes and other activities.

Vancouver

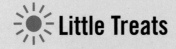 **Little Treats**

Leisurely Bike Ride

Cycle along the **Stanley Park Seawall** (➤ 52) and take in some of the city's best views, sights and attractions.

Japanese Snack

Downtown (➤ 63) and feeling hungry? **Try a trendy Japadog** – a hotdog with teriyaki sauce, mayo and seaweed – from a street food vendor.

Shaken, not Stirred

Nightlife and cocktails go hand in hand, and for an excellent selection of drinks head to **The Diamond** (➤ 81) in Gastown.

Getting Your Bearings

Sydney would disagree, Rio too, and San Francisco might demur, but it's hard to think of a city more beautiful than Vancouver – or one where it must be such a pleasure to live. Set between ocean and mountain, the city is scenically unrivalled, the waters of the Pacific bounding the downtown core, the peaks of the Coast Mountains rearing majestically in the near distance.

Hedonism among locals is unbridled, and no wonder, for Vancouver's lucky, multicultural residents can ski, sail, sunbathe (Vancouver even has beaches), hike, fish, dive and much more, all within a few minutes of the city centre. Wilderness – literally – is just a bus ride away, in the mountains above North Vancouver, while the world-class winter and summer resort of Whistler is a mere 90 minutes away by road.

Whether or not you take advantage of this natural playground, it's hard to resist Vancouver's summer allure, when the city's café and cultural life – vibrant at the best of times – takes to the streets and parks (Vancouver's infamous rain can put a damper on things the rest of the year).

Outstanding museums, galleries, gardens and shops also abound, but you could simply revel in the cityscapes and still have a great trip – the vibrant port that underpins the city's prosperity, the natural splendour of Stanley Park, the high-rise Downtown, the busy market on Granville Island, the beach at Kitsilano and the grittier and more historic corners of Gastown and Chinatown. You can see Vancouver in three days but you'll probably want to stay longer.

Museum of Anthropology

B C University Grounds

TOP 10

Don't Miss

At Your Leisure

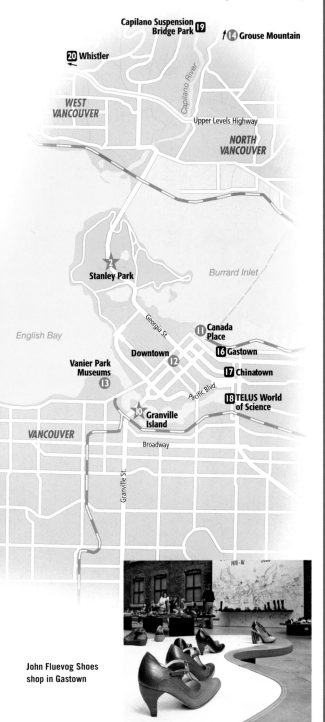

Getting Your Bearings

Capilano Suspension Bridge Park 19   ↑14 **Grouse Mountain**

20 **Whistler** ←

Capilano River

WEST VANCOUVER

Upper Levels Highway

NORTH VANCOUVER

2 **Stanley Park**

Burrard Inlet

English Bay

Georgia St.

11 **Canada Place**

Downtown 12

16 **Gastown**

Vanier Park Museums 13

17 **Chinatown**

Pacific Blvd.

18 **TELUS World of Science**

10 **Granville Island**

VANCOUVER

Broadway

Granville St.

John Fluevog Shoes shop in Gastown

Vancouver

Three Perfect Days

If you're not quite sure where to begin your travels, this itinerary recommends a practical and enjoyable three-day tour of Vancouver, taking in some of the best places to see. For more information see the main entries (►52–75).

Day 1

Morning

Visit the Vancouver TouristInfo Centre (►34) to book trips, buy passes and tickets, or to pick up brochures and information, then cross Canada Place Way outside the visitor centre to the waterfront and stroll around ❶ **Canada Place** (left; ►60). Walk to the Harbour Centre and take the elevators for stunning city views from The Lookout. Explore ❶ **Gastown** (►72), breaking for lunch in the **Water Street Café** (►80) or one of the many other cafés and restaurants nearby. After lunch you might walk to ❶ **Chinatown** (below; ►73), following the well-signed Silk Road Route.

Afternoon

Explore the heart of ❶ **Downtown** (►63) around Hornby, Howe or Burrard streets. Shop or visit the **Vancouver Art Gallery** (►63), with a break for refreshments in the **Gallery Café** (►81). Walk east on Robson Street to look at the **Vancouver Public Library** (►182) near the corner of Homer Street and Robson Street. Consider an early evening walk to the trendy **Yaletown** district nearby for a drink or early supper.

Day 2

Morning

Take a bus or ferry to ⭐ **Granville Island** (►58) to explore the city's soul. Catch a ferry to Heritage Harbour and visit one or more of the ❶ **Vanier Park museums** (►66). Return by ferry to Granville Island for lunch: buy a picnic from the market stalls or food concessions at the Public Market (►82), or try one of the island's restaurants, such as **Dockside** (►79).

Afternoon

Take a bus or taxi to downtown and continue to
⭐ **Stanley Park** (➤ 52) where you can spend the afternoon relaxing, visiting the **Vancouver Aquarium** and exploring the park on foot, bus or bike.

Evening

Have a break and something to drink or eat in one of several cafés around the park, or walk down Denman Street – which has several cafés and bars – for a stroll along **English Bay Beach**.

Day 3

Morning

Buy a public transportation **DayPass** (➤ 37) and travel by SkyTrain to Waterfront. Take the SeaBus to Lonsdale Quay in North Vancouver and then, if the weather is fine, catch a bus to the cable-car station at the foot of ⑭ **Grouse Mountain** (above; ➤ 68) followed by a possible visit to **Capilano Suspension Bridge Park** (➤ 74) with its Cliffwalk attraction. Return to Lonsdale Quay for lunch at the Quay's market (➤ 82), then take the SeaBus to downtown.

Afternoon

Take a bus to the ⑮ **Museum of Anthropology** (➤ 70). Pass a full afternoon viewing the museum's magnificent collection of First Nations' artifacts, as well as important collections from India, China and Southeast Asia.

Capilano Suspension Bridge Park ⑲ ⑭ Grouse Mountain

⑳ Whistler

⭐ Stanley Park
Canada Place
Downtown ⑪ Gastown
⑫ ⑯
Vanier Park Museums ⑬ ⑰ Chinatown
⑱ TELUS World of Science
⑩ Granville Island

⑮ Museum of Anthropology

★ Stanley Park

Stanley Park is one of the world's great city parks. At more than 350ha (865 acres) – an area greater than the whole of downtown – it rates among North America's largest urban parks, containing not only beaches, formal gardens and a remarkable semi-wilderness of forest, but also plenty of hiking and bicycle trails and one of western Canada's leading attractions – the Vancouver Aquarium.

Water surrounds the park on three sides, cradling a heart of virgin forest, tangled woodland glades and a criss-cross of trails. A 10.5km (6.5mi) road and parallel path and bicycle route run around the perimeter seawall, offering magnificent views, while on the park's eastern fringe are more manicured gardens and a medley of sights and attractions. These include the **aquarium** (▶ below), **Hallelujah Point** (a collection of painted totems, pictured right), the 5,000-bush **Rose Gardens**, **Royal Vancouver Yacht Club** and **Lost Lagoon**, the last a shallow tidal haven for a host of birds.

A typical totem pole in Stanley Park

How you visit Stanley Park – and a visit is essential – will depend on your energy levels. The best way is to rent a bicycle or Rollerblades from one of several outlets at the eastern end of Denman Street and follow the seawall for all or part of its circuit. **Prospect Point** offers superlative views, as does **Ferguson Point** to its west, while the track between the two runs through old-growth forest of western red cedar, hemlock and Douglas fir. Finish on one of the beaches lining the park's western edge – the most convenient is **English Bay Beach** at the southern end of Denman Street. Near by, **Second Beach**, to the north, has a saltwater swimming pool.

Insider Tip

Insider Tip

🐋 Vancouver Aquarium

More than a million people a year visit the Vancouver Aquarium, which makes it Canada's most popular visitor attraction west of Toronto's CN Tower. It is the third largest – and one of the best – in North America, with more than 8,000 living creatures representing over 600 different marine species. The prize attractions are the whales and performing dolphins, and though the aquarium has been the target of animal rights campaigners, upset, in particular, by the dolphin shows and the restricted space available to the whales, environmentalists support its commitment to education and conservation.

Above and below: Exhibits in Vancouver Aquarium

Displays are themed around several basic habitats: **Arctic Canada**, where you can watch animals of the cold Canadian north such as beluga whales, seals and walruses; the **Pacific Northwest Centre**, filled with beavers, otters and other creatures associated with the waters of British Columbia; the climate-controlled **Graham Amazon Gallery**, where a tropical deluge is unleashed on the hour above sloths, iguanas, piranhas, crocodiles and other rain-forest creatures; and the Tropical Pacific Gallery, which re-creates the coral reefs of Indonesia's Bunaken National Park, complete with angelfish and blacktip reef sharks. Be sure to call ahead for current feeding times for the sharks and sea otters. **Aquaquest – the Marilyn Blusson Learning Centre** is a facility that was designed according to strict ecological criteria and completed in 2006. It has exhibits of unique sea creatures, an environmental newsroom with the latest conservation news, an educational family play area and a viewing gallery where visitors can watch aquarium staff engaged in research projects.

SAVED FOR POSTERITY

Stanley Park was created thanks to the foresight of the city's first council. In the 1860s the area was partly logged, lumbermen being attracted by the vast 800-year-old trees. It was then turned into a military reserve as border tensions rose between Britain and the US. In 1886, within a month of Vancouver's foundation, the city council petitioned for the area to be turned into a permanent park. This took its name from Lord Stanley, Canada's Governor General between 1888 and 1893.

Vancouver

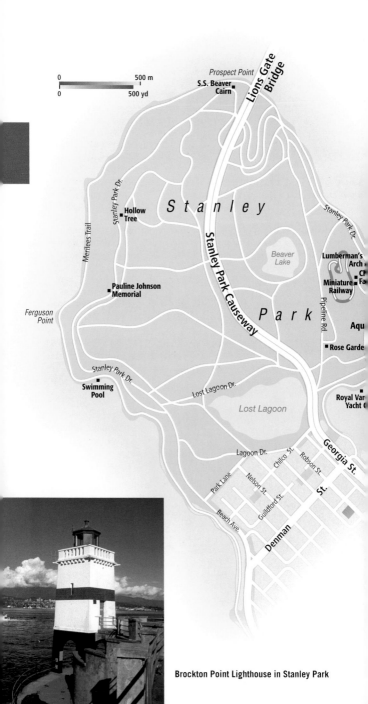

0 — 500 m
0 — 500 yd

Prospect Point
S.S. Beaver
Cairn

Lions Gate
Bridge

S t a n l e y

Stanley Park Dr.

Stanley Park Dr.

Hollow
Tree

*Beaver
Lake*

Lumberman's
Arch

Ch
Fa

Miniature
Railway

Merilees Trail

Pauline Johnson
Memorial

P a r k

*Ferguson
Point*

Pipeline Rd.

Aqu

Rose Garde

Stanley Park Dr.

Swimming
Pool

Lost Lagoon Dr.

Lost Lagoon

Royal Var
Yacht C

Lagoon Dr.

Chilco St.

Robson St.

Georgia St.

Park Lane

Nelson St.

Guildford St.

St.

Beach Ave.

Denman

Brockton Point Lighthouse in Stanley Park

TAKING A BREAK
Cafés along the seawall, at Prospect Point and Ferguson Point.

Stanley Park Vancouver Parks Board
➕ 204 B5 ✉ 2099 Beach Avenue ☎ 604/873-7000

Vancouver Aquarium
➕ 204 C5 ✉ 845 Avison Way, Stanley Park
☎ 604/659-37474 or 604/659-3552 for bookings; www.vanaqua.org
🕐 Mon–Fri 10–5, Sat, Sun 9:30–6
🍴 Upstream Café ($) and gift shop 🚉 Skytrain: Burrard, then bus 19
🚌 19 on West Pender or Georgia
💵 CDN$31

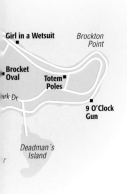

Vancouver's aquarium is a premier attraction

INSIDER INFO

- Stanley Park is generally safe – one of the biggest dangers is getting lost – but as much of it is so wild you should leave before nightfall.
- **Don't walk from downtown** – it's a long and uninteresting trek. Save your energy for walking around the park.
- If you're not a walker, just **visit the aquarium** and the gardens near Lost Lagoon. You can rent a bicycle at the corner of Denman and West Georgia.
- In summer, when funds are available, the free **Stanley Park Shuttle** (mid-Jun to late Sep daily 10–6:30) circles the seawall, connecting all the major attractions. Buses, fuelled by propane gas, leave approximately every 12–15 minutes, and the full circuit takes about 45 minutes. The **19 bus** from downtown connects with the shuttle.

Insider Tip

City Set Between Ocean & Mountain

Western Canada's metropolis on the Pacific is one of the most scenic cities in the world. Vancouver seduces its visitors with an imposing backdrop of the Coastal Mountains, extensive parks and impressive harbour facility, the restored Gastown historic area and the futuristic elegance of its downtown buildings.

❶ Maritime Museum: Focuses on seafaring, harbours, fishing, and marine memorabilia and research.

❷ Museum of Vancouver: The ethnographic collection on the First Nations of the Northwest Coast deserves special attention.

❸ Granville Island: The buzzing historic area of converted old warehouses and waterfront houseboats attracts visitors with its theatres, artists' studios and galleries, restaurants and shops, lovely pockets of greenery and great food markets.

❹ BC Place Stadium: The stadium features a gigantic air-inflated domed roof.

❺ Rogers Arena: Known by the locals as "the Garage", the arena is the venue for the home games of the Vancouver Canucks NHL ice hockey team.

❻ Sam Kee Building: It is hard to get lost in one of the narrowest commercial buildings in the world.

❼ Steam Clock: A grandfather clock that lets out some steam on the hour and whistles on the quarter hour.

❽ Harbour Centre: The locals have nick-named the Harbour Centre, one of the city's tallest buildings, "the urinal" because of its distinctive flying saucer shaped top. Take the glass SkyLift up to The Lookout for stunning views of the city.

❾ Tourism Vancouver Info Centre: This is the place to stock up on all of the city's tourism information.

❿ Marine Building: An art deco building with terracotta bas-relief designs on the facade that portray Vancouver's relationship to trade and the ocean.

⓫ Stanley Park: The green heart of the city, this urban forest includes a lake with water-fowl, the zoo, the Lost Lagoon, the aquarium, world-famous totem poles, a canon that is fired every day at 9pm, and much, much more…

⓬ Hotel Vancouver: This historic building (or one of its predecessors) has been the

Vancouver Aquarium's prize attractions are the whales and performing dolphins

A modern take on Rome's Colosseum: the Vancouver Public Library

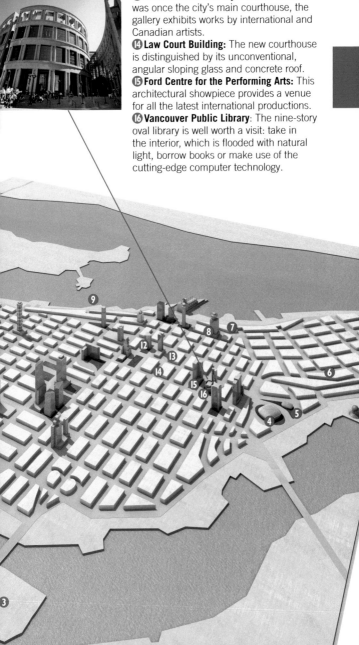

luxurious home away from home for such illustrious guests as Mark Twain, Rudyard Kipling, Winston Churchill, Indira Gandhi and Queen Elizabeth.

⓭ Vancouver Art Gallery: Housed in what was once the city's main courthouse, the gallery exhibits works by international and Canadian artists.

⓮ Law Court Building: The new courthouse is distinguished by its unconventional, angular sloping glass and concrete roof.

⓯ Ford Centre for the Performing Arts: This architectural showpiece provides a venue for all the latest international productions.

⓰ Vancouver Public Library: The nine-story oval library is well worth a visit: take in the interior, which is flooded with natural light, borrow books or make use of the cutting-edge computer technology.

⭐10 Granville Island

Granville Island is Vancouver's heart and soul, a small redoubt of renovated semi-industrial buildings and waterfront on the southern edge of the downtown peninsula. It contains one of the world's great food markets and a medley of galleries, wharves, walkways, galleries, specialty shops, restaurants, artists' studios – even a small brewery.

Transportation

The quickest way to get here is by taxi or a 50 bus from Gastown or bus stops on the west side of the Granville Street Bridge. You'll be dropped underneath the girders of the bridge on the island side, from where you walk back straight onto the largely pedestrianized island. If you have a car, don't dream of driving – parking is all but impossible. Don't walk over the Granville Street Bridge – it's a long, dull hike.

The slower but more enjoyable approach is to walk to the foot of Hornby Street and pick up one of the tiny ferries that ply to the island across False Creek. These same ferries will carry you from the island to Vanier Park (➤66), the next logical stage of any Vancouver itinerary. Allow at least a couple of hours before moving on.

Regeneration

The island is a triumph of urban regeneration. It was originally reclaimed from swampland in 1917 and used as the site of an iron and shipbuilding factory. By the 1960s it was a derelict wasteland and rubbish dump, and might have stayed that way but for a federally funded project, begun in 1972, that successfully transformed it into an inspired "open-plan" mixture of commercial, residential and light industrial use.

The high-rises of downtown tower over Granville Island

A trip here is rewarding at any time, but especially fun at weekends, when half of Vancouver descends on the island to buy food in the glorious covered **food market**, grab a cappuccino, people-watch, eat brunch outdoors, stroll among the **shops and wharves**, or sit in the sun watching the numerous street performers. Also worth a look is the **Granville Island Brewing**, which has a store and offers tours with tastings of its additive-free beer, such as Gastown Amber Ale and Brockton Black.

The island's also good in the evening, when you can sit and watch the sunset, sip a beer, eat in the restaurants, or take in a revue, play or cabaret at the **Arts Club Theatre** (➤84).

A waterside restaurant on Granville Island

TAKING A BREAK

The popular, laid-back **Backstage Lounge** (tel: 604/687 1354; www.thebackstagelounge.com) at the Arts Club (► 84) has a waterfront view, occasional live music and good, inexpensive snacks and meals. Or, try **Granville Island Keg** at 1499 Anderson Street (tel: 604/685-4735; www.kegsteakhouse.com).

⊞ 204 C1
✉ Granville Island Infocentre, 1661 Duranleau Street
(and kiosks around the island May–Sep)
☎ 604/666-5784 or 604/666-6655; www.granvilleisland.com
🕐 Island: 24 hours. Public market: daily 9–7
🚌 50 ⛴ Aquabus, False Creek Ferries (► 38)

Granville Island Brewing
⊞ 204 C1
✉ 1441 Cartwright Street, Granville Island
☎ 604/687-2739; www.gib.ca
🕐 Store: daily 10–8; brewery: tours daily noon, 2 and 4 🎟 CDN$9.75

INSIDER INFO

- The island is extremely busy at weekends, so if you'd prefer to avoid the crowds **come during the week**. Note that many of the shops are shut on Mondays, as, too, is the market during winter.

Insider Tip

- The **Granville Island Infocentre** (tel: 604/666-5784; www.granvilleisland.com), can be found upstairs at 1661 Duranleau Street. There are also summer-only kiosks around the island that have maps and details of various attractions.
- **Heading back to downtown** you should take a 50 bus from the stop beside the island's single road entrance, not the 51 from the stop on the island on Cartwright Street.

Insider Tip

In more depth You can 🚣 **rent canoes** from several outlets to paddle around False Creek, or stroll along the waterfront to Sea Village, where you can take some photographs of the charming houseboats.

⓫ Canada Place

Canada Place makes a stunning introduction to Vancouver. Begun in 1986 as the Canadian Pavilion for Expo '86, the long pier offers sensational views of the city's port, the ranks of downtown skyscrapers and the mountains above North Vancouver. Dotted around its panoramic promenades are information boards that offer fascinating insights into the history and background of what you're seeing.

The huge complex juts into the harbour in the manner of a ship, an architectural trick complemented by the distinctive white Teflon roof, designed to resemble the sails of a ship at sea. The complex comprises of a medley of shops, restaurants, convention centre, exhibitions, and attractions such as 🏙 **FlyOver Canada**, which is a virtual flight over Canada's most spectacular landscapes. To enjoy the complex's magnificent views you can take a wander on the "decks" – the promenades that encircle the building. Allow an hour or so.

Right: One of the decorative sails of Canada Place

Insider Tip

First Port of Call
Canada Place lies on the waterfront at the foot of Howe and Burrard streets, on the northern edge of downtown, making it easy to find and easily accessible on your first morning in Vancouver. It's also just a minute's walk from the city's excellent main visitor centre, or **TouristInfo Centre** (▶ 34).

Superb Scenery
From the promenades you can watch the buzz of activity scattered across one of North America's busiest ports. Helicopters swoop over the water, floatplanes pull themselves into the sky, and boats of all shapes and sizes criss-cross the spectacular mountain-backed harbour. To the west, the waterfront curves to meet **Stanley Park** (▶ 52), downtown's glorious crown of forest and wilderness. Below you there's likely to be at least one cruise ship moored at the pier – the terminal here handles some 120 cruise ships and around 600,000 passengers annually.

Inside Canada Place

As you walk, pause to read the 44 information boards that deal with everything from the history of the city to the different types of ships and cargoes on the water. The port sprang to life in 1864, when it started exporting fence

INSIDER INFO

Insider Tip

- **The Lookout** in the Harbour Centre is nearly always busy so in peak season consider visiting it before Canada Place to avoid the crowds.
- Tickets are valid all day, so come back to The Lookout in the evening to **enjoy the city lights by night**.

Vancouver

pickets to Australia. Today it processes some 3,000 ships a year from over 100 different countries, handles over 83 million tons of cargo, and turns over $40 billion of trade every year. The port's Interpretive Centre has some fun, hands-on exhibits.

Canada Place juts out into the harbour

If the views from Canada Place aren't enough, then walk to the nearby Harbour Centre Building, where in just 60 seconds all-glass SkyLifts carry you 170m (558ft) to **The Lookout**, with a magnificent 360-degree view of the city.

TAKING A BREAK

For lunch, try the inexpensive **café** at the tip of Canada Place ($); in the evening, check out the formal restaurants of the Pan Pacific hotel ($$$) nearby.

✚ 205 E3 ✉ Canada Place, 100–999 Canada Place
☎ Information 604/665-9000; www.canadaplace.ca 🕓 24 hours
🍴 Café ($) 🚉 Waterfront 🚌 4, 6, 7, 8 or 50 north on Granville Street

FlyOver Canada
✉ 201-999 Canada Place
☎ 604/620-8455; www.flyovercanada.com 🕓 Daily 10–9
🚉 Waterfront 🚌 4, 6, 7, 8 or 50 north on Granville Street
🎟 CDN$19.95

The Lookout at Harbour Centre
✉ Harbour Centre, 555 West Hastings Street
☎ 604/689-0421; www.vancouverlookout.com
🕓 May to mid-Oct daily 8:30am–10:30pm; mid-Oct to Apr 9–9
🍴 Food court ($) and restaurant ($$)
🚉 Waterfront 🚌 4, 6, 7, 8, 10, 16, 20 or 50 north to Granville Mall
🎟 CDN$15.75

⑫ Downtown

Vancouver's downtown core looks much like any other North American city – lots of sleek high-rise buildings, malls, offices and shops – but it has two important differences: the views and the setting. Turn almost any corner and you're greeted with startling panoramas of the sea and mountains, a constant reminder of the spectacular scenery that frames one of the world's most beautiful cities.

Downtown's heart is the grid of streets on and around Robson, Granville and Burrard, though as Vancouver's smart centre is spreading rapidly – particularly to the east. Robson Street is the key thoroughfare, full of shops and restaurants: On summer evenings this is the place to be, part of a vibrant throng and colourful street life. Granville Street is less smart – at its southern end it's downright seedy – but it is also a focus for bars, cinemas and entertainment. Burrard Street is the smartest of the three streets, and the stretch down to the waterfront and **Canada Place** (▶ 60) contains some of the city's grandest – and most expensive – hotels, shops and offices.

Cafés and bars in Gastown

Head West or East
West of the downtown core lies the West End, a predominantly residential district. Beyond that again is **Stanley Park** (▶ 52), an area of near wilderness wonderfully at odds with the concrete, glass and steel of downtown. Heading east you come to **Gastown** (▶ 72), an only partly successful piece of city rejuvenation, and then a grittier, more down-at-the-heels district that merges into **Chinatown** (▶ 73).

What to See
On your first downtown venture make for the **Vancouver Art Gallery**, a former city courthouse that has been transformed into a handsomely presented gallery. The gallery's collection totals 10,000 works (not all on show at one time), including paintings by BC's most acclaimed artist, Emily Carr. Works by

Vancouver

Carr are usually on view. Much of the gallery is given over to changing exhibitions of international artists that can be dramatic and challenging. The Gallery Store sells Carr merchandise and handicrafts by local artists while the Gallery Café has a delightful patio. Plans were announced in early 2008 for a new venue for the gallery in a waterside setting on False Creek's Plaza of Nations.

Downtown is filled with malls and department stores. The most interesting are the Hudson's Bay store and the Sinclair Centre mall (▶ 83); for more details of these and other downtown stores).

Inside the former courthouse that is now Vancouver Art Gallery

TAKING A BREAK
The **Gallery Café** (▶ 81), with its large outdoor area, is one of downtown's nicest places for lunch or a coffee.

✚ 205 D2

Vancouver Art Gallery
✉ 750 Hornby Street
☎ 604/662-4719 for 24-hour information; www.vanartgallery.bc.ca
🕐 Art gallery: daily 10–5 (Tue until 9). Café: Mon–Fri 9–9, Sat, Sun 9:30–6
🍴 Gallery Café 🚇 Burrard or Granville 🚌 3, 5 & 15 west on Robson Street
🎫 CDN$21

INSIDER INFO

■ To see the best of downtown's dynamic new buildings, walk east
along Robson Street to the magnificent **Vancouver Public Library**
complex (▶ 57, 182) – a modern take on Rome's Colosseum.

■ Follow the **Vancouver city walk** (▶ 180) to uncover hidden cor-
ners, including such as architectural gems as Christ Church
Cathedral and the Marine Building, or the **Bill Reid Gallery** of
Northwest Coast Art (639 Hornby Street at Dunsmuir; tel:
604/682-3455; www.billreidgallery.ca) devoted to the art of
Haida artist Bill Reid (▶ 15, 70).

Downtown
Vancouver
seen from
Davie Street

⑬ Vanier Park Museums

Vanier Park contains three of Vancouver's four major museums: the Museum of Vancouver, which recounts the history of the city; the Maritime Museum, which contains a wealth of maritime displays and memorabilia; and the H R MacMillan Space Centre, which is dedicated to the science and exploration of space. All lie close to one another, and all are ideally suited to visit from Granville Island (► 58), which is connected to the park by ferry.

Maritime Museum

Arriving by ferry from Granville Island – by far the best approach to Vanier Park – you disembark at Heritage Harbour, a small quay containing beautiful old boats. These provide the perfect prelude to the nearby Maritime Museum, which is dedicated to Vancouver's strong seafaring traditions.

Pride of place among the somewhat dated displays at Heritage Harbour goes to the *St Roch*, a Royal Canadian Mounted Police (► 24) schooner that in 1944 became the first vessel to make a single-season voyage across the Northwest Passage (a 1,497km/930mi traverse between Baffin Island and Alaska's Beaufort Sea). Other highlights – for which you should allow an hour at the most – include many period photographs, models and maritime artifacts, as well as the 🚸 **Children's Maritime Discovery Centre** and **Pirates' Cove**, with activities designed to teach children about maritime issues.

Museum of Vancouver

Vancouver's main civic museum suffers by comparison with Victoria's Royal British Columbia Museum (► 96), which covers British Columbia's First Nations and other history in a more impressive manner. However, the museum intends to re-define its content and curatorial role toward a greater focus on Vancouver in a modern context. Plans include a possible move to the heart of downtown: the Vancouver Art Gallery building in Hornby Street is being considered when it is vacated. Current highlights include re-created Edwardian and Victorian rooms, an old Hudson's Bay Company post, a **Canadian Pacific Railway car** and the immigration section. The last contains an eye-opening mock-up of the conditions endured by those traveling in "steerage," the cheapest way of crossing the Atlantic from Europe.

Ben Franklin, a mini submarine in the Maritime Museum

🏛 H.R. MacMillan Space Centre

Admission to this excellent high-tech space centre, observatory and planetarium buys you, among other things, a "virtual" trip to Mars in a full-motion simulator, during which you ride close to the sun, tangle with a meteor shower and save a settlement of space colonists. Then you can admire one of the huge motors from **Apollo 17** and wander through the Cosmic Courtyard, which is stuffed with interactive displays – have a go at designing a spacecraft or guiding a lunar robot. The **H.R. MacMillan Planetarium** offers a variety of star and laser shows. Other parts of the centre have changing exhibitions and shows.

Exhibits in Vancouver Museum

Maritime Museum
✛ 204 B2 ✉ Vanier Park, 1905 Ogden Avenue
☎ 604/257-8300; www.vancouvermaritimemuseum.com
🕐 Daily 10–5 🍴 Vending machines
🚌 2 or 22 (Macdonald) from Burrard Street or West Pender Street to Chestnut Street or Cornwall Street
💲 CDN$11

Museum of Vancouver
✛ 204 B2 ✉ Vanier Park, 1100 Chestnut Street (150m from the Maritime Museum)
☎ 604/736-4431; www.museumofvancouver.ca
🕐 Daily 10–5 (Thu until 8)
🚌 2 or 22 (Macdonald) from Burrard Street or West Pender Street to Cornwall Street 💲 CDN$15

Right: The fountain outside Vancouver Museum

H.R. MacMillan Space Centre
✛ 204 B2 ✉ Vanier Park, 1100 Chestnut Street ☎ 604/738-7827 (call for evening star and laser show times); www.spacecentre.ca
🕐 Mon–Fri 10–3, Sat, Sun and public holidays 10–5
🚌 2 or 22 (Macdonald) from Burrard Street or West Pender Street to Chestnut Street or Cornwall Street
💲 CDN$18. Admission includes complex and one Virtual Voyage, subject to health and minimum height requirement of 1m (3ft). Additional Voyages: CDN$11

INSIDER INFO

■ By far the best way to visit the Vanier Park museums is on one of the tiny **ferries** (▶ 38) from Granville Island. Some boats go directly to the small landing stage close to the Maritime Museum; others require a change of ferry en route. It's a straightforward procedure – simply ask your ferry operator. Pay your fare on the boat.

■ Choose the Museum of Vancouver if you have **time for just one** of the park's three museums. If you're traveling with children, however, the H.R. MacMillan Space Centre is the best single choice.

⑭ Grouse Mountain

On a first visit to Vancouver there are only two reasons for making the 40-minute journey across the Burrard Inlet from the city's downtown peninsula to North Vancouver: one is the journey itself – views from the SeaBus are impressive – and the second is Grouse Mountain, a high mountain eyrie reached by a cable car, which offers a stupendous panorama of Vancouver and its surroundings.

Two Swiss-built **cable cars –** among North America's largest – run from the cable-car station (290m/950ft) to the upper station (1,250m/4,100ft) in about 10 minutes. Once up the mountain, you could spend a few minutes in the **Interpretive Centre**, where your cable-car ticket covers entry to the theatre for an impressive video presentation that takes you on an eagle's-eye ride over southern BC. Also here is a restaurant, bistro, snack bars and gift shop, but save these for later (▶ Insider Info).

HIGHLIGHTS
There are a variety of Grouse Mountain **helicopter tours packages** (tel: 604/980-9311; www.grouse mountain.com/helitours) ranging from the 8-minute **Crown Mountain** (CDN$89.95) to the 20-minute **Coastal Scenic Tour** (CDN$189.95). A **Fly, Dine and Drive** trip flies you from downtown to dine at the Observatory, with a chauffeured limousine back (prices on request).

Summer Activities
All manner of activities are laid on in the summer – wilderness it is not. You can join easy **guided strolls** through the woods (they run hourly and last around 30 minutes) or sign

A view of Vancouver from Grouse Mountain

Above: Grouse Mountain cable car

up for **helicopter rides** (➤ panel left), **paragliding**, **ziplining** and **guided mountain bike rides**. Free attractions include a children's **playground** and the "**World Famous Lumberjack Shows**", which involve chopping and other lumberjack displays. All activities are in the area near the Interpretive Centre. Just beyond, a smaller **Peak Chairlift** rumbles upward for eight minutes to Grouse Mountain's summit (the ride is included in the cable-car ticket). On a clear day, the **views** are truly extraordinary. You can see more of Vancouver and across to the San Juan Islands from the glass viewing pod of the 58m (190ft) high wind turbine, the Eye of the Wind (daily).

🚪 198 A1 ✉ 6400 Nancy Greene Way
☎ 604/980-9311; www.grousemountain.com 🕐 Daily 9am–10pm 🍴 Cafés ($) and restaurants ($$) 🚇 SkyTrain to Waterfront, then SeaBus to Lonsdale Quay, then 236 bus from Lonsdale Quay or 232 from Phibbs Exchange 💵 Combined tickets from CDN$44

INSIDER INFO

- Pick a good day so as to be able to enjoy the views from the summit, and set off early to avoid **long lines** at the cable-car station.
- Consider **reserving a table** at the Observatory Restaurant (daily 5–10; tel: 604/980-9311; $$$) for dinner – cable-car rides are free with a reservation – and enjoy the experience of dining in the evening with the lights of Vancouver laid out below.

In more depth Get off the bus on the way back to Lonsdale Quay to explore the **Capilano Suspension Bridge Park** (➤ 74).

Insider Tip

⑮ Museum of Anthropology

Vancouver's finest museum is a half-hour bus or taxi ride from downtown, but don't let that deter you, for the Museum of Anthropology is a magnificent modern gallery filled with a striking collection of totem poles and other artifacts created by, and associated with, BC coastal First Nations peoples.

Architecture

The museum forms part of the huge University of British Columbia campus, well to the west of central Vancouver. The impressive building was designed in 1976 by the distinguished North American architect Arthur Erickson. Its big, bright concrete-and-glass structure was inspired by the post-and-beam wooden dwellings of the region's First Nations peoples, whose art and culture it showcases.

Right: A totem pole outside the Museum of Anthropology

First People's Cultural Art and More

The museum exhibits a collection of cultural products from the Northwest Coast First Nations, including the world-famous sculpture *The Raven and the First Man* by Haida artist Bill Reid (► 15), which is on display in the rotunda named after him. The breathtaking Great Hall houses the **world's finest collection of totem poles**, most of which belonged to the Haida, Salish, Tsimshian and Kwakiutl, Aboriginal peoples who shared many common cultural and artistic traits. Through the large glass windows you look onto more totem poles, framed by the waters of the Georgia Strait. Also here are two **longhouses** overlooking Point Grey, built according to Haida methods and aligned on the traditional north–south axis.

Below: Statues in the museum

Renewal Project

Vancouver's finest museum has seen extensive renovation and expansion through its Renewal Project. The museum has been extended by 50 percent and was

Museum of Anthropology

relaunched in January 2010. The project includes a new **Major Exhibit Gallery** for touring exhibitions and a pleasant new café.

The **Multiversity Galleries** (replacing the Visible Storage Galleries), display cases featuring artifacts from the museum's unrivalled collection of more than 35,000 artifacts (some in cabinets with removable trays), including many from India, China and Southeast Asia. There are computer terminals that provide additional information, images, audio and video about the objects on display.

There is also a **new South Wing** housing a community research suite and a state-of-the-art archaeology facility; a redesigned research centre; and revitalized public amenities. Funds also covered the cost of digitization of 35,000 objects to enhance online research access, a project on view to visitors in the Digitization Studio.

Insider Tip

➕ 204 off A1
✉ 6393 NW Marine Drive
☎ 604/822-5087; 604/822-3825 for recorded information; www.moa.ubc.ca
🕐 Tue 10–9, Wed–Sun 10–5;
Café: Mon 10:30–2, Tue–Sun 10–4:30
🍴 Café $
🚌 4, 9, 17, 25, 41, 43, 44, 49, 84, 258, 480
💲 CDN$16.75

INSIDER INFO

■ Take a **4 or 10 bus** to the end of the line and on the campus follow the tree-lined East Mall from the bus stop and then turn left into NW Marine Drive. It's about a 15-minute walk.

In more depth While on the UBC campus, turn right out of the museum for a five-minute walk to the small **Nitobe Memorial Garden**, considered the world's most authentic Japanese garden outside Japan (1895 Lower Mall, http://botanicalgarden.ubc.ca; 15 Mar to Oct daily 11–4:30; CDN$7; Nov to 14 Mar Mon–Fri 10–2; donation; combined ticket with UBC Botanical Garden: CDN$13). Beyond it at 16th Avenue and SW Marine drive lies the larger university **UBC Botanical Garden** (6804 SW Marine Drive; tel: 604/822-4208; daily 9:30–4:30; CDN$9; Nov to 14 Mar: donation). This has five separate gardens: Asian, Alpine, Food, Herb and BC Native.

Insider Tip

At Your Leisure

16 Gastown

Gastown is a rejuvenated city district five minutes' walk east of Canada Place (► 60). Full of cafés, bars, converted warehouses and interesting shops, it's a busy and major fixture on the tourist trail: It's also close to the seedier and, at times, downright unpleasant parts of the city en route to Chinatown (► opposite).

The area contains some of Vancouver's oldest buildings, for it was here that the city was born – the district grew up around a tavern established by "Gassy" Jack Leighton, from whom the quarter's present name derives (► 17).

Fire ravaged the area in 1886, but the coming of the railroad in 1887 saw a new building boom. By the 1970s, however, Gastown was a sad, seedy and semiderelict Skid Row, but one whose historic buildings and proximity to downtown made it an obvious candidate for renovation.

Today the area is not quite as dynamic a city space as its planners hoped, and certainly less successful than the similar Granville Island redevelopment (► 58). This said, it's easy to see and well worth a stroll for an hour or so. Look for the plaques identifying 23 historic buildings. Most of what there is to see centres on **Water Street**, which, before Vancouver's port developed, was on the waterfront. Here you'll find a famous steam-powered clock (1977; pictured left), whose old paddle-steamer whistle hoots and shrieks every 15 minutes, and a series

The Gastown steam clock is connected to the district's heating network

---

👫 FUN AND GAMES IN VANCOUVER

There is plenty to amuse children in Vancouver, but there are several attractions aimed specifically at younger visitors. Both the water slides and play areas at **Granville Island Waterpark** (tel: 604/257-8195; www.falsecreekcc.ca/waterpark.htm) and the adventure rides and roller coasters at **Playland** (tel: 604/252-3583; www.pne.ca) are popular with children. In Stanley Park the **Miniature Railway** and **Children's Farmyard** (tel: 604/257-8531; http://vancouver.ca/parks-recreation-culture/stanley-park-miniature-train.aspx) add to the fun for youngsters. The train rides feature replicas of historic engines and the farmyard has goats, cows and llamas. A 30-minute drive east of the city centre, in Aldergrove, is the **Greater Vancouver Zoo** (604/856-6825; www.gvzoo.com) and in North Vancouver, 10 minutes' drive from downtown, **Maplewood Farm** (604/929-5610; www.maplewoodfarm.bc.ca).

FIRST NATIONS CRAFT

If you are looking for **interesting souvenirs** to take home, there are some excellent, if somewhat pricey, First Nations craft galleries in the Gastown area of Vancouver. Alternatively, you may find some unusual and authentic pieces sold by licensed street artists in the area.

of specialty shops, galleries, cafés and restaurants, of which the best are the Water Street Café (➤ 80), the Old Spaghetti Factory and the Inuit Gallery of Canada (➤ 82).

➕ 205 E2 🚇 Skytrain: Waterfront

🚌 3, 4, 6, 7, 8, 50

🔟 Chinatown

Chinatown is full of tiny, crowded streets, vibrant markets, and shops full of Oriental foods and medicines. It lies east from Gastown, from where the best walking route is south on Cambie, then left on Pender Street. If starting from downtown, you can follow the **Silk Road Route** from Library Square, a self-guiding walking route marked by colourful banners and street signs. This encircles Chinatown and takes in all the main attractions.

With a population of more than 100,000, this is the third largest Chinatown in North America after San Francisco and New York. It dates to around 1858, when Chinese immigrants flocked here during the Fraser Valley gold rush. Others followed to work on the railroad, gravitating to a district where special clan associations assisted the newcomers.

Discrimination was rife – legal rights and citizenship, for example, were denied to the Chinese until 1947, and during the 1930s white women were forbidden to work in Chinese restaurants because, in the words of the local police chief, "it is almost impossible for them to be so employed without falling victim to some immoral life."

Today Vancouver is far more racially integrated, but Chinatown retains its ethnic integrity: All the signs are in Chinese, all the buildings have a distinct Eastern tinge, and just about every resident is Chinese.

The area is mostly enclosed by Pender, Carrall, Gore and Main streets. Many people make first for the **Sam Kee Building** at the corner of Pender Street and Carrall Street, one of the world's narrowest buildings at 1.8m (6ft) wide.

Also worth a visit is the **Dr Sun Yat-Sen Classical Chinese Garden**, named after the founder of the first Chinese Republic, a regular visitor to Vancouver. The garden was created for Expo '86 with the help of 950 crates of materials from the People's Republic. It was the first authentic Chinese garden created outside China, and one that emulated Suzhou's classical gardens of the Ming dynasty (1368–1644). All the garden's elements, such as hard and soft, big and small, smooth and rough,

Peaceful Dr Sun Yat-Sen Classical Chinese Garden

Vancouver

and flowing and static, carefully balance. At first sight the effect is austere, but after a while, you begin to notice the subtleties, and the city outside is subsumed by the garden's peace and tranquillity.
➕ 205 E2

Dr Sun Yat-Sen Classical Chinese Garden
✉ 578 Carrall Street near Pender Street
☎ 604/662-3207; www.vancouverchinese garden.com 🕐 Daily, May to mid-Jun and Sep 10–6; mid-Jun to Aug 9:30–7; Oct–Apr 10–4:30
🍴 Café ($) 🚌 19 or 22 east on Pender Street
🚇 Skytrain: Stadium-Chinatown 💵 CDN$12

🅱 🍴 TELUS Science World

Science World's big silver geodesic dome forms a prominent part of the Vancouver skyline. Built as a pavilion for Expo '86, it now contains science-oriented displays, with plenty of hands-on exhibits guaranteed to appeal to kids. In many ways, the displays don't quite live up to the splendour of

Science World's geodesic dome

the setting and you'll need to make a special journey from downtown to get to the site. This said, if you have children in tow, the laser and 3D shows, the big-screen films in the Omnimax Theatre, and the various drum and musical synthesizer displays are all excellent.

Capilano Suspension Bridge

➕ 205 E1 ✉ 1455 Québec Street
☎ 604/443-7440; www.scienceworld.ca
🕐 Mon–Fri 10–5, Sat, Sun 10–6
🍴 Triple O's by White Spot ($)
🚇 SkyTrain to Science World-Main Street
🚌 3 and 8 north on Granville Mall or 19 on Pender Street
💵 CDN$23.25

🔟 Capilano Suspension Bridge Park

The **Capilano Suspension Bridge** is among the most visited attractions in the province, with around 750,000 people coming annually to cross the 137m (450ft) swaying footbridge 70m (230ft) above the river. Having acquired a taste for the vertiginous thrill, they can move on to the **Treetops Adventure**, crossing seven bridges suspended 30m (100ft) above the forest floor in the rain forest canopy. The complex also includes a Living Forest exhibit and the new cliffwalk.

It's very touristy, and very busy at peak times, and those who prefer more tranquil surroundings are advised to continue north for the short distance to the free **Capilano River Regional Park**, off Nancy Greene Way. You can walk and see the river scenery for free, and it also allows you to visit the

fascinating **salmon hatchery** there (signed from the entrance), built in 1977 to help spawning salmon and thus restore dwindling stocks.

The best way to include the park in a visit is to see Grouse Mountain (➤ 68) and then walk or take a bus 1km/0.5mi to the main entrance (there's another entrance at the Cleveland Dam near Grouse Mountain at the park's northern limit). The **Capilano Pacific trail** (1.5km/1mi) runs from the dam to the hatchery, one of several easy forest and river walks in the park. Alternatively, follow riverside trails from the hatchery to Dog's Leg Pool (1km/0.5mi).

The park is the most accessible of several similar parks in the forests and mountains above North Vancouver: contact the visitor centre for details on access, trails and other activities in Lynn Canyon,

Whistler is now an all-year resort

At Your Leisure

Mount Seymour, Cypress Park and Lighthouse Park.
✚ 204 B5
✉ 3735 Capilano Road, North Vancouver
🚌 236, 239 or 246 west on Georgia Street

Suspension Bridge
☎ 604/985-7474; www.capbridge.com
🕐 Jan to mid-Mar, early Oct to late Nov 9–5; mid-Mar to mid-Apr, Sep to early Oct 9–6; mid-Apr to May 9–7, Jun to early Sep 8:30–8; late Nov to early Jan 11–9

Hatchery
☎ 604/666-1790 🕐 Daily from 8am 🎟 Free

⓴ Whistler

Whistler lies 125km (77.5mi) north of Vancouver amid stunning mountain scenery and is known as one of North America's finest ski resorts. So good, in fact, that it was chosen as the venue for the 2010 Winter Olympic Games. During the summer, visitors come here to cycle, horseback ride, play golf, ride mountain bikes or hike 18 incredible trails, including a glacier walk. Cable cars and ski lifts give access to some easy high-level walks. The resort is about 1.5 hours by car or bus from Vancouver, so a day trip is feasible. Accommodations are plentiful if you want to stay overnight, but can be expensive. Contact Vancouver's TouristInfo Centre (➤ 34) or the Whistler Infocentre (tel: 604/935-3357) for further information.
✚ 198 A2 🔢 604/932-3928; www.whistler.com

Insider Tip

Vancouver

Where to...
Stay

Prices
Expect to pay per double room per night excluding breakfast and taxes:
$ under CDN$100 $$ CDN$101–$200 $$$ CDN$201–$300 $$$$ over CDN$300

Barclay House $$
From the first sight of its bright exterior, this heritage-home bed-and-breakfast at the West End is simply stunning. Its character sets off interior furnishings and decor that are luxurious, ultramodern and supremely stylish. Most of the bedrooms have a personal lounge area, and all come with bathrobes, quality toiletries, coffee maker, WiFi, and much more. Continental and hot breakfasts are available.

➕ 204 C3
✉ 1351 Barclay Street at Jervis Street, V6E 1H6
☎ 604/605-1351 or toll free 1-800/971-1351; www.barclayhouse.com

The Fairmont Hotel Vancouver
$$$–$$$$
The 556-room Canadian Pacific Hotel Vancouver has been a prominent fixture of the city's central downtown area for many years. Although now somewhat overshadowed by newcomers on the waterfront like the Fairmont Waterfront (▶ right), it is the accommodation of choice if you prefer a luxury hotel with a more traditional feel. Modernization has added 21st-century amenities, such as internet access and spa. Superior Entrée Gold rooms offer still more comfort and services. General facilities include a health club with indoor swimming pool, whirlpool, sauna and massage.

➕ 205 D3
✉ 900 West Georgia Street, V6C 2W6
☎ 604/684-3131 or 1-866/540-4452; www.fairmont.com/hotel-vancouver

The Fairmont Waterfront
$$$–$$$$
The 23-story hotel popularly known as "The Waterfront" forms part of the spectacular Canada Place development (▶ 60). About 70 percent of its 489 rooms enjoy views over the port and Burrard Inlet to the mountains above North Vancouver. Staff are friendly and knowledgeable and rooms are stylishly appointed with blond-wood furnishings and modern Canadian art. Facilities include a restaurant, health club and outdoor pool, but it's the views and fabulous location that make this one of the city's foremost hotels.

➕ 205 E3 ✉ 900 Canada Place Way, V6C 3L5
☎ 604/691-1991 or toll free 1-866/540-4509; www.fairmont.com/waterfront-vancouver

Four Seasons $$$$
This 372-room hotel sits at the top of the Pacific Centre mall (▶ 83). Behind its anonymous entrance lies a luxurious interior. Rooms are fairly small, but more spacious deluxe rooms and suites are also available. The health club, swimming pool and fitness centre are the best of any hotel in the city. Attention is paid to the tiniest of details – children get milk and cookies at bedtime, and pets have mineral water.

➕ 205 D2 ✉ 791 West Georgia Street, V6C 2T4
☎ 604/689-9333; toll free 1-800/819-5053; www.fourseasons.com/vancouver

Listel Hotel $$–$$$
The Listel lies at the heart of West End Vancouver and is an attractive

boutique hotel that has great style in everything from amenities to contemporary coastal artwork. The amenities include free WiFi and long-distance calls and the trendy in-house restaurant, Forage, serving BC's best regional cuisine made with fresh local produce.

🚩 205 off D3
✉ 1300 Robson Street at Jarvis Street, V6E 1C5
☎ 604/684-8461 or toll free 1-800/663-5491; www.thelistelhotel.com

Sandman Hotel Vancouver City Centre $$–$$$

Sandman is a good mid-price chain group. Its 302-room Vancouver hotel lies a little to the east of the main downtown area, close to the Vancouver Library and the Queen Elizabeth Theatre, but it is still within comfortable walking distance of Gastown (➤ 72) and the central sights. Rooms are predictable and comfortable in the manner of a chain hotel – some of them include kitchenettes. Facilities include a couple of restaurants, a sauna and indoor swimming pool and whirlpool.

🚩 205 E2
✉ 180 West Georgia Street, V6B 4P4
☎ 604/681-2211; toll free 1-800/726-3626; www.sandmanhotels.ca

Sylvia Hotel $$

The Sylvia has a reputation for being hip and bohemian, thanks to its restful, laid-back and faintly arty look and atmosphere; to its trendy address – on the beach at English Bay near Stanley Park and Denman Street; and to its appearance – it's an eight-story, ivy-covered mansion in attractive weathered gray stone.

Built in 1912 as an apartment building and named for the builder's daughter, this is one of the city's oldest buildings and was western Canada's tallest structure until World War II. The beachside bar, which opened in 1954, was Vancouver's first cocktail bar. The 120 rooms are competitively priced – another reason for its popularity – and decorated in a variety of styles from each of the last four decades of the 20th century. The best are on the upper floors (which have great views), and there are 18 suites with kitchens that are suitable for families. The rooms in the 1980s annex are a little smarter, but have less period appeal. The hotel is a fair walk or bus ride to central downtown. To stay here in summer you'll need to make a reservation many weeks in advance.

🚩 204 B3 ✉ 1154 Gilford Street, V6G 2P6
☎ 604/681-9321; www.sylviahotel.com

Holiday Inn Hotel & Suites Vancouver Downtown $$$

This modern, 245-room (plus 28 suites) hotel is not as central as some downtown accommodations, but it is convenient for the shops, bars and restaurants of Yaletown and Granville Island. It is also better-positioned than similar nearby chain hotels such as the cheaper Howard Johnson Hotel Downtown on the less attractive southern reaches of Granville Street. Room rates vary considerably, but are relatively high for the chain and the location, though the higher rates buy numerous facilities, including a swimming pool, sauna, children's activity centre, as well as the option of rooms with well-equipped kitchenettes for self-catering.

🚩 205 D2
✉ 1110 Howe Street between Davie and Helmcken streets, V6Z 1R2 ☎ 604/684-2151 or 1-800/663-9151 in the US and Canada; www.holidayinnvancouverdowntown.com

BED-AND-BREAKFAST

For information on bed-and-breakfast options check out the BC Breakfast Innkeepers' Guild (www.bcsbestbnbs.com) or visit www.bedandbreakfast.com or www.bbcanada.com, which has links to some 10,000 bed-and-breakfasts.

Where to…
Eat and Drink

Prices
Expect to pay for a three-course meal for two, excluding drinks and service
$ under CDN$50 $$ CDN$50–$100 $$$ over CDN$100

RESTAURANTS

Bishop's $$$
Bishop's has topped just about every Vancouver restaurant poll for many years and is where the celebrities dine. Don't let this discourage you, though, as restaurants of this class and caliber ensure that everyone receives a warm and professional welcome. The food is described as "contemporary home cooking," which in practice means a modern fusion of a whole range of cuisines – Italian, French, West Coast and Far Eastern. Note that it's some way from downtown, in the northeast corner of 4th and Yew, and you'll need to make a reservation a long time in advance.

➕ 204 A1 ✉ Kitsilano, 2183 West 4th Avenue near Yew Street, V6K 1N7
☎ 604/738-2025; www.bishopsonline.com
🕐 Daily 5:30–11

Blue Water Café + Raw Bar $$

This large and pleasantly bustling restaurant is a fixture of the Yaletown dining scene. It owes its success to the food – high-quality sushi, fish, and seafood – and to the friendly, unpretentious service and setting. The main room is a long, low-lit space of exposed beams and brick, with an open kitchen that provides the main menu. There's also a less expensive "raw" bar for smaller dishes and an ice bar for chilled vodka, fresh fruit juices and other drinks. The restaurant is a member of the Ocean Wise initiative (➤ 29).

➕ 205 D2 ✉ 1095 Hamilton Street at Helmcken Street, V6B 5T4
☎ 604/688-8078; www.bluewatercafe.net
🕐 Restaurant daily 5–11 (late menu to midnight), bar 6:30pm–1am

Cactus Club Café $
Vancouver's 15 or so Cactus Club restaurants are the latest in a line of excellent mid- and low-price price chain outlets that include Earls (➤ 79), Milestone's (➤ 106), and White Spot (➤ 74, 80).

Key to its success are the excellent dining rooms – which are invariably bold and contemporary while remaining warm, romantic, and inviting – and the reliably good West Coast Coast food that is served along with popular staple dishes from Italy, Mexico and Asia.

➕ 205 D3
✉ 1136 Robson Street at Thurlow Street, V6E 1B2
☎ 604/687-3278
➕ 205 D2
✉ 357 Davie Street at Hamilton Street, V6B 1R2
☎ 604/685-8070; www.cactusclubcafe.com
🕐 Daily 11am–late

Café Medina $
This restaurant takes no reservations and always has a long line of guests waiting outside because it is one of the best breakfast and brunch spots in town. Try the delicious cassoulet with homemade sausage or Israeli couscous with toasted almonds and marinated beets. Everything is made with organic ingredients and spices that are locally sourced.

+ 205 D2 ✉ 780 Richards Street, V6B 3A4
☎ 604/879-3114; www.medinacafe.com
🕐 Mon–Fri 8–3, Sat, Sun 9–3

Cardero's $$

In a great setting, on the inner harbour waterfront just off the Stanley Park Seawall, Cardero's offers an interesting menu of mostly seafood dishes. Starters might include mussels in lemongrass, coconut curry sauce, honey molasses back ribs or a fishermen's platter that's perfect for sharing. After that, there are wok dishes, salads, chops and steaks, pasta, pizzas, and the house specialties: cedar-plank salmon, cooked in the wood oven, and baked lobster with lemon drawn butter.

+ 204 C3
✉ 1583 Coal Harbour Quay, V6G 3E7
☎ 604/669-7666; www.vancouverdine.com
🕐 Daily 11:30am–midnight

Chambar $$

For more than 10 years this restaurant has been the place to go to for a relaxed, fine dining experience and in that time Chambar's cuisine has remained impossible to define. Moroccan, French, and Asian influences make dishes such as Thon Frit (tuna with tamarind and jalapeno pistou) or Moules Congolaise (mussels with coconut cream and smoked chilli) delicious discoveries that befit this multi-cultural city.

+ 205 E2
✉ 568 Beatty Street, V6B 2L3
☎ 604 8 79 71 19; www.chambar.com
🕐 Daily 5pm–11pm; breakfast Mon–Fri 8–11:30; brunch Sat, Sun 8–3

CinCin $$

Steps lead up from Robson Street into a locals' favourite, a tasteful oasis with terracotta tiles, muraled walls, a scattering of statues and an open kitchen with alderwood-fired grill that adds subtle flavours to meat, fish and game. The food is mainly Italian – *cin cin* is Italian for "cheers" – but you can also choose between paella and a variety of other international dishes. The bar is open between meals for antipasti (appetizers) and pizza from the wood-fired oven. Wines are excellent, and all pastries, bread and ice cream are home-made.

+ 205 D3
✉ 1154 Robson Street near Bute Street, V6E 1B5
☎ 604/688-7338; www.cincin.net
🕐 Restaurant and bar 5pm–midnight; late menu 11pm–midnight

Le Crocodile $$–$$$

Cooking at Le Crocodile looks to hearty French bistro traditions merged with BC-sourced ingredients to produce such dishes as Provençal-style slow-braised lamb shank, fresh fettuccine with grilled tiger prawns and lobster meat, and rich, calorie-laden desserts. Standards are high and the clientele smart.

+ 205 D2 ✉ 100–909 Burrard Street (entrance on Smithe Street), V6Z 2N2
☎ 604/ 669-4298;
www.lecrocodilerestaurant.com
🕐 Mon–Sat 11:30–2, 5:30–10

Dockside Restaurant and Brewing Company $$

The popular and bustling Dockside is part of the Granville Island Hotel. There's a wood grill serving up delicious steaks or, if you're there for dinner, you can settle for the finest salmon. If you are there earlier in the day, the Dockside also caters for breakfast and lunch as well. There's a waterfront patio, floor to ceiling windows and a big aquarium to entertain.

Insider Tip

+ 205 D2 ✉ 1253 Johnston Street, Granville Island, V6H 3R9
☎ 604/685-7070; www.docksidevancouver.com
🕐 Daily 7am–10pm

Earls Restaurant on Top $–$$

Wherever you find an Earl's – and there's one in most western Canadian towns – you're guaranteed

Vancouver

a good, mid-priced meal in the company of happy locals. The Earl's in Vancouver enjoys a central location on Robson Street, the city's main thoroughfare. Service is brisk, staff are enthusiastic, the atmosphere buzzy but not too buzzy, and the eclectic menu contains ideas borrowed from Italian, North American, Mexican and Far Eastern cuisines.

🚌 205 off D3 ✉ 1185 Robson Street, corner of Bute Street, V6E 1B5
☎ 604/669-0020; www.earls.ca
🕙 Daily 11:30am–1am

The Flying Pig $

Relaxed bistro-style restaurant in the heart of Gastown serving delicious seasonal dishes such as pan seared Haida Gwaii halibut and maple and mustard pork rack. Also a popular weekend brunch spot.

🚌 205 E3 ✉ 102 Water Street
☎ 604/559-7968; www.theflyingpigvan.com
🕙 Daily 11:30am–midnight

Lombardo's Ristorante Pizzeria $

Don't be deterred by the mall location. You'll be rewarded with crispy brick-oven pizzas that have been rated the best in Vancouver. There are also pasta dishes, salads and sandwiches. Carry-out is available.

🚌 Off map
✉ 120–1641 Commercial Drive, V5L 3A4
☎ 604/251-2240; www.lombardos.ca
🕙 Mon–Sat 11–11, Sun 11–10

Pink Pearl Chinese Restaurant $

No visit to Vancouver is complete without a Chinese meal, and the Pink Pearl – though east of downtown (take a cab) – is one of the most authentic places to go. It's been in business for over 25 years, and you can expect to eat in the company of Chinese–Canadian families in a busy but fun atmosphere. Food has a Cantonese slant, and dim sum is a good bet, with excellent clams in black-bean sauce and spicy prawns, among

many other options. Service is brisk and often unsmiling, but efficient.

🚌 205 off F2 ✉ 1132 East Hastings Street near Glen Drive, V6A 1S2
☎ 604/253-4316; www.pinkpearl.com
🕙 Daily 9am–10pm

Water Street Café $

Like any tourist area, Gastown has its share of bland or uninspiring cafés and restaurants. The Water Street Café is a notable exception. Right on the main street near the famous steam clock, it has a pleasant patio eating area for good weather (book ahead to be sure of a place here or by the windows inside) and good tasty bistro-style food. You can sample creative pastas, super-fresh seafood (great oysters), the homemade focaccia and daily specials.

🚌 205 E3
✉ 300 Water Street at Cambie Street, V6B 1B6
☎ 604/689-2832; www.waterstreetcafe.ca
🕙 11:30–11pm or later

West $$–$$$

West's decor is chic modern, with leather-panelled walls, mirrors and subtle lighting complementing the intimate dining experience and the superlative West Coast cuisine. Start with fresh seared scallops or a warm salad of Vancouver Island octopus, beetroot, potato and cucumber. Follow with mains such as Fraser Valley veal tenderloin or grilled lobster. There are also three tasting menus, including vegetarian. The wine list is suitably outstanding.

🚌 204 C3 ✉ 2881 Granville Street near West 13th Ave, V64 3J4
☎ 604/738-8938; www.westrestaurant.com
🕙 Mon–Sat 11:30–11, Sun 5:30–11

White Spot $–$$

This restaurant chain has branches across Vancouver and western Canada (www.whitespot.com). Dishes on offer are basically high-quality fast food, and offer superb value, variety and reliability. The

Insider Tip

surroundings are also bright and modern, with a touch of style. Standards of service are equally good. These restaurants are excellent for families. *Insider Tip*

🔲 204 C3 ✉ 1616 West Georgia Street at Cardero Street, V6G 2V5
☎ 604/681-8034 🕓 Daily 6:30am–11pm

CAFÉS & BARS

The Backstage Lounge

For something a touch quieter on Granville Island try the Backstage Lounge, part of the Arts Club theatre complex. The food's good and there's live music some nights.

🔲 204 C1
✉ 1585 Johnson Street, Granville Island
☎ 604/687-1354; www.thebackstagelounge.com
🕓 Mon–Sat noon–2am, Sun noon–midnight

Bodega on Main

This is an updated and contemporary version of the long-established La Bodega Spanish bar and lounge, which is has moved to Main Street. The tapas are still the best in the city and deservedly popular, but most people come here to drink and chat.

🔲 205 F2 ✉ 1014 Main Street, V6A 2W1
☎ 604 5658815; www.bodegaonmain.ca
🕓 Mon–Fri 11am–midnight, Sat, Sun from 4:30pm

The Diamond

Located not far from Maple Leaf Square in Gastown, The Diamond is one of the coolest cocktail bars in the city. The first floor space was once a brothel but today bartenders serve the most unusual cocktails, including the Sazerac, one of the oldest cocktails in the world.

🔲 205 F3 ✉ 6 Powell Street, Gastown
☎ 604/209-7490; www.di6mond.com
🕓 Mon–Thu 5:30pm–1am, Fri, Sat until 2am, Sun until midnight

Caffè Artigiano

The baristas here "paint" motifs on the final pour of your latte or cappuccino with deceptive skill.

Brick laid tables and Italian decor enhance the creative vibe and there's an outside patio. Tasty snacks and cakes are available.

🔲 205 D2 ✉ 763 Hornby Street (and branches at 1101 West Pender Street, 740 West Hastings Street, 574 Granville Street
☎ 604/694-7737; www.cafesrtiggiano.com
🕓 Hornby Street: Mon–Fri 5:30am–9pm, Sat, Sun 6:30am–8pm

Gallery Café

The café at the Vancouver Art Gallery (►63) is a great central place for coffee, lunch or snacks whether you're visiting the gallery or not. It also has a restful garden patio.

🔲 205 D2
✉ Vancouver Art Gallery, 750 Hornby Street
☎ 604/688-2233; www.thegallerycafe.ca
🕓 Mon, Wed, Fri 9–6, Tue, Thu 9–9, Sat 9:30–6, Sun 10–6

900 West

The restaurant, big bar and wine bar of the central Fairmont Hotel Vancouver (►76) is a favourite place to meet for a drink or snack. Fifty wines are available by the glass.

🔲 205 D3 ✉ 900 West Georgia Street
☎ 604/669-9378 🕓 Sun–Thu 11:30am–midnight, Fri, Sat 11:30am–1am

Sylvia

The bar in the Sylvia Hotel (►77) is low key, but that's one of the things that make it popular. Close to the beach, it's a relaxing place for a rendezvous and a quiet drink.

🔲 204 B3 ✉ Sylvia Hotel, 1154 Gilford Street
☎ 604/681-9321; www.sylviahotel.com
🕓 Daily 11:30am–midnight

Yaletown Brewing Company

A vast pub-restaurant-brewery on a sizable part of the Yaletown district.

🔲 205 D2 ✉ 1111 Mainland Street
☎ 604/681-2739;
www.markjamesgroup.com/yaletown
🕓 Daily 11:30am–midnight
(and Thu until 1am, Fri, Sat until 3am)

Where to...
Shop

INDIGENOUS ART STORES

Coastal Peoples Fine Arts Gallery
This leading gallery showcases the art of the Northwest Coast First Nations. A light, airy space, it sells artworks and artifacts by established and emerging artists. It is particularly recommended for its exquisite gold, silver and other jewellery.

➕ 205 E3 ✉ 312 Water Street
☎ 604/684-9222; www.coastalpeoples.com
🚌 2, 15, 17

Hill's Native Art
This is the largest of four Hill's galleries, with three floors of First Nations arts and crafts, including a huge range of clothing, Inuit sculptures, jewellery, carvings, blankets, drums and books. Everything in the store has been purchased direct from the artist or artisan. Worldwide shipping is available.

➕ 205 E3 ✉ 165 Water Street
☎ 604/685-4249; www.hillsnativeart.com
🕐 Daily 9–9 🚌 1 or 50 🚉 Waterfront

Inuit Gallery of Canada
This gallery has been a Gastown fixture for years, its exhibits representing some of the best Inuit and other aboriginal art in Canada. Prices are high – justifiably so, given the quality – but even if you can't afford to make a purchase it's worth coming here just to look.

➕ 205 E3 ✉ 206 Cambie Street, Gastown
☎ 604/688-7323; www.inuit.com 🚌 1 or 50

FOOD MARKETS

Granville Island Public Market
This is one of North America's finest food markets – visit even if you just look at the stunning displays of meat, fish, cheese, fruit, wine and specialist food. Buy lunch and eat outdoors overlooking False Creek.

➕ 204 C1 ✉ Granville Island
☎ 604/666-5784; www.granvilleisland.com
🕐 Daily 9–7 🚌 50, 51

Lonsdale Quay Market
A trip across Burrard Inlet is an essential part of a visit to Vancouver. The ferry docks at Lonsdale Quay just steps away from this market. Not quite as impressive as Granville Island's food hall, it is still a great place to explore and eat with views over the water. Craft, book and gift stores are on the upper levels.

➕ 200 off C5 ✉ Lonsdale Quay, 123 Carrie Cates Court, North Vancouver
☎ 604/985-6261; www.lonsdalequay.com
🕐 Daily 9–7 🚢 SeaBus from Waterfront

SPECIALTY STORES

Chapters
This huge modern bookstore has forced traditional Vancouver bookstores from the city centre. Big, bright and browser-friendly with a vast stock of books and helpful staff. Make this your first stop in the city for all books, maps and guides.

➕ 205 D2 ✉ 788 Robson Street, corner of Howe ☎ 604/682-4066; www.chapters.ca
🕐 Daily 9am–10pm 🚌 5, 17, 20 on Robson

Chintz & Company
This large store just north of trendy Yaletown is crammed with treasures for the home: fabrics, furnishings, accessories, giftware and antique or original beds, wardrobes, tables and other pieces of furniture. It also sells smaller items such as candles, lamps and assorted objets d'art.

➕ 205 D2 ✉ 950 Homer Street
☎ 604/689-2022 or 1-888/648-0889;
www.chintz.com 🚌 2, 15, 17

Edible British Columbia
Based in Granville Public Market, and fast-growing in popularity, this unique take on sustainability offers terrific local produce from best

wines to preserves, spices and sauces. It also does take-out meals.

🏠 204 C1 ✉ 565, 1596 Johnston Street
☎ 604/558-0040; www.ediblecanada.com
🚌 51

Lululemon Athletica

Fashion meets fitness at this temple to stylish tech clothing for yoga, dance and running. And you don't need to be a sports fanatic to look good in the svelte range that includes tank tops and hoodies, yoga pants, running hats, tote bags and many other accessories.

🏠 205 D3 ✉ 970 Robson Street
☎ 604/681-3118; www.lululemon.com

MacLeod's Books

Independent MacLeod's stubbornly – and successfully – defends itself against the digital tide with its dizzying selection of rare collector's editions (and with tacky mass produced books) that are stacked here in shelves that go right up to the ceiling.

🏠 205 E3 ✉ 455 West Pender Street
☎ 604/681-7654
🕐 Mon–Sat 10–6, Sun 11–6 🚌 22

Murchie's Tea & Coffee

Vancouverites have been coming to Murchie's for their tea and coffee for more than a century. It also sells china, crystal and a selection of teapots and coffeemakers.

🏠 205 D3 ✉ 825 West Pender Street
☎ 604/669-0783; www.murchies.com 🚌 8

Seafood City

This one-stop salmon outlet offers great products, including delicious wild sockeye smoked salmon and even smoked-salmon candy soaked in maple syrup and sprinkled with black pepper. For take-home gifts the best bet is salmon jerky, long-smoked and with a long shelf life.

🏠 204 C1
✉ 1689 Johnston Street (Granville Island)
☎ 604/688-1818; www.seafoodcitygi.com
🕐 Daily 9–7 🚌 50, 51

MALLS & DEPARTMENT STORES

Hudson's Bay

The chain is a direct descendent of the trading post of the Hudson's Bay Company. Its Vancouver store is in a tired-looking, period building but the merchandise is of high quality.

🏠 205 D2 ✉ 674 Granville Street at West Georgia Street ☎ 604/681-6211; www.thebay.com 🚇 Granville 🚌 8

The Landing

The Landing, housed in a 1905 warehouse, is a small mall conveniently located in Gastown. It contains mainly upmarket food, souvenir stores and designer outlets, notably Roger's Chocolates and Jade.

🏠 205 E3 ✉ 389 Water Street ☎ 604/453-5050; www.vancouverkiosk.ca/the-landing.php

Pacific Centre Mall

One of Vancouver's best malls, this three-block affair has more than 200 shops and links underground to the Vancouver Centre mall at 650 West Georgia Street, which has a further 115 stores.

🏠 205 D2 ✉ 609 Granville Street
☎ 604/688-7235; www.cfshops.com/pacific-centre.html 🚇 Granville

Holt Renfrew

The Vancouver branch of the Canadian chain of high-end department stores has everything that the sophisticated shopper is accustomed to, including wares by Canadian fashion designers such as Wayne Clark, Trout and Lida Baday.

🏠 205 D3 ✉ 737 Dunsmuir Street at Granville Street ☎ 604/681-3121; www.holtrenfrew.com
🕐 Mon, Tue 10–7, Wed–Fri 10–9, Sat 10–7, Sun 11–6 🚇 Granville

Sinclair Centre

This sophisticated mall combines four converted historic buildings. Stores include fashion and accessories. There is a food court.

🏠 205 E3 ✉ 757 West Hastings Street
☎ 604/488-0672; www.sinclaircentre.com
🕐 Mon–Sat 10–5:30 🚇 Waterfront

Where to...
Go Out

CLASSICAL MUSIC

The **Vancouver Symphony Orchestra** (tel: 604/876-3434; www.vancouversymphony.ca) generally performs at the Orpheum Theatre (801 Granville Street).

The **Vancouver Opera** (tel: 604/683-0222; www.vancouver opera.ca) holds its October–June season of performances at the Queen Elizabeth Complex (600 Hamilton Street).

Smaller but well-respected-ensembles include the **Vancouver Chamber Choir** (tel: 604/738-6822; www.vancouverchamberchoir. com); **Early Music Vancouver** (tel: 604/732-1610; www.earlymusic. bc.ca); **Vancouver Recital Society** (tel: 604/602-0363; www.vanrecital. com); and the **Vancouver New Music Society** (tel: 604/663-0861; www.newmusic.org).

THEATRE

A popular theatre company is the **Arts Club Theatre** (tel: 604/687-1644; www.artsclub.com) on Granville Island, which has a

425-seat main auditorium and smaller Revue Stage.

Also popular in summer are the **Bard on the Beach** (▶ 32; tel: 604/739-0559 or 1-877/739-0559; www.bardonthebeach.org) outdoor shows in Vanier Park (early June to late Sep).

There are many fringe companies: look out for productions at the **Firehall Arts Centre** (280 East Cordova Street; tel: 604/689-0926; www.firehallartscentre.ca).

CINEMAS

The most central multiplex screens are on Granvillet. For classic, foreign and alternative films, try the **Pacific Cinémathèque** (1131 Howe Street; tel: 604/688-8202; www.cinematheque.ca), also the HQ of the **Vancouver International Film Festival** (late Sep to mid-Oct; tel: 604/685-0260; www.viff.org).

CLUBS & LIVE MUSIC

Vancouver's club, dance and music scene is vibrant, which means the coolest places change regularly.

At **Caprice Nightclub** (967 Granville Street; tel: 604/685-3288, www.capricenightclub. com) there is live music as well as DJs playing the latest top hits and electro music.

For live music, visit the **Roxy** (932 Granville Street; tel: 604/331-7999; www.roxyvan.com) or the **Commodore** (868 Granville Street at Mithe Street; tel: 604/739-4550; www.commodore ballroom.ca).

Fashionable venues include nightclub **Bar None** (1222 Hamilton Street; tel: 604/689-7000; http://donnellygroup.ca/bar-none) and stylish bar **Afterglow** (1082 Hamilton Street at Helmcken Street; tel: 604/602-0835; www. glowbalgrill.com).

INFORMATION & TICKETS

The main listings magazines are the weekly *Georgia Straight* (www.straight. com) and monthly *Vancouver Magazine*, both free from bookstores, libraries, venues and curbside boxes (www. vanmag.com). Half-price and last-minute, same-day tickets are available via **Tickets Tonight** outlets (www.tickets tonight.ca) including the main visitor centre (▶ 34). Or buy tickets for many events through **Ticketmaster** (www. ticketmaster.ca).

Victoria

 **Little Treats**

Tasty Memories

The Bengal Lounge at the **Empress Hotel** (➤ 104) scores points with its Victorian splendour – and the best curry buffet in town.

Early Evening in Tofino

There is a particularly peaceful atmosphere on the **pier at the harbour** at sunset as the sun sinks into the sea (➤ 92).

A Water Taxi to Hot Springs Cove

Treat yourself to a relaxing soak in the thermal springs in **Maquinna Provincial Parks** (➤ 92).

Getting Your Bearings

Victoria has evolved from its longstanding incarnation as a Little England overseas into a vibrant cosmopolitan city. Its role as the capital of British Columbia is belied by its modest size and absence of urban angst, overwhelming skyscrapers or frantic traffic. Life revolves around the natural harbour and between the stately enclave of the Parliament Buildings and the attractive downtown area around Government Street.

To some extent, of course, Victoria still promotes a rather stagy Britishness overlaid with sentimentality. Never has there been a taller, more elegant makeover of Queen Victoria than the statue that stands in front of the Parliament Buildings. Expensive afternoon tea is still a major feature of the Empress Hotel and the Union Jack flag still pops up here and there. But modern Victoria is a unique Canadian city that mixes the best of tradition with up-to-date style and that boasts outstanding attractions.

Foremost among these are the Royal British Columbia Museum, one of Canada's finest museums, and the glorious Butchart Gardens, but the city is equally renowned for its whale-watching, its mellow climate, its fine cafés and restaurants and – best of all – the pedestrian-friendly appeal of its old-fashioned streets and hidden historic corners.

0   400 m
0   400 yd

Government St.

Douglas St.

Blanshard St.

Centennial
Square

Market
Square

Johnson St.
Bridge

Johnson St.

Douglas St.

St.

Art Gallery of Greater Victoria 26
Craigdarroch Castle 29 →

Inner
Harbour

Wharf St.

Government St.

Old Town 21

Blanshard

Pioneer
Square

Pioneer
Square

an's Wharf

**Miniature
World** 25

Burdett Ave.

Belleville St.

Humboldt St.

**Royal British
Columbia Museum** 22

Helmcken House 27

Superior St.

St.

Southgate St.

St.

Government

Simcoe St.

Toronto St.

Douglas St.

Goodacre
Lake

28

Beacon Hill Park

Victoria

Two Perfect Days

If you're not quite sure where to begin your travels, this itinerary recommends a practical and enjoyable two-day tour of Victoria, taking in some of the best places to see. For more information see the main entries (➤ 90–103).

Day 1

Morning
Walk to the ⭐**Inner Harbour** (➤ 90) first and call in at the Visitor Centre. If you'd like to go **whale watching**, book a trip here for the afternoon or following afternoon. Spend the morning exploring the Inner Harbour and the ㉑**Old Town** (➤ 94). You could squeeze in the ㉒**Royal British Columbia Museum** (➤ 96) – particularly if you're whale-watching on a boat on day 2– but it's best kept for the afternoon if you're not going whale-watching, or for the morning of day 2.

Lunch
For a light lunch, try the **Rebar** (➤ 107) or a café such as **Murchie's Tea & Coffee** (➤ 107).

Afternoon
Devote the afternoon either to a whale-watching trip or the Royal British Columbia Museum, and if you choose the latter consider a break from sightseeing with tea in the **Empress Hotel** (above; ➤ 104) or, if that's too expensive, in the museum's own attractive café.

Evening
Take an early dinner close to the Inner Harbour Good but busy choices in town are **Il Terrazzo** (➤ 106) and **Pagliacci's** (➤ 106). If the weather's fine spend time after dinner wandering around the Inner Harbour to take in the sunset, the people-watching opportunities and the street performers.

Pacific Rim National Park

Butchart Gardens ㉓

Day 2

Inner Harbour
Art Gallery of Greater Victoria **26**
Craigdarroch Castle **29**
Old Town **21**
Miniature World **25**
Royal British Columbia Museum **22**
Helmcken House **27**
Fisherman's Wharf
Beacon Hill Park **28**

Morning
After a whale-watching trip or a visit to the **22** Royal British Columbia Museum (▶ 96), look around **27** Helmcken House (▶ 102) just outside in Thunderbird Park. If you are traveling with children, explore the **24** Miniature World (▶ 101).

Lunch
Take lunch in the Museum Café, or eat in one of the Old Town's harbour side pubs or cafés (▶ 107). Better still, eat a picnic on Inner Harbour or in Beacon Hill Park.

Afternoon
Spend the afternoon whale-watching – most trips take about three hours – or visit the **23** Butchart Gardens (▶ 99), devote an hour or two to strolling in **28** Beacon Hill Park (▶ 102) or visit other more outlying sights such as **29** Craigdarroch Castle (▶ 103).

Evening
Return to Vancouver or enjoy a leisurely dinner in one of Victoria's restaurants before continuing your travels the next day.

☷ WHALE-WATCHING COMPANIES
- **Eagle Wing Whale Watching Tours** (tel: 250/384-8008, toll free 1-800/708-9488; www.eaglewingtours.com)
- **Five Star Whale Watching** (tel: 250/388-7223 or toll free 1-800/634-9617; www.5starwhales.com)
- **Orca Spirit** (tel: 250/383-8411 or toll free 1-888/672-6722; www.orcaspirit.com)
- **Prince of Whales Whale Watching** (tel: 250/383-4884, toll free 1-888/383-4884; www.princeofwhales.com)
- **SpringTide Whale Watching & Eco Tours** (tel: 250/384-4444, toll free 1-800/470-3474; www.victoriawhalewatching.com)

Victoria

⭐3 Inner Harbour

The lovely Inner Harbour is the heart of Victoria, a sweeping water-front that contains several of the city's best-known landmarks – the Empress Hotel, Parliament Buildings and Royal British Columbia Museum – but is equally pleasant just to wander, particularly in the evening, when the gardens and promenades are full of people and street entertainers.

Early Settlement
The harbour area was Victoria's focus from earliest times. The region's original Salish people lived in 10 scattered villages, and it was the site's perfect anchorage as well as its beautiful natural surroundings that persuaded James Douglas, head of the powerful Hudson's Bay Company, to create a new headquarters for the company here in 1842. In time, a settlement grew up around the company fort. Initially named Fort Camosun, it was later renamed Fort Victoria to honour the British queen. During the 1850s, the settlement boomed on the back of the gold rush.

By the time the gold rush faded, Victoria was firmly on the map, and in 1866 was an obvious candidate for the capital of the new Crown Colony of British Columbia. The Colony of Vancouver Island and the mainland Colony of British Columbia were united in 1866 and the united colony was incorporation into the Canadian Confederation in 1871.

Explore the Area
First stop on any tour of Victoria should be the **Visitor Centre**, which has a wealth of information on the city, its surroundings and Vancouver Island in general. Spend some time exploring the harbour area and Old Town (►94) before seeing the Royal British Columbia Museum (►96). Opposite the Visitor Centre is a city landmark, the massive **Empress Hotel** (►104), which opened in 1908. Wander through some of the lobbies and lounges to soak up their colonial splendour. The veranda has fine views over the Inner Harbour, and the Crystal Ballroom and Bengal Lounge, with its conservatory filled with tropical plants, are worth seeking out.

Above: The Parliament Buildings are often illuminated at night

Parliament Buildings
A short walk away on the harbour's southern edge are the Parliament Buildings, BC's provincial legislature, as prominent a landmark as the Empress. The two structures were designed by Francis Rattenbury. Free and absorbing **guided tours** of the interior are available in summer, although, for most people, it's enough just to enjoy the gardens and the

Insider Tip

The Inner Harbour

exterior. Notice the **statue on top of the dome** – George Vancouver – and the two figures guarding the main door: One is Sir James Douglas, the other Judge Sir Matthew Baillie Begbie, who acquired the nickname of the "Hanging Judge" for his severity during the turbulent days of the gold rush.

TAKING A BREAK

If you want to take tea – one of Victoria's key rituals – you could try the **Empress Hotel's Tea Lobby**. It's expensive and touristy, however, and there's a dress code.

Visitor Centre

🞢 203 A4   ✉ 812 Wharf Street
☎ 250/953-2033; accommodations reservations toll free in Canada and the US 1-800/663-3883; www.tourismvictoria.com
🕙 May–Sep daily 8:30–8:30; Oct–Apr daily 9–5   🚌 5, 6, 27, 28, 30, 31

Parliament Buildings

🞢 203 A4   ✉ 501 Belleville Street   ☎ 250/387-3046 or toll free in BC 1-800/663-7867   🕙 Tours (45 minutes) Mon–Fri 8:30–5 but hours vary according to Parliament business   🚌 5, 27, 28 or 30   💲 Free

INSIDER INFO

- Be sure to visit the waterfront in the evening to watch the sun go down and enjoy the **street life**.
- Take a ride in one of the tiny **ferries** (tel: 250/708-0201; www.victoriaharbourferry.com) that buzz around the harbour.

Insider Tip

In more depth The upper promenade wall above the inner harbour features a series of fascinating plaques, known as the **"Parade of Ships"** that detail famous vessels and maritime events. A handsome statue of the great seaman James Cook holds centre stage. Hugely entertaining buskers perform nightly on the lower promenade.

★7 Pacific Rim National Park

Vancouver Island's national park is 319km (198mi) from Victoria – you need at least one or two nights here to do it justice – but its mountains, rain forest and wild coastal landscapes and whale-watching opportunities make it well worth a trip.

It stretches some 130km (81mi) along Vancouver Island's western coast and has three principal components: the Broken Group Islands, an archipelago of tiny islets only really accessible to sailors and kayakers; the West Coast Trail, an increasingly popular but tough long-distance footpath; and Long Beach, which stretches between Tofino to the north and Ucluelet to the south.

Tofino, the most attractive base, is at least a morning's drive or six-hour bus journey from Victoria (Ucluelet is as convenient but less picturesque). Prettily positioned looking out on Clayoquot Sound, the former fishing village is busy in the summer, its hotels full of visitors making trips.

Five basic boat trips (prices vary) are possible from the village, the closest being **Meares Island** (15 minutes by boat), whose ancient forests have long been the subject of bitter dispute between conservationists and logging companies. The Big Cedar Trail (3km/2mi) winds through some of the oldest and most impressive trees. Other boat and light plane excursions include the islands of **Flores** and **Vargas**, and to the popular thermal pools at Hot Springs Cove located in **Maquinna Provincial Park** in the Clayoquot Sound (see Tofino Infocentre).

A walking or driving trip you can organize yourself is down **Long Beach**, 16km (10mi) of crashing surf and empty sands backed by forest-clad mountains. The water's too cold for swimming, but the area is a favourite among beachcombers and hikers, who can wander virtually at random on the waterfront or follow one or more of eight trails – all 5km (3mi) or less and signposted from Highway 4 and the spur to Ucluelet, road links that back the beach for most of its length.

Drift logs washed up on Long Beach in Pacific Rim National Park

Insider Tip
But before doing anything else, visit the **Kwistis Visitor Centre** (May, Sep to mid-Oct daily 10–5; Jun to early Sep daily 8–7; Oct–Apr Tue–Sat 9–5), also signed off Highway 4, for information on the park and Insider Tip the trails. Some of the best paths take you to Florencia Beach (trails 1, 2, 3 and 5), also known as Wreck Beach, or to South Beach (trail 4), famed for its huge breakers.

Pacific Rim National Park

Also, be sure to walk up **Radar Hill** (96m/315ft) close to Tofino, which offers one of the region's best overall panoramas.

✚ 202 A1

National Park Visitor Centre
✉ Long Beach, off Highway 4
☎ 250/726-4212; www.pc.gc.ca
🕐 May, Sep to mid-Oct daily 10–5;
Jun to early Sep daily 8–7; Tue–Sat 9–5 rest of year
💲 Park fee: CDN$7.80

Relaxing in
Tofino's
thermal pools

Tofino Infocentre
✉ 455 Campbell Street ☎ 250/725-3414 or toll free 1-888/720-3414;
www.tourismtofino.com 🕐 May–Sep daily 9–8/9; Oct–Mar Mon–Fri 9–4

INSIDER INFO

- The best way to visit the **Broken Group Islands** is aboard the MV *Frances Barkley*, a freighter that makes more or less daily sailings year-round to Ucluelet or Bamfield (south of the Broken Group Islands). The boat leaves from Port Alberni, east of Long Beach, and takes all day to make the round trip. The excursions are very popular, so make reservations (tel: 250/723-8313; www.ladyrosemarine.com).
- If you want to walk the 77km (48mi) **West Coast Trail** you'll need to set aside seven to ten days and plan well in advance. Reservations are available in peak season (mid-Jun to mid-Sep) and can be made up to 90 days in advance (www.pc.gc.ca; tel: 250/387-1642 or 1-800/435-5622. Open: Mon–Fri 7am to 9pm from Apr–Sep). Anyone requiring an overnight permit must take part in one of the orientation sessions.

㉑ Old Town

Victoria is barely a city at all – which is one of its great charms –
but rather an intimate, old-fashioned-looking town with none of
the rigid street grids and high-rise buildings of most other North
American cities. Its most charming corners lie in the handful of
streets behind the Inner Harbour (▶ 90), notably Wharf, Government
and Douglas, just a few minutes' stroll away. For details of a walk
around the Old Town turn to the Walks section (▶ 183). Alternatively,
wander north from the Visitor Centre and harbour on Wharf Street
and begin your exploration in Bastion Square, an ensemble of old
streets and buildings built close to the site of the northeasternmost
bastion of the Hudson's Bay Company's original Fort Victoria.

Maritime Museum

Among the square's many
pretty buildings is the former provincial **courthouse**
(1889), site of the city jail
and the spot where public
hangings took place. These
days it plays host to the
Maritime Museum, home to
a good collection of model
boats, photographs, ships'
bells and other maritime
memorabilia. The old courthouse is on the top floor,
reached by a special open
elevator, which was com-
missioned by Chief Justice
Davie in 1901, reputedly
because he was too portly
to get up the stairs.

Market Square

From the museum, walk
to Government Street and
head north, turning left onto
Johnson Street and Market
Square (www.marketsquare.
ca). Today the latter is a
wonderfully restored period
complex filled with cafés,

A sculpture by
Luis Merino in
Market Square

restaurants and interesting little shops, but in 1858 it was
the turbulent heart of the Old Town. The square's central
courtyard area is sunk down, the depression marking the
site of a former ravine. To its north lay Chinatown, the oldest
such enclave in western North America. The whole area
was once filled with brothels, stores and opium dens, not to
mention some 23 factories that turned out around 44 tons
of opium a year (the trade, legal until the 20th century,

The Bridgman Building

constituted one of BC's most lucrative exports).

Chinatown

Today's Chinatown, off Fisgard Street, is smaller and tamer than in times past. Its best street is **Fan Tan Alley,** full of tiny stores: don't miss the two stone chimeras by the **Gate of Harmonious Interest**. They were a gift from Suzhou in China, and legend says they will come to life when an honest politician walks between them – they remain stubbornly petrified.

Government Street

Not much to the north of Fisgard Street is really worth the walk, so head south on Government Street or Wharf Street toward the **Inner Harbour** (▶90). Government Street is busier, and is lined with most of Victoria's major stores. Three, at least, are worth making a special point of seeing: **Old Morris Tobacconist** (www.oldmorris.com) at 1116 Government, a lovely old cigar and tobacco shop, little changed since it was founded in 1892; **Murchie's Tea & Coffee** (www.murchies.com), almost next door at 1110, which has been the source of Victoria's best tea, coffee, cakes and snacks since 1894; and at 1108 is **Munro's Books** (www.munrobooks.com), founded in 1963 by the writer and Nobel Prize winner Alice Munro and her husband Jim, certainly the most civilized bookstore in the city.

Insider Tip

TAKING A BREAK

The best place to relax over coffee, if the weather is good, is **Bastion Square,** where there are several cafés.

✚ 203 B4

Maritime Museum
✉ 28 Bastion Square
☎ 250/385-4222; www.mmbc.bc.ca
🕐 Sun–Wed, Fri, Sat 10–9
🍴 ReBar or Murchie's Tea & Coffee (▶107)
🚌 5
💰 Donation

㉒ Royal British Columbia Museum

This superb museum has been called the best in Canada and one of the top 10 in North America. Its displays embrace the myriad strands of BC's social, cultural and natural history, with emphasis on the province's aboriginal peoples and many natural habitats. It also hosts major touring exhibitions.

Visiting the Museum

You could easily spend a morning or more here, but to do the collection justice – and to escape the tortures of museum fatigue – it may be better to make two separate visits: one to the **Natural History Gallery** and **First Peoples Gallery**; the other to the **Modern History Gallery**. None of the galleries should really be missed.

Insider Tip

The Natural History Gallery

The Gallery opens in tremendous style – with a life-size woolly mammoth complete with ominous tusks. Behind it is a skilfully painted landscape evoking the animal's one-time domain, a device that sets the tone for the wonderfully evocative series of dioramas, or re-created landscapes of BC's many habitats, that follow.

Laid out before you in huge rooms are shorelines, delta landscapes and temperate, coastal, subalpine and boreal forest environments. Each has the animals, trees, vegetation – even the sounds and temperature – appropriate to the individual habitats. Linked with the displays is a welter of audio-visual information explaining the natural nuances of a province that contains Canada's warmest coastline – all 25,599km (15,906mi) of it – wettest mountains, deepest

A replica of part of HMS *Discovery* in the Modern History Gallery

snowfall and driest interior. Don't skip the film on the life of the beaver.

The **Ocean Station** focuses on the surprisingly colourful marine life of British Columbia. The gallery has been designed like a Captain Nemo-style submarine, complete with hatches and controls, from where visitors can peer through portholes at sea creatures and scan the underwater scene with a periscope. A huge hexagonal hatch looks out on a sea-wall diorama populated by all kinds of marine life, and there are lots of hands-on exhibits, from computer games to dry sea stars. The IMAX theatre has a companion film, *Deep Sea*, narrated by Johnny Depp and Kate Winslet.

Insider Tip

A re-created home brings the past to life

Just as memorable are the exhibits of the **First Peoples Gallery**. Many museums in North America tackle First Peoples, or aboriginal culture, but none as successfully as this one – the displays provide an account of the history and culture of the region's Pacific coastal peoples.

The exhibits divide into two sections: one relating to the era before the coming of European settlers, the second to the period after settlement, when aboriginal culture was devastated by disease and land treaties that remain controversial to this day. The thousands of exhibits are dimly lit, and the background colours deliberately muted, creating a reverential and occasionally sombre mood that seems somehow appropriate to the material displayed.

The highlights are numerous, but don't miss the short film footage from 1914 entitled *In the Land of the War Canoes* and the reconstructed plankhouse of Chief Kwakwabalasami, in which there's an excellent audio-visual display evoking shamanic, superstitious and other aboriginal beliefs through song, dance and costume. As a complement to this section, spend some time in **Thunderbird Park**, the ground in front of the museum. It contains a reproduction tribal "bighouse," or ceremonial hall, built in 1953, and several totems. The park is also home to Helmcken House (➤ 102).

Insider Tip

Victoria

The Modern History Gallery

The museum's third floor contains most of the Modern History Gallery, whose striking and extensive displays explore BC's history after the arrival of European settlers. The gallery is arranged in reverse chronological order.

A replica Chinatown street

If the arrangement of displays is somewhat eccentric, however, the displays themselves are superb. Numerous dioramas are used to fine effect, with tableaux that reproduce a full-size Victorian street, Chinatown, an old movie theatre, an early fish-canning factory and many more. All aspects of the province are explored, from farming and fishing to logging, mining and the gold rushes of the 19th century. Each theme is illustrated with a wealth of period artifacts, memorabilia and interesting audiovisual displays.

✚ 203 B3
✉ 675 Belleville Street
☎ 250/356-7226 or 1-888/447-7977; www.royalbcmuseum.bc.ca
🕐 Daily 10–5 🍴 Café ($) 🚌 5, 27, 28, 30, 31
💲 CDN$16 or CDN$25.95 with IMAX

INSIDER INFO

Insider Tip

- If time is limited, check whether your visit coincides with one of the 1.5-hour **Highlights** tours of the museum (four or five a month).
- **Wheelchairs and strollers** are available free of charge from the coat check.
- 🧩 **Kids' activity sheets** can be downloaded and printed from the website.
- Guided tours focussing on either the First Peoples Gallery, the Modern History Gallery or the Natural History Gallery are available on certain days.

㉓ Butchart Gardens

The Butchart Gardens lie about 21km (13mi) north of central Victoria, and represent the single most impressive gardens in a city that is often called the "City of Gardens." In 2006 they were designated a National Historic Site of Canada, and are unmissable, even if you have only a passing interest in things horticultural.

Wonderful borders run alongside paths in Butchart Gardens

The gardens were begun by Jenny Butchart to landscape an exhausted limestone quarry belonging to her husband, Robert Pim Butchart, a mine owner and one of the pioneers of Portland cement in Canada and the US. Jenny's earliest efforts resulted in the Sunken Gardens, opened to the public in 1904. Japanese, rose and Italian gardens soon followed. Today the site is run by the couple's grandson, covers some 22ha (55 acres), and attracts around 500,000 visitors a year.

The floral display is spectacular – you'll see glorious pictures of the gardens all over Victoria – and embraces around 700 different species and more than a million individual plants, trees and shrubs.

If you come here in the summer months you'll be able to enjoy various other attractions, especially at night when the gardens are illuminated. Entertainments include firework displays and nightly concerts or shows on the Lawn Stage.

TAKING A BREAK

There's a choice of three refreshment places: the in-expensive **Coffee Shop**, the **Blue Poppy** cafeteria and the smart **Dining Room restaurant** in the Butcharts' elegant former home.

➕ 202 C1 ✉ 800 Benvenuto Avenue, Brentwood Bay
☎ 250/652-4422; recorded information 250/652-5256; www.butchartgardens.com
🕐 Daily from 9am; hours adjusted seasonally 🍴 Coffee Shop ($), Blue Poppy Restaurant ($–$$), Dining Room ($$$) 🚌 75 Central Saanich; Gray Lines shuttle May–Oct (700 Douglas), Pacific Coach Lines mid-Apr to mid-Oct daily 9:30; tickets for both services include admission to gardens 💰 CDN$21–33

The Butchart Gardens are a brilliant spectacle at any time of the year

INSIDER INFO

- Be warned that **the gardens are busy** – late afternoons are generally the quietest time to visit during summer, except fireworks nights.
- Most of the plants are labelled, but it's well worth picking up **leaflets** (in 18 different languages) at the visitor centre.
- From mid-June until the end of September thousands of tiny lights illuminate the gardens during **specially extended evening opening times**. During the same period free musical and variety entertainments are held in the evenings from Monday to Saturday, while on Saturday evenings in July and August the gardens are the setting for spectacular **fireworks** displays.

- You should pay a visit to the on-site **Seed & Gift Store**, which, as well as selling seeds of some of the gardens' plants, has an impressive range of books, gardening imple-ments, cards, calendars, plant catalogues and numerous other gifts.

At Your Leisure

24 Fisherman's Wharf

Located just on the other side of Inner Harbour, Fisherman's Wharf is one of the favourite stops of the small Victoria Harbour Ferry. The old wharf is a vibrant mix of colourful houseboats, fishing boats coming and going, and a noisy colony of seals. There are some small local suppliers offering kayaking and whale watching excursions, such as Eagle Wing (► 89), and if you feel like having a snack or a meal there are handful of food stalls offering freshly caught fish and seafood.

🚇 203, west A3 ✉ 1 Dallas Road
ℹ http://fishermanswharfvictoria.com

25 Miniature World

Like Pacific Undersea Gardens, this is a children's favourite. In the Empress Hotel complex (► 104), its highlights are the world's largest dollhouse – a 50-room affair built in 1880 – and the world's longest model railroad. The latter compresses the 8,000km (5,000mi) of Canada's transcontinental railway into 34m (112ft). It took 12,000 working hours to build and cost $100,000. Other exhibits include miniature tableaux of famous battles, Charles Dickens' London, a circus and the Wild West.

🚇 203 B3 ✉ 649 Humboldt Street
☎ 250/385-9731; www.miniatureworld.com
🕐 May to early Sep daily 9–9;
early Sep–Apr daily 10–5
🚌 5, 27, 28 or 30
🍴 Empress Hotel ($$$)
🎟 CDN$15, children CDN$8

26 Art Gallery of Greater Victoria

Victoria's public gallery is a delightful venue and one of Canada's finest smaller art museums. It's located about 1.5km (1mi) inland to the east of the harbour but is an easy walk and there is a nearby bus connection. The gallery is housed in a modern complex attached to a handsome old mansion. There is a large permanent collection of art from Asia, Europe and North America, but the work on display is mainly from Canada and Japan. There is, inevitably, a focus on Emily Carr, the doyen of Canadian women artists, and the small, intimate Drury room at the heart of the gallery is devoted to her compelling paintings of the British Columbian wilderness. Typically dark, swirling works, such as *Lone Cedar*, are matched by such brighter, more optimistic works as *Brittany Coast*, 1911, reflecting Carr's time spent in Brittany and Cornwall. There is also a permanent exhibition of Japanese art. Primarily the gallery has a program of changing exhibitions, often of bold, innovative work by modern artists. The adjoining **Gyppeswick House** has period furnishings and a delightful small garden.

🚇 203 off C3 ✉ 1040 Moss Street
☎ 250/384-4171; www.aggv.bc.ca
🕐 Mid-May to early Sep Mon–Wed, Fri, Sat 10–5, Thu 10–9, Sun noon–5; early Sep to mid-May same hours but closed Mon
🚌 11 🎟 CDN$13

Insider Tip

Gulliver, one of Miniature World's intricate exhibits

Victoria

27 Helmcken House

Helmcken House is one of the oldest home on Vancouver Island. Located in the shadow of the Royal British Columbia Museum (▶96), it was built in 1852 by Dr John Helmcken, Fort Victoria's doctor, for his bride Cecilia, daughter of Governor James Douglas (who donated an acre of land to the couple). It's worth seeing for its pretty furniture, artifacts and Victorian knick-knacks.

Behind the house is the white **St Anne's Pioneer Schoolhouse**, former home to four Québec nuns who came to teach in Victoria in 1858. Admission is included with a Royal British Columbia Museum day ticket.

Insider Tip

✚ 203 B3 ✉ Thunderbird Park, Douglas and Belleville streets ☎ 250/361-0021
🕓 Visit the events calendar at www.royalbcmuseum.bc.ca/exhibits/tbird-park/html/early/earlhelm.htm for further details
🚌 5, 30, 31

28 Beacon Hill Park

Too many people miss Victoria's magnificent city park, despite the fact that it's only a few minutes' walk up the hill behind the Royal British Columbia Museum. This is one of North America's most appealing parks, not merely because of its pretty mixture of parkland, woods, leafy glades and open meadow, but also because it affords superlative views on its southern flanks across the Juan de Fuca Strait to Port Angeles at the foot of the Olympic Mountains of Washington State.

The 81ha (200-acre) park dates from a gift of land made by the Hudson's Bay Company to the city back in 1882. Like Vancouver's rambling Stanley Park (▶52), much of the area still has the feel of virgin forest, with some impressive stands of trees and lots of unkempt and semiwild areas where you can enjoy a real walk and quickly escape the hubbub and crowds of the Inner Harbour (▶90).

Inside Tip

Interspersed with these wilder corners are manicured lawns and flower beds – some 30,000 flowers are planted here annually – plus well-worn paths, ponds and lakes scattered with ducks. Among the many attractions for children are a 🏠 **Children's Farm**, with sheep, goats and pot-belly pigs, a playground and a wading pool (the last is near the Dallas Road entrance). The park also contains two great symbols of Englishness – a cricket pitch and lawn bowling green – as well as a pitch-and-putt course,

Idyllic autumnal waterfall scene in Beacon Hill Park

The Gothic grandeur of Craigdarroch Castle

the world's tallest totem pole (carved in 1956) and the **Mile Zero marker** of the Trans-Canada Highway, the road that begins here and crosses the country from west to east.

The park is generally safe, but take the usual precautions to protect yourself. Women should avoid the area at night if alone.

🞤 203 C2 ✉ Bounded by Dallas Road, Douglas Street, Heywood and Southgate Street ☎ 250/361-0364 🕐 24 hours 🔲 5 🎫 Free

29 Craigdarroch Castle

Craigdarroch Castle is the pick of several historic buildings on the fringes of Victoria, although "castle" rather overstates what is a large

---

🐾 **PETTING ZOO**
If you have kids, try taking them to **Beacon Hill Children's Farm** (tel: 250/381-2532; www.beaconhillpark.ca) or the tiny **Victoria Bug Zoo** on Courtney Street (▶ 185).

Gothic house, built in fulfilment of a promise made by Robert Dunsmuir to his wife – the prospect of an extravagant home was reputedly the only way he could tempt her away from their native Scotland.

Dunsmuir moved to Canada in 1851 as an employee of the Hudson's Bay Company, but by 1869 had opened his own coal mine and become a business magnate in his own right. The business and political practices of this robber baron were sharp, to say the least, and involved strike-breaking, the hiring of cheap Chinese labour, and election to the provincial legislature against a candidate backed by his employees. Safety measures in his mines were notoriously lax, and in 1887, 150 men died in an explosion near Nanaimo on Vancouver Island. Strikes were put down with government connivance, and miners ruthlessly evicted from their homes.

Profits from Dunsmuir's enterprises to the tune of $200,000 were sunk into Craigdarroch, which means a "rocky oak place" in Gaelic. No expense was spared: the best marble, granite and sandstone were imported from abroad, and finely worked ceiling panels were crafted for the main hall and staircase. The finished house is an extravagance of stained-glass, paintings, sculptures and precious carpets that extends over four floors and 39 rooms. Dunsmuir, however, never enjoyed its splendour – he died before its completion in 1890. In 1919 Craigdarroch was used as a war veterans' hospital and from 1921 until 1946 was part of McGill University at Montreal.

🞤 203 C3
✉ 1050 Joan Crescent, Rockland
☎ 250/592-5323; www.thecastle.ca
🕐 Summer (usually mid-Jun to early Sep) daily 9–7; winter (usually early Sep to mid-Jun) 10–4:30 🔲 11 or 14 to University from Fort Street, followed by a short walk up hill
🎫 CDN$13.95

Where to...
Stay

The Magnolia Hotel & Spa $$$

The Magnolia broke the mould of Victoria hotels, its boutique size and style in marked contrast to larger, more traditional accommodations. It has the look and feel of a British, Edwardian-era club, without being stuffy, and, with just 63 rooms, is pleasantly intimate. The spa is one of Victoria's best. The more expensive rooms have harbour views.

✚ 203 B3 ✉ 623 Courtenay Street, V8V 1B8
☎ 250/381-0999 or toll free 1-877/624-6654;
www.magnoliahotel.com

Swans Suite Hotel $$

Swans is on the northern edge of the Old Town. Its 30 rooms and onsite brewpub (➤ 107) were once an 1880s grain store; some exposed beams and open brickwork remain in the loft-style spaces of the public areas and some of the rooms. The two-bedroom suites are ideal for families, accommodating up to six people. All have kitchenettes.

✚ 203 B4
✉ 506 Pandora Avenue at Store Street, V8V 1N6
☎ 250/361-3310 or toll free 1-800/668-7926;
www.swanshotel.com

Best Western Carlton Plaza $$

Hotels in the Best Western group are invariably reliable, and the Carlton Plaza is no exception, its 103 modern, air-conditioned and well-equipped rooms providing a comfortable base close to the main sights and shops. Suites are available, as are units with kitchens – useful if you're spending a few days here and want to self-cater.

✚ 203 B4 ✉ 642 Johnson Street, V8W 1M6
☎ 250/388-5513 or toll free 1-800/663-7241;
www.bestwesterncarltonplazahotel.com

Fairmont Empress $$–$$$$

Absolutely the first choice for a treat, the redoubtable Empress is a Victoria institution. Opened in 1908 by the Canadian Pacific Railway, it embodies the city's sense of tradition and is still the first choice of visiting dignitaries and VIPs. It belongs to the Canadian Pacific chain.
    The hotel's central position overlooking the Inner Harbour is perfect, but note that it is a big, busy hotel with some 477 rooms. Service is excellent, as are the facilities, notably the health club. The many lounges and dining rooms are splendid, but are also busy – afternoon tea is served to some 80,000 visitors a year.

✚ 203 B3 ✉ 721 Government Street, V8W 1W5
☎ 250/384-8111; toll free 1-866/540-4429;
www.fairmont.com/empress

Haterleigh Heritage Inn $$–$$$$

Rivalling the Empress Hotel on price, the Haterleigh is a beautiful

1901 "heritage building" two blocks from downtown. It has six rooms and is a self-styled "bed-and-breakfast," though very upscale. The rooms are spacious, decorated with antiques, all with private bathrooms. Rates include breakfast, afternoon refreshments and small treats at check-in.

➕ 203 off A3 ✉ 243 Kingston Street, V8l 1V5
☎ 250/384-9995 or toll free 1-866/234-2244;
www.haterleigh.com

James Bay Inn Hotel & Suites $$

A few blocks from the Inner Harbour, this is Victoria's third-oldest hotel, opening in 1911. Rooms are spacious, modern and comfortable; the "heritage house" annex next door offers four luxury suites with elegant antique furnishing and full kitchens.

➕ 203 B2 ✉ 270 Government Street, V8V 2L2
☎ 250/384-7151 or toll free 1-800/836-2649;
www.jamesbayinn.bc.ca

The Royal Scot Suite Hotel
$$–$$$

Set in its own attractive grounds, the Royal Scot offers a good selection of comfortable and well-appointed rooms and suites in a convenient location for Victoria's Inner Harbour and downtown. Facilities include a restaurant, pool, fitness room and a gift shop offering arts and crafts and gourmet foods.

➕ 203 A3 ✉ 425 Quebec Street, V8V 1W7
☎ 250/388-5463 or toll free 1-800/663-7515;
www.royalscot.com

Where to...
Eat and Drink

Prices
Expect to pay for a three-course meal for two, excluding drinks and service

| $ under CDN$50 | $$ CDN$50–$100 | $$$ over CDN$100 |

RESTAURANTS

10 Acres Kitchen $$
Located near Inner Harbour, this restaurant has a reputation as one of the very best fish and seafood restaurants in the city.

➕ 203 B3
✉ 614 Humboldt Street
☎ 250/385-4512; http://10acreskitchen.ca
🕐 Daily 5pm–11pm

Café Brio $–$$
Despite the "café" name, this restaurant has consistently been ranked as one of the best on the island. Expect skilfully prepared Italian cuisine made with the best regional produce and a wine list featuring 300 selections from around the world. Reservations accepted by telephone only.

➕ 203 C3 ✉ 944 Fort Street
☎ 250/383-0009 (toll free 1-866/270-5461);
www.cafe-brio.com
🕐 Daily from 5:30pm

Canoe Brewpub Marina Restaurant $–$$
The striking interior of this popular pub and restaurant, with its re-doubtable walls and vast beams, owes much to its role as a former power station, built in 1894. The outside patio is attractive, with views across the harbour moorings and the Johnson Street Bridge. Choose between unfussy cooking with locally sourced ingredients in the loft-style restaurant – braised

 Insider Tip

lamb shanks, BC halibut or sirloin steak, for example – and the simpler bar snacks and good pub food in the brewpub.

🚹 203 B4 ✉ 450 Swift Street, V8V 1S3 ☎ 250/361-1940; www.canoebrewpub.com ⏰ Sun–Wed 11:30–11, Thu 11:30–midnight, Fri, Sat 11:30am–1am

L'École $$

This modern bistro offers fine French cuisine, using the best local produce, at prices that won't break the bank. The decor is persuasively French – white linen tablecloths and dark hardwood floors. You can treat yourself to starters of oysters or mussels followed by delicious mead-braised duck legs, sauerkraut, capers and chestnuts, or such fish dishes as grilled tuna with leek and peppercorn ragout. The wine list is excellent and there's a terrific selection of beers.

🚹 203 B4 ✉ 1715 Government Street, V8W 1Z4 ☎ 250/475-6260; www.lecole.ca ⏰ Tue–Sat 5:30–11

Milestone's Grill & Bar $–$$

Milestone's is a part of a good mid-market chain, and has one of Victoria's finest central locations – right by the visitor centre overlooking the Inner Harbour. Prices are reasonable, and the food more ambitious than you might expect (Italian, West Coast and Asian options). Lunch might include hot spinach and artichoke dip or crispy honey Phyllo shrimp, and dinner wild coho salmon or steaks and prime rib.

🚹 203 B3 ✉ 812 Wharf Street, V8W 1T3 ☎ 250/381-2244; www.milestonesrestaurants.com ⏰ Mon–Thu 11–9:30, Fri 11–11, Sat 10am–11pm, Sun 10am–9:30pm

Pagliacci's $$

Pagliacci's opened back in 1979 when it was impossible to find a cappuccino or Italian food in Victoria. Since then it's been one of the city's favourite restaurants – so popular, in fact, that you can't reserve a table but have to wait in line until a table becomes free. The success is partly due to the food – an eccentric Italian, Jewish, West Coast, Brooklyn mixture, with everything, including bread, made on the premises – and partly to the lively and very genial atmosphere. There's always a buzz of animated conversation, supplemented most nights by live music. Informal to a fault, this is a place where both adults and children can have fun.

Inside Tip

🚹 203 B4 ✉ 1011 Broad Street, V8V 2A1 ☎ 250/386-1662; www.pagliaccis.ca ⏰ Mon–Thu 11:30–10, Fri, Sat 11:30–11, Sun 10–10

Spinnakers Gastro Brewpub & Guesthouses $

Although not central, Spinnakers is worth a journey for its harbour views, food, occasional live music and home-brewed beers (and occasional tours of the brewery). Most ingredients are locally sourced (herbs come from its garden, for example) and you can choose from snacks that are "Perfect with a Pint", soups, salads and staples such as pastas, burgers, pizzas, pies and fish and chips. Leave room for the excellent desserts, such as blueberry crisp with white lavender ice cream.

🚹 203 off A4 ✉ 308 Catherine Street off Esquimalt Road, V9A 3S8 ☎ 250/386-2739 or toll free 1-877/838-2739; www.spinnakers.com ⏰ Daily 11–10:30 🚌 23 to Esquimalt Road

Il Terrazzo $$

Il Terrazzo lies in a small alley off another small alley, but makes light of its cramped and hidden location with a spacious interior of bare brick walls, lots of plants and big windows that give an airy, alfresco feeling. The restaurant is a favourite among visitors and Victorians alike, who flock here for good Italian food in pretty, contemporary surroundings. Dishes range from reasonably priced small pizzas to more expensive main-course classics such as local halibut, pork scaloppine and shank of lamb.

➕ 203 B4 ✉ 555 Johnson Street, off Waddington Alley, V8V 1M2

☎ 250/361-0028; www.ilterrazzo.com

🕐 Mon–Sat 11:30am–3, daily 5–10pm. Closed Sat lunch Oct–Apr

CAFÉS & PUBS

Murchie's Tea & Coffee

Taking English afternoon tea is something of a ritual among some visitors to Victoria, albeit a rather self-conscious one. If you don't want to spend $60 plus taxes each at top spots, the Empress Hotel (➤ 104) or Blethering Place at 2250 Oak Bay Avenue, try Murchies, a central café that's been in business since 1894.

➕ 203 B4 ✉ 1110 Government Street

☎ 250/383-3112; www.murchies.com

🕐 Mon–Sat 7:30–6, Sun 8–6

Rebar

Rebar serves a bewildering range of healthy and exotic drinks, as well as excellent organic vegetarian snacks and meals. It's a funky place, great for breakfast, lunch or short break.

➕ 203 B4

✉ 50 Bastion Square at Langley Street

☎ 250/361-9223; www.rebarmodernfood.com

🕐 Mon–Thu 11–10

Sticky Wicket

Victoria is filled with mostly poor imitations of British pubs, but the Wicket is by far the best, and certainly most favoured by locals. It has a pleasant rooftop patio area and occasional live music. There are rooftop volleyball courts and you can head downstairs for some late night clubbing.

➕ 203 B3 ✉ 919 Douglas Street

☎ 250/383-7137; www.strathconahotel.com

🕐 Mon–Fri 11:30am–2am, Sat 9am–2am, Sun 9am–midnight

Swans Brew Pub

Victoria's most popular pub-restaurant is housed in a converted 1913 warehouse. Swans offers 10 beers from its brewery (such as Pumpkin Ale, and Smooth Sailing Honey Ale) and excellent food (including salads, nachos, fish and chips and shepherd's pie). The complex includes a small hotel and basement nightclub.

➕ 203 B4

✉ 506 Pandora Avenue, corner of Store Street

☎ 250/361-3310; www.swanshotel.com

🕐 Mon–Fri 11am–1am, Sat 9am–1am, Sun 9am–midnight

Willie's Bakery Café

This rambling café and bakery, dating from 1887, is BC's oldest bakery, and still occupies part of a pretty heritage building. It serves full breakfasts and lunches daily, using mostly local and organic produce, and is well-placed close to Market Square, immediately to the north. The flower-filled conservatory and courtyard are especially attractive on a sunny day.

Insider Tip

➕ 203 B4 ✉ 537 Johnson Street

☎ 250/381-8414; www.williesbakery.com

Where to...
Shop

Victoria's main shopping areas are **downtown** – behind the Inner Harbour – and the Old Town core centred on **Market Square**. The streets containing the main stores and largest number of small specialty shops, mingled with various bland souvenir shops, are **Government** and **Douglas**, but interesting shops and stalls can also be found in Market Square itself and small side streets such as **Trounce Alley**.

The key department store is **Bay Centre** (1150 Douglas Street; tel: 250/952-5690), with a huge selection of goods at reasonable prices. Head to **Murchie's** (➤ above) for tea, coffee and cakes, and **Rogers'**

Chocolates (913 Government Street; tel: 250/881-8771; www.rogers chocolates.com) for sublime chocolates. For Canadian wine, drop in on the **Artisan Wine Shop** (644 Broughton Street; tel: 250/384-9994; www.artisanwineshop.ca/locations/ victoria).

First Nations crafts can be found at **Cowichan Trading** (1328 Government Street; tel: 250/383-0321; www.cowichantrading.com), along with a plethora of souvenirs, including textiles, pewter, jewellery, art, masks, T-shirts and blankets.

Try **Artina's** for handmade jewellery by Canadian artists, the pieces by First Nations artisans merit particular attention (1002 Government Street; tel: 250/386-7000; www. artinas-jewellery.com).

A good selection of small boutiques and little specialist stores is found in and around **Market Square** (www.marketsquare.ca).

The best stock of books is held by **Munro's** (1108 Government Street; tel: 250/382-2464; www. munrosbooks.com). **Fort Street** is a good place to start looking for antiques and galleries.

Where to…
Go Out

PERFORMING ARTS

Victoria has its own orchestra, the **Victoria Symphony Orchestra** (610–620 View Street; tel: 250/385-6515; www.victoriasymphony.ca, open Mon–Fri 9–4), its own opera company, the **Pacific Opera Victoria** (925 Balmoral Road; tel: 250/382-1641; www.pov.bc.ca), and its own musicals and light opera society, the **Victoria Operatic Society** (744 Fairview Road; tel: 250/381-1021; www.vos.bc.ca). All perform mainly at the **McPherson Playhouse** (3 Centennial Square; tel: 250/386-6121 or 1-888/717-6121; www. rmts.bc.ca).

The **Belfry Theatre** (1291 Gladstone Avenue; tel: 250/385-6815; www.belfry.bc.ca) stages around five productions annually (Oct–Apr), and the **Intrepid Theatre Company** (1609 Blanshard Street; tel: 250/383-2663; www.intrepid theatre.com) organizes two major theatrical festivals: the **Victoria Fringe Festival** (late summer); and the **Shakespeare Festival** (Aug), held near the Inner Harbour.

JAZZ

The best club for live music is **Hermann's** (753 View Street, near Blanshard; tel: 250/388-9166; www.hermansjazz.com).

The **Victoria Jazz Society** (345 Quebec Street; tel: 250/388-4423; www.jazzvictoria.ca) will have details of all events, including the major **Jazzfest International**.

BARS & CLUBS

Victoria is full of pubs and bars. Try the **Irish Times** bar (1200 Government Street; tel: 250/383-7775; www.irishtimespub.ca) with live music that echoes of Irish footstomping pubs; the pretty **Swans Pub** (▶ 107); **Spinnaker's** (▶ 106), or **Bartholomew's** (777 Douglas Street; tel: 250/388-5111; www. executivehouse.com). **Lucky Bar** (517 Yates Street; tel: 250/382-5825; www.luckybar.ca) is a longstanding Victoria favourite, with the best in club music, from rock and punk to hip hop, folk and jazz.

INFORMATION & TICKETS
Head for the **Visitor Centre**, or consult the listings pages of local newspapers and free sheets such as the *Monday Magazine* (www.mondaymag.ca).

British Columbia

 Little Treats

Cinnamon Buns, Nanaimo Bars and More
Fort Steele Heritage Town (► 125) is known far and wide for having the best bakery in the area.

Salmon Run
In late summer you can watch thousands of salmon leaping as they swim upstream in vthe **Fraser Canyon** (► 124) to spawn.

Fine Ferry Ride
The scenic crossing of **Kootenay Lake** (► 121) to Balfour is not only picturesque but it is also free!

British Columbia

Getting Your Bearings

Imagine Canada and the chances are you'll imagine British Columbia. This is the province where the country is seen at its glorious best, where the mountains, forests and lakes are on the grandest scale, where flora, fauna and landscape are at their most dramatic and diverse, and where the towns and cities – notably Vancouver – are at their most beautiful and cosmopolitan.

No short visit can do justice to the region's immensity – it covers an area larger than the US states of California, Washington and Oregon combined. Aim to explore a couple of its most distinctive corners – the Kootenays for some of the region's loveliest lakes and mountains, Wells Gray for a taste of its wilderness, or the Okanagan for a glimpse of its more pastoral corners.

The distances you'll cover will be considerable, and many of the interior towns, though beautifully located, are of relatively little interest – Nelson in the Kootenays being a notable exception. Neither fact should put you off, for in a region where spectacular scenery is almost universal, it's a pleasure simply to drive from place to place.

Touring by bus, car or RV is easy: the roads are excellent, and most towns and villages have at least one hotel or motel. Your only problem will be resisting the many scenic temptations en route, not to mention the countless opportunities for outdoor activities such as hiking or horseback riding.

The chances are you'll find too much to do and see, but you can always come back – most people do.

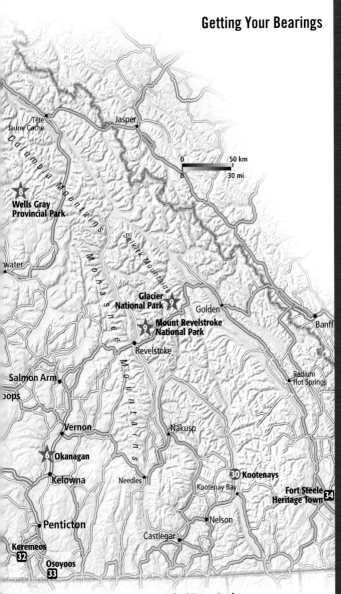

Five Perfect Days

If you're not quite sure where to begin your travels, this itinerary recommends a practical and enjoyable five-day tour of British Colombia, taking in some of the best places to see. For more information see the main entries (►114–123).

Day 1

Leave Vancouver at dawn and head east on Highway 1 to Hope and then drive north to Lytton via the dramatic **31 Fraser Canyon** (► 124) with breathtaking views of the river and mountains. More spectacular mountain panoramas are also revealed on the drive to Kamloops via Cache Creek and north on Highway 5 to Clearwater, the best base for ★ **Wells Gray Provincial Park** (► 116). If you do not stay in Kamloops and want take a full day to explore Wells Gray Provincial Park, continue north on Highway 5 to Mount Robson and **Jasper National Park** (► 146) in the Rocky Mountains, or drive from Lytton to the ★ **Okanagan** (► 114) via Merritt.

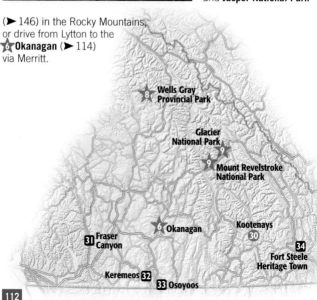

Day 2

If you decide against Wells Gray Provincial Park, then spend time exploring the Okanagan, leaving yourself the option of spending Day 3 in the region at the **O'Keefe Ranch** (➤ 115) for recreation.

Day 3

From the Okanagan you have yet more choices. One is to head north to Salmon Arm from Vernon and then east on the Trans-Canada Highway (Highway 1) to see ☆**Glacier and Mount Revelstoke National Parks** (➤ 118). From here it's a straightforward drive on Highway 1 through Yoho National Park (left; ➤ 150) to Lake Louise (➤ 142) and Banff National Park (➤ 139). If you feel the Rockies can wait, then on Day 3 or 4 head east on Highway 6 from Vernon to Needles, Nakusp and New Denver. This is a delightful drive in its own right, and leaves you well placed for exploring ㉚**The Kootenays** (Kootenay Lake, above; ➤ 120).

Day 4

Spend the day driving to or exploring the Kootenays, overnighting in **Kaslo** or **Nelson**. Villages not to be missed include **Kaslo** and **New Denver**, while some of the most scenic stretches of road are Highway 31A between Kaslo and New Denver and Highway 3A from Balfour to Creston.

Day 5

Leave the Kootenays via Creston and then follow Highway 95 north toward Cranbrook and the heritage town of ㉞**Fort Steele** (➤ 125). Continue north on Highway 93–95 to Radium Hot Springs and **Kootenay National Park** (➤ 153), a far prettier route east than Highway 3 over the Crowsnest Pass to Fort Macleod and southern Alberta.

⭐6 The Okanagan

The Okanagan region is the last thing you'd expect of British Columbia. Instead of the province's familiar mountain and forest landscapes, this is an almost Mediterranean region of vine-covered hills, beaches, dulcet lakes, orchards and pastoral river valleys. Vacationers flock here to enjoy its mild climate, wine, water sports and other recreational activities.

Kelowna

The main centre is Kelowna, best approached from the west across Okanagan Lake – a much prettier route than Highway 97. In town, the lakefront centre is a lovely mixture of parks, gardens, beaches and well-ordered streets lined with cafés, galleries, interesting stores and good restaurants. **Rotary Beach**, **Boyce Gyro Park** and **Bear Creek Provincial Park**, just over a kilometre away across  the curious floating bridge that spans Okanagan Lake, are the main beaches. For good views, take the five-minute drive up to **Knox Mountain** just to the north.

Insider Tip

The marina on the west bank of Lake Okanagan in Kelowna

Wine-growing Region

You can also visit some of the region's **vineyards**. There's a signposted **Wine Route** that starts at Salmon Arm, on Shuswap Lake, and heads south on Highway 97 through Vernon, Kelowna, Peachland, Kaleden and Osoyoos. Most of the 40 or so wineries on the route are south of Kelowna. The majority sell wines direct, and some offer tours. One of the most interesting is the organic **Summerhill Pyramid Winery** (4870 Chute Hill Road; tel: 250/764-8000 or toll free 1-800/667-3538; www.summerhill.bc.ca), where they use a pyramid to mature the wines. They also have a good lakeside restaurant.

You can pick up details of the route from visitor centres and stop by at the **BC VQA Wine Information Centre** (tel: 250/490-2006; www.pentictonwineinfo.com), which shares the premises of the **Penticton visitor centre**. Penticton, south of Kelowna, takes its name from a Salish phrase meaning "a place to stay forever," a reference to a blessed climate and

ORCHARDS

Kelowna and the rest of the Okanagan owe much of their prosperity to **fruit-growing**. Credit for planting the trees goes to Father Charles Pandosy, a member of an Oblate mission founded close to Kelowna in 1859. You can undertake any number of orchard, juice, fruit and food tours – obtain details from visitor centres.

Vineyards swathe much of the Okanagan Valley

idyllic surroundings. It is fairly pretty at its centre and also has beaches (Skaha and Okanagan are the best), water sports and tours.

Vernon

The same goes for Vernon, north of Kelowna, whose appeal is enhanced by its tree-lined streets and 500 or so heritage buildings. It's also close to the region's major point of historical interest, the **O'Keefe Ranch** (12km/7.5mi to the north), a fascinating collection of original buildings and equipment that evokes the flavour of 19th-century frontier life.

➕ 199 E2

Kelowna Visitor Centre
✉ 544 Harvey Avenue
☎ 250/ 861-1515; toll free in North America 1-800-663-4345; www.tourismkelowna.com
🕐 Mid-May to Jun Mon–Sat 9–5, Sun 10–3; Jul, Aug daily 9–6; Sep, Oct Mon–Sat 9–6, Sun 10–3; Nov–Apr Mon–Fri 9–5, Sat 10–3

Vernon Visitor Centre
✉ 3004 39th Avenue
☎ 250/542-1415; toll free in North America 1-800/665-0795; www.vernontourism.com
🕐 Mid-May to late Jun daily 9–5; Jul, Aug daily 8:30–6; Sep to mid-Oct Mon–Sat 8:30–4:30; mid-Oct to mid-May Mon–Fri 8:30–4:30

Historic O'Keefe Ranch
✉ 12km (7.5mi) north of Vernon, 9380 Hwy 97N ☎ 250/542-7868; www.okeeferanch.ca 🕐 May, Jun and Sep daily 10–5; Jul, Aug daily 10–6
🍴 Café ($) 💵 CDN$13.50

Penticton & Wine Country Visitor Centre
✉ 553 Vees Drive ☎ 250/276-2170; toll free in North America 1-800/663-5052; www.visitpenticton.com
🕐 Mon–Sat 8–7, Sun 9–6

INSIDER INFO

- Don't follow the **busy roads** on the east side of Okanagan Lake; take the quieter and prettier roads on the west side, away from the main towns.
- Come to the Okanagan **off season** if possible to sample its charms – fruit trees in blossom, lakeside villages and vineyard tours – without the crowds.

British Columbia

⭐⑧ Wells Gray Provincial Park

Wells Gray and its medley of mountains, waterfalls, lakes, torrential rivers and deep forests is one of the finest of British Columbia's parks, although it is less visually rugged and mountainous than the Rockies national parks to the east. Some of the best scenic highlights can be seen easily from a road that penetrates the park's lonely heart.

It's debatable whether you'd make a special journey here on a short visit to BC, but if you're traveling from **Jasper** and **Mount Robson**, then it's easy to spend a night in Clearwater and then a day exploring the park. Clearwater's excellent visitor centre, on the highway outside the village proper, is the place to pick up details about the park's trails and attractions. It also has details of whitewater rafting and canoeing trips on the Clearwater River and other outdoor activities in the park.

Right: At more than twice the height of Niagara, Helmcken Falls impresses in both summer and winter

Driving the Park Route
If all you're doing is sightseeing from a car, then just follow the 62.5km (39mi) Wells Gray Park Road off Highway 5 into the park. All the sights along the road are signposted. The first is **Spahats Creek Provincial Park**, 8km (5mi) from Clearwater, where a short trail from the parking area leads to the 61m (200ft) **Spahats Falls**. The next is the **Green Mountain Lookout**, accessed via a winding side road just after the main road crosses the Wells Gray Park boundary. At the lookout is a sensational view of some of BC's wildest reaches: so wild that many of the peaks remain unnamed.

Below: Ray Farm is now mostly ruined

Back on the main park road, the next stop is **Dawson Falls**. Where other waterfalls derive their beauty from high, graceful arcs of water, the drama here is provided by the sheer volume and power of cascading water. The falls are 91.5m (300ft) wide, but just 5m (16ft) high. The waterfalls in the park are all a result of glaciers receding during the last ice age.

A waterfall of the graceful variety, **Helmcken Falls**, the park's centre-piece, is reached on a signposted access road soon after Dawson Falls. At 137m (450ft), these falls are two- and-a-half times the height of Niagara, their height comple-

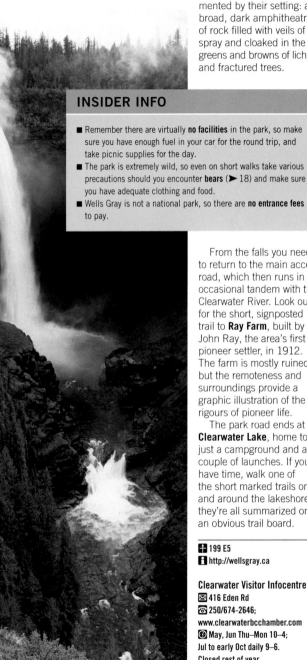

mented by their setting: a broad, dark amphitheatre of rock filled with veils of spray and cloaked in the greens and browns of lichens and fractured trees.

INSIDER INFO

- Remember there are virtually **no facilities** in the park, so make sure you have enough fuel in your car for the round trip, and take picnic supplies for the day.
- The park is extremely wild, so even on short walks take various precautions should you encounter **bears** (➤ 18) and make sure you have adequate clothing and food.
- Wells Gray is not a national park, so there are **no entrance fees** to pay.

From the falls you need to return to the main access road, which then runs in occasional tandem with the Clearwater River. Look out for the short, signposted trail to **Ray Farm**, built by John Ray, the area's first pioneer settler, in 1912. The farm is mostly ruined but the remoteness and surroundings provide a graphic illustration of the rigours of pioneer life.

The park road ends at **Clearwater Lake**, home to just a campground and a couple of launches. If you have time, walk one of the short marked trails on and around the lakeshore: they're all summarized on an obvious trail board.

➕ 199 E5
ℹ️ http://wellsgray.ca

Clearwater Visitor Infocentre
✉️ 416 Eden Rd
☎️ 250/674-2646;
www.clearwaterbcchamber.com
🕐 May, Jun Thu–Mon 10–4;
Jul to early Oct daily 9–6.
Closed rest of year.

British Columbia

★ 9 Glacier & Mount Revelstoke National Parks

The mountain ranges immediately to the west of the Rockies are just as spectacular as the Rockies themselves. Glacier and Mount Revelstoke national parks protect a fragment of these ranges, the Columbia and Selkirk mountains, which offer as seductive a medley of landscapes as their famous neighbours.

Glacier National Park

The national park owes its existence to the Canadian Pacific Railway. Before its arrival, the region's terrain was so inhospitable as to be almost deserted. Neither explorers nor aboriginal peoples ventured into its icy interior, which is ringed with peaks such as **Mount Dawson** (3,392m/11,128ft), as imposing as the Rockies' peaks to the east.

Some 14 percent of the area has permanent snow cover, with more than 420 glaciers, including at least 68 that have re-formed on previously vanished ice sheets, an unusual phenomenon – most glaciers are in retreat. The railway was driven through in 1885 via **Rogers Pass** (1,383m/4,534ft), named after the chief engineer, Major Albert Rogers.

Tourists filled the Pass hotel until 1916, when repeated avalanches led the railway to use a new tunnel. Visitor numbers dropped, only recovering in 1962 on the opening of the Trans-Canada Highway (Highway 1). Today the road is the best way to see the park – much of the interior is the preserve only of experienced mountaineers. Stop at the park **visitor centre**, a kilometre west of Rogers Pass, to get details of shorter walks. Just south of the centre you should also stop off to admire the views of the **Illecillewaet Neve**, one of the park's most visible and impressive glaciers.

On the trail of the giant cedar, Mount Revelstoke National Park

Mount Revelstoke National Park

This national park lies 16km (10mi) west of Glacier. It is smaller and was created 1916, largely to protect the floral meadows on **Mount Revelstoke**. Main access is on the **Meadows in the Sky Parkway** (25.5km/16mi), near the western entrance and the town of Revelstoke (a good base for both parks).

Looking from Mount Revelstoke to the town of the same name

There are trails at the top, notably the paved **Meadows in the Sky Trail** (0.8km/0.5mi) and longer **Miller Lake Trail** (6km/3.7mi one way). Other short trails start from the main Trans-Canada Highway – the best are the **Giant Cedars** (half a mile) and **Skunk Cabbage** (1.2km/0.7mi) trails, respectively 0.5 and 6km (0.3 and 3.7mi) from the eastern gate.

WALKS IN GLACIER

There are eight hikes in the park, from a gentle stroll to a challenging full-day mountain hike, all leading out from the Illecillewaet Campground. The shortest are the 1km (0.5mi) **Bear Falls Trail** and **Meeting of the Waters Trail**, and one of the easiest, though longer, is the 1885 **Rails Trail** (3.8km/2.3mi each way), following the disused line of the Canadian Pacific Railway. Best of the strenuous hikes are the **Great Glacier**, **Avalanche** and **Abbott's** ridge trails.

➕ 200 A4

Rogers Pass Discovery Centre
✉ Rogers Pass ☎ 250/837-7500; www.pc.gc.ca/lhn-nhs/bc/rogers/visit/visit2.aspx
🕐 17 May–11 Jun and 10 Sep–13 Oct 9–5, 12 Jun–9 Sep 8–7; 21 Nov–30 Apr 7–4; closed 1–16 May and 14 Oct–20 Nov
💷 Park: free

Revelstoke Town Visitor Centre
✉ 204 Campbell Avenue ☎ 250/837-5345 or toll free 1-800/487-1493; www.seerevelstoke.com
🕐 Jul, Aug daily 9–7; Sep to mid-Oct until 5; mid-Oct to Jun, Mon–Fri 8:30–4:30

INSIDER INFO

- Park **passes** are required for both Glacier and Revelstoke. Buy them from park centres – prices are a dollar or two less than for the four Rockies national parks. (Visit www.pc.gc.ca for more on park passes in Canada's national parks.)
- Glacier marks the border between **Mountain and Pacific time**. Remember to set your watches back an hour traveling west, forward an hour traveling east.
- You can't drive all the way up the Mount Revelstoke road or Meadows in the Sky Parkway – park at Balsam Lake and catch a **shuttle bus** for the 2km (1.3mi) route to the summit area. *Insider Tip*
- **Weather** can be poor in Glacier, even in summer, so drive carefully – road conditions can change quickly.
- **Interpretation talks** (mid-Jun to Aug, daily at 7pm) and occasional guided walks at the campground cover subjects such as the park's wildlife, geology and vegetation; contact the Rogers Pass Discovery Centre (see above).

30 The Kootenays

The Kootenays are a sublime pocket of lakes and mountains in British Columbia's southeast corner, an unspoiled and relatively unvisited enclave of tiny villages, parks, historic sites, forests, ghost towns, spectacular highways and lakeside hamlets set amid some of the province's loveliest landscapes.

NAME ORIGIN
The Kootenays take their name from an indigenous word meaning "people from beyond the hills," probably a reference to the hunting sorties made by the Kutenai or Kootenai tribes.

Best Approach

Kootenay Country, as it's often called, is loosely based on two major river valleys – the Kootenay and Columbia – their huge lakes (Kootenay and Arrow lakes) and the three colossal mountain ranges that divide and bind them: the Purcells, Selkirks and Monashees.

What you see of the region depends on your itinerary. From the west the best approach is on Highway 6 from Vernon to Needles, **a majestic drive** (► 186), while from the Rockies and the east the journey is more circuitous but almost equally beguiling via Fort Steele, Yahk and Creston. **Fort Steele** (► 125) has a well-sited reconstructed pioneer village, while Creston is noted for the **Creston Valley Wildlife Management Area** (9.5km/6mi northwest of town; tel: 250/402-6908; www.crestonwildlife.ca; visitor centre 9–4, mid-May to Jun Tue–Sat; Jul, Aug daily; Sep Wed–Fri), a haven for birds and wildlife, including one of the world's largest nesting osprey populations.

Nelson

The biggest and most obvious base in the region is Nelson – "Queen of the Kootenays" – a likeable place with a close-knit community feel, pretty streets, lots of cafés, galleries and bookstores, and more than 350 quaint wooden "heritage" buildings. The town and its surroundings have been used as locations for many film and television productions, most famously as the setting for comedian Steve Martin's film *Roxanne*. Brochures detailing walks around the buildings can be obtained from the visitor centre – don't miss the old town Courthouse, designed by Francis Rattenbury, architect of the Empress Hotel (▶104) and Parliament Buildings in Victoria (▶90).

Like most Kootenay settlements, Nelson sprang to life at the end of the 19th century following the discovery of silver, copper and gold in the hills nearby. Much of the area's mining heritage is recalled in the **Mining Museum** (215 Hall Street; tel: 250/352-5242), best seen with the **Touchstones Nelson Museum of Art and History** (502 Vernon Street; tel:

There are a lot of idyllic places along the more than 160km (100mi) of the Kootenay Lake shoreline

250/352-9813; www.touchstonesnelseon.ca; 15 May–14 Sep Mon–Sat 10–5, Thu until 8, Sun until 4; Wed–Sat 10–5, Thu until 8 rest of year; CDN$8), whose most interesting displays deal with the Doukhobors, a pacifist sect that settled across the region. To learn more about the sect and its way of life, visit the **Doukhobor Discovery Centre** in Castlegar.

Kaslo

While Nelson is an excellent base, with plenty of hotels, you might want to stay in one of the region's charming smaller villages. Best of these is urbane little **Kaslo**, a too-good-to-be-true spot on Kootenay Lake, with as picturesque and homey a collection of heritage buildings and gardens as Nelson. The village also boasts North America's oldest paddle steamer, or stern-wheeler, the SS *Moyie*, launched in 1898. This was one of many such vessels that once plied the Kootenays' lakes, loading and unloading minerals and other goods.

Insider Tip

Kaslo is delightful in its own right, but it also has a glorious mountain-ringed setting, with plenty of opportunities for sightseeing by car, walking and other outdoor activities. The hamlet of **Argenta**, 35.5km (22mi) to the north, makes a good target, as does the **Kokanee Glacier Provincial Park**, a mountain park with marked hiking trails accessed from several points on highways 6, 31 and 3A.

Kootenay Lake's rugged shoreline

Lakeside Centres
Other pretty centres include **New Denver**, only slightly less picture-perfect than Kaslo, and **Nakusp**, noted for its hot springs, a well-signposted natural spa with outdoor pools approximately 13km (8mi) northeast of the village.

The Kootenays

Both towns have small museums, devoted mainly to mining.

However, it's the scenery, in particular the region's beautiful ensembles of mountain, lake and forest, that you'll remember from the Kootenays. Much of the landscape can be enjoyed from the road, notably Highway 3A north of

In the valley of the Kootenay River

Creston, which runs alongside Kootenay Lake to the "world's longest free ferry crossing" (9km/5.5mi) at Kootenay Bay. En route, you'll pass all kinds of tucked-away bed-and-breakfast homes, good alternatives to staying in Nelson or the smaller villages – contact local visitor centres for details. You'll also pass the wonderfully eccentric **Glass House**, 6.5km (4mi) south of Boswell on Highway 3A, built in 1955 by a former mortician from 500,000 bottles. Beyond the ferry, 14.5km (9mi) north of Balfour, you might want to take a soak in the **Ainsworth Hot Springs**.

Insider Tip

➕ 200 B2

Nelson Visitor Infocentre
✉ 91 Baker Street, Nelson, BC, V1L 4G8
☎ 250/352-3433 or 1-877/663-5706; www.discovernelson.com
🕑 Jan–May, Sep–Dec Mon–Fri 8:30–5; Jun, Aug Mon–Fri 8:30–5:30, Sat, Sun 9–6

Kaslo Visitor Infocentre
✉ 324 Front Street
☎ 250/353-2525; www.klhs.bc.ca
🕑 Mid-May to mid-Oct daily 9–5. Closed rest of year

Nakusp Visitor Infocentre
✉ 92 6th Avenue NW
☎ 250/ 265-4234 or 1-800/909-8819; www.nakusparrowlakes.com
🕑 Jul, Aug daily 9–5. Times vary rest of year

New Denver Visitor Infocentre
✉ Silvery Slocan Museum, 202 6th Avenue
☎ 250/358-2719; www.slocanlake.com
🕑 Early Jul to early Sep daily 10–6. Times vary rest of year

INSIDER INFO

- You'll **need a car** to see the Kootenays: public transportation takes you only to the main centres.
- **Planning a route** through the Kootenays' twists and turns is difficult. The best of the region's towns and villages are Nelson, Kaslo and Nakusp.
- The most **scenic drives** are from Vernon to Needles, Creston to Kaslo, and Kaslo or Nakusp to Revelstoke via the ferry crossing at Galena Bay.
- Don't expect much in the way of **facilities** outside the towns and villages – and note that "villages" marked on maps – such as Balfour, Kootenay Bay, Needles, Crawford Bay and so on – usually amount to little more than a small cluster of houses.

Insider Tip

At Your Leisure

31 Fraser Canyon

The most interesting route when driving across British Columbia is the Trans-Canada Highway (Highway 1). It runs through semi desert scenery and shadows the Thompson River before turning south at Cache Creek. Between Lytton and Yale it follows the Fraser Canyon, the highlight of the journey. The road climbs, swoops and clings to the side of the canyon, offering views over the river and the mountains above.

River and canyon take their name from Simon Fraser (1776–1862), an explorer, fur trader and employee (later partner) of the North West Company, who established the first non-native settlements in western Canada and undertook prodigious feats of exploration.

Today the road route is straightforward but exhilarating, especially at **Hell's Gate** (about 9.5km/6mi north of Yale), where the Fraser's flow is squeezed into a seething mass of whitewater some 61m (200ft) deep. Here you can ride the **Airtram** cable car toward the canyon bottom, where a suspension bridge crosses the river, and look at displays detailing the salmon runs up the Fraser.

Yale began life in the 1840s as a Hudson's Bay Company fort. By 1858 it had become the largest town in North America west of Chicago and north of San Francisco, its population swollen by 20,000 gold prospectors. Today barely 200 people live here, but it's worth a stop for the small museum on its main highway dedicated to its gold-rush heyday.

Some 19.5km (12mi) south of Yale is the town of **Hope**, a pleasant place to stop, with another modest museum of pioneer memorabilia and opportunities for walking and – unusually – gliding. For details contact the town's visitor centre.
➕ 198 C2

Airtram
✉ 43111 Trans Canada Hwy, Boston Bar, 9.5km (6mi) north of Yale
☎ 604/867-9277; www.hellsgateairtram.com
🕐 Mid-Apr to mid-May and early Sep to mid-Oct daily 11–4; mid-May to early Sep 10–6
🍽 Cafe ($) 💳 CDN$22

Hope Infocentre
✉ 919 Water Avenue
☎ 604/869-2021 or toll free 1-866/467-3842; http://hopebc.ca/visitor-centre
🕐 Jun–Apr, Oct–Dec Mon–Sat 10–4; May and Sep daily 9–5; Jul, Aug daily 8–8

Over the abyss: the Airtram at Hell's Gate

Yale Museum Visitor Info Booth
✉ 31187 Douglas Street ☎ 604/863-2324
🕐 3 May to 30 Sep, daily 10–5

32 Keremeos

Highway 3 hugs the US border and takes you through some beautiful and varied scenery, beginning with the forests of the Coast Mountains and wild Manning Provincial Park. East of Princeton the scenery remains spectacular, but becomes more pastoral closer to Keremeos, a village beautifully set on a mountain-ringed plain. The local climate here is one of Canada's best, and allows the growing of a wide range of often exotic fruits and vegetables, earning the region the title of "Fruit Stand Capital of Canada."

Keremos Infocentre
🔢 199 E1 ✉ 417 7th Avenue
☎ 250/499-5225; www.similkameencountry.org
🕐 Jan–Jun, Sep–Dec Mon–Fri 9–5;
Jul, Aug daily 9–5

33 Osoyoos

The desert scenery around Osoyoos is some of the most startling in British Columbia. The Nk'Mip Desert is the historic home of the Osoyoos Indian Band (**Nk'Mip**), who still own and manage the land. The Osoyoos have created a thriving vacation resort nearby, but are actively conserving this endangered landscape.

There are self-guiding trails and, at the **Desert Cultural Centre**, visitors can learn about the land and the indigenous people via interactive exhibits, two multimedia theatres and a rattlesnake research program. There's an indoor habitat housing desert "critturs," and a sculpture garden and reconstructions of tribal dwellings. The region has Canada's lowest rainfall and an average annual temperature 10 degrees higher than Nelson.

The town of Osoyoos is also a busy spot when vacationers flock in summer to swim in the lake.
🔢 199 E1

Osoyoos Infocentre
✉ 8701 Main Street ☎ 250/495-5410 or
1-888/676-9667; www.destinationosoyoos.com
🕐 Jan to mid-May, Sep–Dec daily 9–4;
Jun 9–5; Jul, Aug 8–6

Nk'Mip Desert Cultural Centre
✉ 1000 Rancher Creek Road
☎ 250/495-7901 or 1-888/495-8555;
www.nkmipdesert.com
🕐 Late May to early Jul, Sep 1 to mid-Oct daily 9:30-4:30; early Jul, Aug daily 9:30–6; mid–late Oct Tue–Sat 9:30–4. Closed rest of year
💲 CDN$12

34 👥 Fort Steele Heritage Town

Fort Steele is a partly original, partly reconstructed village, put together to resemble how it might have appeared at the end of the 19th century. The original fort was created around 1884 by Inspector Sam Steele of the North West Mounted Police, who was sent to settle a dispute over land and two wrongfully imprisoned members of the Ktunaxa people.

The settlement later prospered as a result of nearby discoveries of silver, lead and zinc, and on the expectation that the transcontinental Canadian Pacific Railway would pass through the area. In the event, the railway passed through nearby Cranbrook instead. As Cranbrook boomed, Fort Steele declined, saved only by its restoration as a heritage site in 1961.

Today, the many old buildings are staffed by people in period dress. Visit an old-time smithy, bakery, general store, printing office and many other "working" enterprises. You can also ride a steam engine, board a stagecoach, and watch bread being baked or quilts being made.
🔢 201 D1 ✉ 9851 Hwy 93/95
☎ 250/417-6000 or 250/426-7352;
www.fortsteele.ca
🕐 May, Jun, early Sep to mid-Oct daily 10–4 (site until 6); Jul to early Sep 10–5 (site until 7); mid-Oct to Apr 10–4
🍽 Café ($) 💲 CDN$12

Where to...
Stay

Prices
Expect to pay per double room per night excluding breakfast and taxes:
$ under CDN$100   **$$** CDN$101–$200   **$$$** CDN$201–$300   **$$$$** over CDN$300

THE OKANAGAN

The Hopeless Romantic B&B Guest Suites $$
Three suites decorated in a wonderfully old-fashioned style, each with a private bathroom. Two of the suites also have a private entrance and overlook Kelowna and Lake Okanagan.

✚ 199 E2
✉ 2735 Lone Pine Drive, Kelowna, V1P 1A1
☎ 250/765-5006, 1-888/765-5006;
www.thehopelessromanticbandb.com

Walnut Beach Resort $$$
Although south of the Okanagan's heartland, and in a dry, near-desert landscape, Osoyoos makes a good base or stopover, thanks to its benign climate, pretty setting and almost guaranteed sunshine. Walnut Beach is one of the newest and smartest resorts, with a large swimming pool and a fine private beach on Canada's warmest lake. The 112 suites are decorated in a pared-down, contemporary style, with clean lines and muted colour. A wide range of outdoor activities is available and several major wineries are a short drive away.

✚ 199 E1
✉ 4200 Lakeshore Drive, Osoyoos, V0H 1V6
☎ 250/495-5400 or toll free 1-877/936-5400;
www.walnutbeachresort.com

Lake Okanagan Resort $$–$$$
This beautiful, self-contained lakeside resort hotel lies 17km (10.5mi) from Kelowna. It is a peaceful place to stay. Facilities include a par 3 golf course, two pools, tennis courts, marina, beach and horseback riding. Most of the 125 rooms are on the lakeside.

✚ 199 E2
✉ 2751 Westside Road, Kelowna, V1Z 3T1
☎ 250/769-3511; toll free in North America 1-800/663-3273; www.lakeokanagan.com

WELLS GRAY PROVINCIAL PARK

Dutch Lake Motel $–$$
A great place to stay if you are visiting Wells Gray, this motel is by the side of Dutch Lake. All the rooms have balconies overlooking the lake and some have kitchens. All are climate controlled, with cable TV and coffee makers. On site, there's a coin laundry, boat rentals, restaurant and RV campground.

✚ 199 E5
✉ 333 Roy Road, Clearwater, V0E 1N8
☎ 250/674-3325 or 1-877/674-3325;
www.dutchlakemotel.com

THE KOOTENAYS

Best Western Plus Baker Street Inn & Convention Centre $$–$$$
Downtown Nelson has a sprinkling of old, rather battered and inexpensive hotels, but it's better to spend a little more to stay in the Baker Street Inn, whose 70 rooms offer a more modern and stylish overnight option. Hotels affiliated to the Best Western chain are invariably reliable.

✚ 200 B1
✉ 153 Baker Street, Nelson, V1L 4H1
☎ 250/352-3525; toll free in North America 1-888/255-3525; www.bwbakerstreetinn.com

Hillside Lodge & Chalets $$–$$$

Superb main lodge and modern, cosy wooden chalets (one- and two-bedroom options) dotted around a wooded setting, with spectacular mountain and river views. This is a convenient base for both Glacier and Yoho national parks, situated 13km (8mi) west of Golden. It's also near Kicking Horse Mountain Resort, so a possible accommodation if you're here in winter and want to ski. Tours and activities can be arranged.

🞢 200 B4 ✉ 740 Seward Frontage Rd, Golden, 500m off Hwy 1, V0A 1H0
☎ 250/344-7281; www.hillsidechalets.com

William Hunter Cabins $–$$

What better way to complete a trip to the Kootenays than to spend the night in a real log cabin? This is no backwoods experience, though. The cabins here are beautiful, with handmade pine furniture, and the queen-size beds have duvets. Each

has a fully equipped kitchenette and a living room with sofa-bed and French doors leading onto a deck.

🞢 200 B2 ✉ 303 Lake Ave, Silverton, V0G 2B0
☎ 250/358-2647 or 250/505-4610;
www.williamhuntercabins.com

GLACIER NATIONAL PARK

Coast Hillcrest Hotel $$–$$$

It's hard to take your eyes off the spectacular views of snow-capped mountains and the Mount Begbie Glacier from this spot, but the hotel foyer is pretty eye-catching too, with its double-height ceiling and massive wooden pillars. Rooms are spacious, and there are some two-floor suites. The health club has whirlpool, steam room, sauna and exercise equipment.

🞢 199 F3
✉ 2100 Oak Drive, Revelstoke, V0E 2S0
☎ 250/837-3322 or toll free 1-800/663-1144;
www.coasthotels.com/hotels/bc/revelstoke/coast-hillcrest-hotel

Where to...
Eat and Drink

Prices
Expect to pay for a three-course meal for two, excluding drinks and service
$ under CDN$50 $$ CDN$50–$100 $$$ over CDN$100

THE OKANAGAN

Raudz Regional Table Restaurant $$

An attractive, contemporary eatery with red brick walls and a relaxed ambience. The superb dishes are all made from fresh, organic produce sourced locally. The menu offers something for everyone – salads, steaks, seafood, and pasta – all prepared in a decidedly modern way.

🞢 199 E2 ✉ 1560 Water Street, Kelowna
☎ 250/868-8805; www.raudz.com ⏲ 5pm–late

Social Lounge & Grill $$

Classic leather booths, excellent daily deals and a good selection of traditional favourites (homemade burgers, aged steaks) and exotic cocktails.

🞢 199 E2 ✉ 242 Lawrence Avenue, Kelowna
☎ 778/484-0242; www.social242.com
⏲ 5pm–midnight, Fri, Sat until 1am

THE KOOTENAYS

All Seasons Café $$

This elegant restaurant is in a heritage home in Nelson and it provides some of the finest dining in the Kootenays. The chef uses the very best local produce, including Ocean Wise seafood (►29) and a superb sheep's-milk **v**, to create truly mouthwatering dishes. Try starters of crispy tiger prawns, then rack of lamb.

✚ 200 B1
✉ 620 Herridge Lane, Nelson, V1L 6A7
☎ 250/352-0101; www.allseasonscafe.com
🕐 Daily from 5pm; Sun brunch 10–2

GLACIER NATIONAL PARK

The Wolf's Den $

The newly refurbished Wolf's Den offers a rustic log-cabin setting, juicy steaks, massive gourmet burgers, substantial salads and, for a small place like Golden, an extraordinary selection of wine, beer and cocktails.

✚ 200 B4
✉ 1105 9th Street South, Golden, V0A 1H0
☎ 250/344-9863; www.thewolfsdengolden.ca

Where to...
Shop

At **Craft Connection** (378 Baker Street, Nelson; tel: 250/352-3006; www.craftconnectin.org) there's the work of 20 local artists.

Another excellent gallery is the **Hazeldean** (105–405 Baker Street; tel: 250/352-0660; www.hazeldean gallery.com).

Or browse for secondhand books in **Packrat Annie's** (411 Kootenay Street; tel: 250/354-4722).

In Kaslo **Your Art's Desire** (423 Front Street; tel: 250/353-7500) and **Figment's Fine Canadian Crafts** (408 Front Street; tel: 250/353-2566) showcase locally made crafts, including silk scarves and bear bells.

Pick up the BC Wine Institute leaflet describing each Okanagan winery.

Where to...
Go Out

THE OKANAGAN

Rose's Waterfront Pub (1352 Water Street, Kelowna; tel: 250/ 860-1141; www.rosespub.com) is popular, as is the bar at the **Hotel Eldorado** (500 Cook Road; tel: 250/763-7500; www.hoteleldoradokelowna.com), which has a lakeside verandah for drinking and occasional live music.

Also good for live music and excellent food is the **The Grateful Fed** (509 Bernard Avenue; tel: 250/ 862-8621; www.thegratefulfed.ca).

For theatre and performing arts, try Kelowna's **Rotary Centre** (421 Cawston Avenue at Water Street; tel: 250/717-5304; www.rotary centreforthearts.com).

In Vernon, **Sir Winston's** (2705 32nd Street; tel: 250/549-3485; www.sirwinstons.ca) is a popular pub.

THE KOOTENAYS

The Kootenays is a hotbed of artistic talent. The **Kaslo Jazz Festival** (tel: 250/353-7577; www.kaslojazzfest. com), held on the last weekend in July, has a gorgeous setting, and many people listen from boats moored on Kootenay Lake.

For art and drama, visit Kaslo's **Langham Cultural Society** (447 A Avenue; tel: 250/353-2661; www. thelangham.ca).

Drop into **Mike's Place Pub** (Hume Hotel, 422 Vernon Street, Nelson; tel: 250/352-5331; www. humehotel.com), a classic tavern, recommended for its selection of local ales.

For a quieter drink, visit the Hume Hotel's **Library Bar.** The **Royal** (330 Baker Street, Nelson; tel: 250/354-7017) has major music acts.

Rocky Mountains

 **Little Treats**

Feed the Chipmunks

Granted, this is something you can do anywhere in Canada, but the turquoise **Moraine Lake** (▶ 144) makes for a particularly beautiful backdrop.

Culinary Gem

There is something quite unexpected in Yoho National Park: fine dining at the **Truffle Pigs Bistro** (▶ 161).

Wildlife Sightings

You will almost certainly spot some wapiti along the way on the drive from Jasper to the nearby **Pyramid Lake** (▶ 147).

Rocky Mountains

Getting Your Bearings

The Canadian Rockies can hold their own in the most exalted mountain company. A byword for scenic splendour, the great range – one of the world's most majestic – is a mighty patchwork of dramatic peaks, pristine forests, emerald lakes and vast swathes of untrammelled wilderness.

For most visitors, the Rockies mean the four national parks of Banff, Jasper, Yoho and Kootenay, four contiguous parks so magnificent they earned designation as a UNESCO World Heritage Site in 1985. Banff is the most famous, Jasper the biggest; Kootenay and Yoho are much smaller. Scenically, however, there's nothing to choose between the four.

All can be seen easily and quickly from the comfort of a car, but you'd be foolish not to linger occasionally and venture beyond the roads – even if it's just a gentle stroll on one of the parks' many hundreds of well-groomed trails.

It's not only the paths that are good. All facilities for visitors are well developed, at least in the main centres – Banff town, Lake Louise and Jasper – but also extremely busy. Elsewhere, there's next to nothing but wilderness.

Don't get the idea that the hotels and tourist razzmatazz spoil the scenery. Canada treasures the Rockies and the parks, which are consummately run, balancing the needs of tourism and conservation to perfection. A week here would only scratch the surface – but what a surface!

Jasper National Park

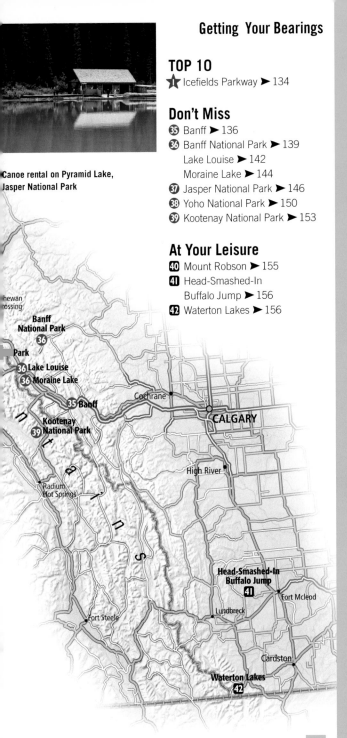

Getting Your Bearings

Canoe rental on Pyramid Lake,
Jasper National Park

Eight Perfect Days

If you're not quite sure where to begin your travels, this itinerary recommends a practical and enjoyable eight-day tour of the Rockies, taking in some of the best places to see. For more information see the main entries (► 134–156).

Day 1

Morning
Explore **35 Banff** (► 136), visiting the park visitor centre, Banff Park Museum and Whyte Museum of the Canadian Rockies. Grab lunch in a café on **Banff Avenue** (► 136).

Afternoon
Continue your exploration of Banff and then either take a half-day walk, ride the **Banff Gondola**, or take a boat trip on **Lake Minnewanka**.

Evening
Relax with a stroll along the Bow River to **Bow Falls** (► 137) and then treat yourself to a drink in the **Fairmont Banff Springs hotel** (► 157). Return to town along the river – the road route back, Spray Avenue, is dull.

Day 2

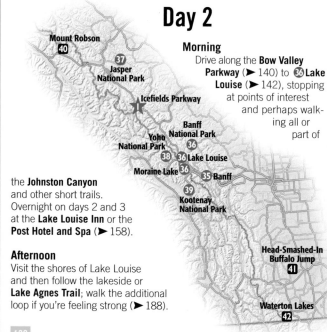

Mount Robson **40**

Jasper National Park **37**

Icefields Parkway

Banff National Park **36**

Yoho National Park **38**

36 Lake Louise

Moraine Lake **36**

35 Banff

Kootenay National Park **39**

Head-Smashed-In Buffalo Jump **41**

Waterton Lakes **42**

Morning
Drive along the **Bow Valley Parkway** (► 140) to **36 Lake Louise** (► 142), stopping at points of interest and perhaps walking all or part of the **Johnston Canyon** and other short trails. Overnight on days 2 and 3 at the **Lake Louise Inn** or the **Post Hotel and Spa** (► 158).

Afternoon
Visit the shores of Lake Louise and then follow the lakeside or **Lake Agnes Trail**; walk the additional loop if you're feeling strong (► 188).

Day 3

Spend the day walking above **36 Moraine Lake** (➤ 144) – the Consolation and more demanding Eiffel Lake–Larch Valley trails are manageable in a day.

Day 4

Travel along the ★**Icefields Parkway** (➤ 134), stopping en route, especially at the **Columbia Icefield** and **Peyto Lake Lookout**. Buy a picnic lunch at Saskatchewan River Crossing. Stay two nights in Jasper at the heart of Jasper National Park.

Day 5

Morning
Drive along Maligne Lake Road to **Maligne Lake** (➤ 147) and take a boat trip on the lake.

Afternoon
Either spend more time exploring **37 Jasper National Park** (➤ 146) or head toward **40 Mount Robson** (above; ➤ 155) for the views and a walk.

Day 6

Enjoy a leisurely drive back along the Icefields Parkway to Lake Louise, exploring the **Mistaya Canyon** and the **Parker Ridge Trail** as you go.

Day 7

Spend the day exploring and walking in **38 Yoho National Park** (left; ➤ 150), returning to Banff or Lake Louise in the evening. Buy lunch at the **Truffle Pigs Bistro** (➤ 161) in Field.

Day 8

Spend the day exploring and walking in **39 Kootenay National Park** (➤ 153), returning to Banff or Lake Louise later. Buy a picnic in Banff for lunch, as there's next to nothing in the park.

Rocky Mountains

★Icefields Parkway

The Icefields Parkway between Lake Louise and Jasper is one of the world's ultimate drives. For some 230km (143mi) this magnificent highway runs through scenery of staggering grandeur, passing vast snowcapped peaks, mighty waterfalls, shimmering lakes, immense icefields, flower-scattered meadows and huge swathes of virgin forest.

Break the Drive
Most of the ride is wilderness, with only two points to pick up food and fuel – **Saskatchewan River Crossing** and **Columbia Icefield** (77km/48mi and 127km/79mi from Lake Louise, respectively). Campgrounds and youth hostels aside, there are only three hotels en route, all invariably booked months ahead.

Walks and natural attractions are signposted, and even if you plan to drive the road in one go, you must stop to admire some of the waterfalls and viewpoints. There are plenty of half- and full-day trails along the way.

Saskatchewan Glacier is part of the Columbia Icefield off the Icefields Parkway

Walk Trails
As you leave Lake Louise, the first major highlight is **Hector Lake**, the park's second largest lake. If you want to walk, carry on a few miles to **Bow Lake** (37km/23mi from Lake Louise), where the Bow Lake and Bow Glacier Falls trail (4km/2.7mi, 55.5m/182ft ascent) offers the best lake walk of the drive. The road climbs to **Bow Summit** (2,082m/6,830ft), the highest point on a Canadian highway, and shortly after passes a sign to **Peyto Lake Lookout**. If you stop nowhere else, stop here, and walk the easy 20-minute trail (91.5m/300ft descent) to the most breathtaking lake view in the Rockies.

Hereafter the road drops, passing the **Mistaya Canyon** – the easy 300m trail is worth exploring – before arriving at **Saskatchewan River Crossing**. Some 134km (83mi) from Lake Louise the road climbs the "Big Hill," a vast curve of highway that offers sensational views. Other viewpoints nearby include the **Cirrus Mountain Lookout** and **Bridal Veil Falls**, the latter providing access to a rough track (0.8km/0.5mi) to the **Panther Falls**, the most impressive of the highway's waterfalls. Five kilometres (3mi) on, a sign marks the start of the **Parker Ridge Trail** (2.5km/1.5mi one way, 214m/700ft ascent) – another walk you shouldn't miss: the ridge offers memorable views.

Peyto Lake is a highlight of the Icefields Parkway

The Saskatchewan Glacier belongs to the **Columbia Icefield**. The road passes the icefield's edge a few kilometres after the Sunwapta Pass (2,035m/6,677ft). Close to the Athabasca glacier is the **Icefield Centre** (tel: 780/852-6288; 7 May to 25 Sep daily 9–5; closed rest of year) with a visitor and interpretive centre, food and lodgings. Brewster Transportation (www.explorerockies.com/columbia-icefield) offers 90-minute, 5km (3mi) rides onto the glacier with a chance to walk on part of the ice as well as trips to the glass-floored **Glacier Skywalk** (daily 10–6; CDN$32) only a few kilometres away. Opened in 2014, the horseshoe-shaped and vertigo-inducing walkway projects out from a cliff edge and offers spectacular views of the Sunwapta Valley.

Two highlights stand out before you reach Jasper (➤ 147): the **Sunwapta Falls** (55km/34mi from Jasper), 15 minutes along an easy path from the road, and the **Athabasca Falls** (30km/18.6mi from Jasper), set just off the Athabasca Parkway, a parallel road that offers an alternative to the Icefields Parkway for the last few miles into Jasper.

✚ 200 A5–C4

INSIDER INFO

- There is a speed limit of 90kmph (55mph) on the Icefields Parkway. Check for further reduced speed limits. There are no services November to March. If you don't have your own vehicle, **Brewster Transportation** (➤ 162) runs several tours and a **daily scheduled bus service** (summer only) along the Icefields Parkway from Banff and Lake Louise.
- The **Peyto Lake Lookout** is an absolute must-see on the Icefields Parkway.
- On no account venture onto the glaciers alone: people die every year from **falling into hidden crevasses**. Sign up for special **guided walks** (three hours) or walk to the toe of the glacier from the parking area at Sunwapta Lake.
- Beyond the Icefield Centre look out for the sign for the **Wilcox Pass Trail** (4km/2.5mi one way, 322m/1,055ft ascent), widely considered one of the Rockies' best shorter walks.

Insider Tip

㉟ Banff

Some 4.6 million visitors a year flock to Banff National Park, and just about all of them visit Banff, making its 7,500 population swell to around 30,000 during the summer months. Statistics suggest the town is the busiest urban area of any national park in the world. So although the town has a superb setting – mountains ring it on all sides – its busy streets, full hotels and buzzing tour buses are a long way from the quiet and wilderness you might expect of the Rockies.

This said, the town offers plenty of reasons to stop: an excellent visitor centre, museums, shops for supplies and souvenirs, and the vast majority of the park's accommodations and restaurants. It's also within easy striking distance of walks and drives – peaceful strolls along the Bow River, for example, start from the town centre. You could easily spend a day or two here, more if you decided to use it as a base.

Banff Avenue with Mount Rundle in the background

Central Banff

Much of what happens in Banff occurs on Banff Avenue, the main street, and near its southern end lies the **Banff Park Museum**, a lovely old building full of stuffed birds and animals indigenous to the Rockies. Hunting game animals was banned in Banff in 1913, but predators such as wolves, lynx and eagles were still pursued until the 1930s. Behind the museum is a park that runs down to the Bow River,

and just a few steps away stands the modern **Whyte Museum of the Canadian Rockies**, with paintings, photographs and temporary exhibitions exploring the Rockies' people and landscapes and the area's emergence as a tourist destination.

Exhibits in
Banff Park
Museum

Farther Afield

It is worth following the riverside path just over the Bow River bridge and walking through the trees to **Bow Falls**, a powerful waterfall also accessible by a quieter trail on the other side of the river. From the first trail you can walk farther up the Spray River to the south or cut up to the **Fairmont Banff Springs** (➤ 157), Banff's famous landmark. Tours for non-residents are available around the 770-room hotel (details in the lobby), but it's enough simply to buy a drink or snack from the café off the main reception area and enjoy the superb views from the terrace.

The **Cave and Basin National Historic Site** is an interpretive centre based around the cave and hot springs discovered in 1883. Two easy strolls start from here: the Discovery Trail (1.2km/0.75mi) takes 15 minutes and the Marsh Loop Trail (2.4km/1.5mi) 25–30 minutes, the latter touching **Vermilion Lakes**, an area rich in flora and fauna despite its proximity to town: drivers can follow the 4km (2.5mi) Vermilion Lakes Drive, which is signed off Mount Norquay Road just south of its intersection with the Trans-Canada Highway.

Banff's other major attractions are a short car or taxi ride away. First choice is the **Banff Gondola** (➤ 138),

INSIDER INFO

- Visit the **Banff Information Centre** (➤ 138), a joint venture between the town's Banff and Lake Louise tourism bureaus, for information on sights, accommodations and the national park (information on trails and other park activities).

- It is essential to **reserve accommodations** in Banff well in advance: the information centre can help. Alternatively, contact one of several agencies, which, for a small fee, will find and reserve accommodations (www.skibanff.com; www.banfflakelouise. com or www.enjoybanff.com).

- **Banff Transit**'s "Roam" Shuttle (route 1), from Banff Avenue, will take you to the **Banff Gondola**. **Brewster Transportation** (tel: 403/762-6700 or 1-866/606-6700; www.brewster.ca) runs a guided sightseeing trip too, and the ticket includes the price of the gondola ride.

- **Rent a bicycle** from one of Banff's many outlets to explore some of the trails and roads close to the town.

- In high summer the best of the Minnewanka boat trips is the **sunset cruise**.

- Inquire at the park centre about **combined tickets** to the Cave and Basin Hot Springs, Banff Park Museum and Whyte Museum.

Insider
Tip

Rocky Mountains

a cable car 3km (2mi) south of town that runs to Canada's highest restaurant, two short trails and stunning views. Not far from the cable car and easily visited are the **Banff Upper Hot Springs**, a swimming pool based on hot springs, with waters at a steamy 32°C (90°F).

Farther afield still, a 25km (15.5mi) round trip, is **Lake Minnewanka**, a lake-reservoir in a mountainous setting. You can take a 90-minute, 48km (30mi) boat trip: contact the Banff Information Centre or Banff Lake Cruise (tel: 403/762-3473; www. explorerockies.com/minnewanka).

The Cave and Basin Hot Springs – sulphur-rich water with therapeutic benefits

---

✚ 200 C4

Banff Information Centre

✉ 224 Banff Avenue
☎ 403/762-8421; 403/762-1550 (park information); www.banfflakelouise.com
🕐 Mid-May to mid-Jun and mid-Sep to end Sep daily 9–7; mid-Jun to mid-Sep 8–8; Oct to mid-May 9–5 💲 Free

Banff Park Museum

✉ 91 Banff Avenue ☎ 403/762-1558; www.pc.gc.ca/lhn-nhs/ab/banff/visit
🕐 Mid-Jan to early Feb Sat, Sun noon–4; mid-May to Jun and Sep to early Oct Wed–Sun 10–5; Jul, Aug daily 10–5, 💲 CDN$3.90

Whyte Museum of the Canadian Rockies

✉ 111 Bear Street ☎ 403/762-2291; www.whyte.org
🕐 1 Jun to 15 Sep daily 9:30–6; 10–5 rest of year; archive Mon–Sat 1–5 💲 CDN$8

Cave and Basin National Historic Site

✉ 311 Cave Avenue
☎ 403/762-1566; www.pc.gc.ca/lhn.nhs/ab/caveandbasin/index.asp
🕐 Jan to mid-May and Oct–Dec Wed–Sun 11–5; mid-May to Jun and Sep to early Oct Tue–Sun 10–5; Jul, Aug daily 10–5 💲 CDN$3.90

Banff Gondola

✉ Mountain Drive ☎ 1-800/760-6934; www.banfflakelouise.com
🕐 Late Nov to mid-Jan daily 10–4; mid-Jan closed; end Jan–Mar 10–5; Apr–late May 8:30–6 (9 on Sat); late May to mid-Aug 8:30-9; mid-Aug to early Sep 8:30–8 (9 on Sat); early Sep to early Oct 8:30–6:30; early Oct–late Nov 8:30–4:30 💲 CDN$39.95

Banff Upper Hot Springs

✉ Mountain Avenue, 5km (3mi) from town centre
☎ 403/762-1515 or toll free 1-800/767-1611; www.pleiadsmassage.com
🕐 Nov to mid-May Sun–Thu 10am–10pm, Fri, Sat until 11pm; mid-May to mid-Oct daily 9am–11pm (closed mid to late Oct) 💲 CDN$7.30

36 Banff National Park

Banff is the most celebrated of the four major national parks that protect the best of the Canadian Rockies. Within its boundaries lie two renowned mountain resorts – Banff and Lake Louise – two grandiose and scenic highways, a plethora of majestic mountains, innumerable lakes, forests and waterfalls, countless magnificent viewpoints, and numerous opportunities to indulge in summer outdoor activities such as hiking, riding, whitewater rafting, golf and mountain biking.

Lake Louise in the national park

The park is easily seen. Most first-time visitors to the region make for the township of **Banff** (▶ 136), just 90 minutes by road from the centre of Calgary, a bustling place that provides everything you're likely to need to explore the rest of the park.

From Banff virtually all visitors make their way to **Lake Louise** (▶ 142, 188–190), a much smaller centre 45 minutes' drive or bus ride to the northwest. Some visitors take the fast and scenic **Trans-Canada Highway** (or Highway 1) route, others follow the parallel and still more beautiful

Rocky Mountains

Bow Valley Parkway (➤ below). Both roads have numerous spectacular view points and trails, long and short, that start from roadside trailheads.

Lake Louise (➤ 142) divides into two: a staggeringly beautiful but much visited lake and a small specially built "village" with a handful of hotels, shops, tour operators and a visitor centre a few minutes' drive from the lakeshore. This, too, makes a good base for walks (➤ 142, 188–190) and car touring, but accommodations are in short supply in peak season and the village is fairly characterless. Less well-known than Lake Louise, but in ways even more captivating, is **Moraine Lake** (➤ 144) just 13km (8mi) to the east. Like Lake Louise it is an excellent base for a wide variety of half- or full-day circular walks. The single hotel here, however – Moraine Lake Lodge – needs to be reserved well in advance.

Further Along the Trans-Canada Highway

From Lake Louise the Trans-Canada Highway runs west into Yoho National Park (➤ 150). Heading north to Jasper National Park (➤ 146) is the scenic Icefields Parkway (➤ 134), one of the world's great drives, a 230km (143mi) odyssey through some of North America's grandest scenery. Most people simply follow the highway as a drive – there are only a handful of hotels, hostels and campgrounds en route – but you should take time to follow at least one of the many trails that start from points along the road.

The Parkway leaves you in Jasper (➤ 147), a perfect base for seeing Jasper National Park, but unfortunately there's no easy return loop to bring you back to Banff. The obvious onward route is to head west on Highway 5 past the 3,956m (12,979ft) Mount Robson, the Rockies' highest mountain (➤ 155), but this commits you to an extended journey to Wells Gray Provincial Park (➤ 116) and the heart of British Columbia. A lot of people simply

Thompson Mountain with a meadow in the foreground

THE BOW VALLEY PARKWAY

Insider Tip

Use Highway 1 to cover the 58km (36mi) between Banff and Lake Louise. You won't be disappointed – the scenery is magnificent. Use the parallel Bow Valley Parkway, however, and you'll be even happier, for the older road between the two centres is lined with lots of turnoffs, **view points and short trails** designed to make the journey even more memorable. The best view points (all signed) are at the Merrent turnoff and Backswamp Viewpoint (8km/5mi) along the highway heading north. The best short walk is the highly recommended Johnston Canyon Trail, which leads over cleverly built catwalks to two sets of waterfalls, 1km (0.5mi) and 2.5km (1.7mi) respectively from the roadside parking area. Alternatively, try the shorter 400m stroll to Lizard Lake. The Muleshoe Picnic Area (21km/13mi southeast of Castle Junction) offers good opportunities to spot birds and other wildlife.

backtrack along the Icefields Parkway – no great hardship given the stunning scenery.

➕ 200 C4
🎫 CDN$9.80 tickets available at road entrances or park visitor centres.

BIRTH OF A PARK

The Canadian Pacific Railway (CPR) was the making of Banff National Park. Before its arrival at the end of the 19th century the area had been the preserve of First Nations peoples, the odd fur trapper and explorers such as Fraser, Thompson and Mackenzie. On November 8, 1883, three railroad workers, laid off when work on the line stopped for the winter, stumbled across a set of warm, sulphurous springs – the present-day Cave and Basin Hot Springs – while prospecting for gold. They failed in their attempts to lay claim to the springs, and in 1885 the government designated the Hot Springs Reserve a protected area. Two years later the reserve was renamed the Rocky Mountains Park, the world's third national park after the Royal in Australia and Yellowstone in the United States.

The government's early interest in the park was only partly environmental. Far more important was the notion that visitors to the region would consolidate and help pay for the government-backed CPR. The railway's vice president, the hard-dealing William Cornelius Van Horne, famously observed of the Rockies that if "we can't export the scenery we'll import the tourists." To this end he embarked on a series of grand railroad hotels to accommodate the hoped-for influx, the antecedents of Banff's present-day Fairmont Banff Springs (➤ 157), the Fairmont Chateau Lake Louise (➤ 142) and Yoho's Emerald Lake Lodge (➤ 152, 162).

Lake Louise

No picture can quite do justice to the matchless beauty of Lake Louise, with its sapphire waters and a majestic backdrop of mountains, glaciers and tumbling forests.

The lake is hidden in the mountains, 5km (3mi) from Lake Louise Village. Most visitors pass though the village, a modest sprawl of hotels, youth hostel, gas station, visitor centre and a small mall, en route for the lake. First impressions of the village may be disappointing, but Lake Louise itself cannot fail to impress. Little detracts from the view, although there's much that should, not least the huge Fairmont Chateau Lake Louise hotel, and the sheer number of visitors – anything up to 10,000 people a day in the height of summer.

The first foreigner to see the lake was Tom Wilson, an outfitter working for the CPR, brought here by a Stoney indigenous guide in 1882 (the Stoney had long known of the lake, which they called the "Lake of the Little Fishes"). Wilson called it Emerald Lake but it was renamed in 1884 in honour of Princess Louise Caroline Alberta, a daughter of Britain's Queen Victoria, who was married to Canada's governor-general. To escape the crowds, take a trail to Lake Agnes (➤ 188 and 189) or the **Plain of Six Glaciers** (➤ 190). You won't have the paths to yourselves – they're the most popular in the Rockies – but, as with the lake, the views are so good it's worth sharing them.

The light-absorbing properties of glacier silt help create the stunning blue of the waters of Lake Louise

WHY ARE THE LAKES SO BLUE?

Lake Louise, Moraine Lake and many other lakes in the Rockies owe their intense colouring to superfine particles of glacial silt, or till, known as rock flour. This glacier-ground till absorbs all colours of incoming light except those in the turquoise-blue spectrum – hence the colour. The particles are washed into the lakes from melting glaciers in the late spring and summer.

✚ 200 C4

Lake Louise Gondola
✉ Off Whitehorn Road, 0.8km (0.5mi) from Lake Louise Village
☎ 403/522-3555 or 1-877/956-8473; www.lakelouisegondola.com
🕐 Mid-May to mid-Jun Mon–Fri 9:30–4, Sat, Sun 9–4; mid-Jun to Jul daily 9–5; Aug to early Sep daily 9–6:30; rest of Sep daily 9:30–4:30
✋ CDN$28.75

Lake Louise Visitor Centre
✉ Samson Mall
☎ Parks Canada: 403/522-3833; www.pc.gc.ca/banff.Banff/Lake Louise Tourism: 403/762-8421; www.banfflakelouise.com
🕐 Mid-Oct to Apr Thu–Sun 9–4:30; May to mid-Jun and Sep to mid-Oct daily 9–5; mid-Jun to Aug daily 9–7

INSIDER INFO

■ Arrive early in the morning, late in the afternoon, or off season to avoid the worst of Lake Louise's crowds. Accommodations are more costly and difficult to find here than in Banff.

■ If you want fantastic views without hiking, take the 👪 **Lake Louise Gondola**, a cable car that runs to 2,088m (6,850ft) on Mount Whitehorn, signed just east of Lake Louise Village at the ski area. While a family outing is quite expensive, you can up-grade to a Ride & Dine Package (just CDN$3 extra), which includes a buffet lunch at the Lodge of the Ten Peaks at the base of the gondola.

Insider
Tip

Moraine Lake

Only a fraction of the number of people who visit Lake Louise visit this lake, just 14km (8mi) south of Lake Louise on Moraine Lake Road. However, it is the equal – many would say the superior – of its more famous neighbour.

The water is a deeper blue, the stupendous snow-dusted Wenckchemna Mountains of the Wenckchemna Valley more spectacular as a backdrop. The name, though, is a misnomer, for the "moraine" that appears to dam the lake at its northern end – a moraine is the debris gouged up or deposited by a glacier – is actually a landslip.

The lake has just one beautifully integrated hotel, café and restaurant, the Moraine Lake Lodge, which offers canoe rental and walks (lake strolls, two-hour, half-day and full-day hikes) that make this one of the best bases in the park if you want to spend two or three days walking. The best stroll is along the lakeshore; the best short walk is to Consolation Lake; and the best half- or day-walk is the Moraine Lake–Larch Valley–Sentinel Pass trail, with an additional spur to Eiffel Lake.

Above: Reflections in the still waters of Moraine Lake

Right: Walks range from short to multiday routes

➕ 200 C4

ROAD CLOSURES
The 14km (12mi) Moraine Lake Road is **closed** from mid-October until snow clears (usually mid-May).

WALKING IN THE ROCKIES

Walking in Banff and the other national parks is simple. Banff alone has nearly 1,600km (1,000mi) of trails, the vast majority of them well kept, well marked and well walked. Standards vary from easy strolls around lakeshores to multiday backpacking routes. Luckily you don't need to be super-fit and super-equipped to enjoy most of the paths – the vast majority don't require maps, as all popular trails are named, signed and well worn: Simply turn up with boots and bad-weather clothing and start walking. The main problem is knowing which of the many trails to choose. One is mapped on ► 188, and brief accounts of the best other walks are dotted throughout the text. Staff in visitor centres are trained to advise on hikes, and if you want to tackle more demanding walks there are numerous trail guides.

The best known trail guide is the widely available *Canadian Rockies Trail Guide* (Summerthought Books, 9th edition 2011) by Brian Patton and Bart Robinson, which contains most of the major trails in the four national parks.

⟨37⟩ Jasper National Park

In terms of visitor numbers, Jasper ranks second to Banff, but covers an area – 1,067km² (412mi²) – greater than the other main three Canadian Rockies' parks combined. It's also a wilder and quieter park than Banff, and the atmosphere of its more modest main centre, Jasper, retains far more of the frontier spirit. The wilderness landscapes and opportunities for outdoor activities, however, remain as enticing as any in North America.

Above: Patricia Lake

Where Banff town (▶ 136) is all hustle and bustle, Jasper Townsite, or Jasper, is quieter and more small-town in feel and appearance. It's also less immediately striking, for here the mountains lie at some distance from the townsite. This makes it more of a base rather than somewhere to spend time for its own sake – the outdoor activities aside, the Jasper Tramway cable car is the only real local attraction.

You'll need to join a tour or have transportation to get the most from the rest of the park, whose main points of interest centre on the **Maligne Valley**, southeast of Jasper, and **Miette Hot Springs** (a pool complex based around the Rockies' hottest thermal springs). There are fewer short hikes than in Banff, but Jasper scores heavily in its many **river** and **whitewater rafting** possibilities. These include water-based adventures to suit all levels of adrenaline rush, from rides down raging torrents to gentle river trips. Jasper also makes a perfect base for visiting Mount Robson (▶ 155), the Rockies' highest peak, 16km (10mi) west of the Jasper National Park boundary off the Yellowhead Highway (Highway 16).

Jasper

Jasper takes its name from Jasper Hawes, an employee of the North West Company, which established a trading post here after it was opened up by explorers at the beginning of the 19th century. The town's present-day origins, however, date back to the first years of the 20th century, when the Grand Trunk Pacific Railway sought to emulate the success of the Canadian Pacific Railway by building a rail route across Canada. Like the CPR it hoped to use the scenery as a bait for travellers, and in 1908 the Jasper Forest Park was duly established, followed in 1911 by a tent city on Jasper's present site (known as Fitzhugh after the company's vice president). The name Jasper was formally adopted soon after, when the site was officially surveyed. Jasper National Park was established in 1930.

Today the town gathers around two main thoroughfares, **Connaught Drive** and **Patricia Street**, the former home to the railway station and bus terminal, the excellent park visitor centre (50m/164ft east of the station), the Chamber of Commerce and town information centre, and most of the shops, hotels and restaurants. Maligne Tours, the town's main tour operator (➤ 162), is also on Connaught Drive about 135m/440ft south of the station.

Take a cruise on Maligne Lake, or rent kayaks or canoes to go fishing

The only real in-town attraction is the **Yellowhead Museum and Archives**, whose modest displays relate to the history of Jasper and the surrounding area. The best short walk to take is the Old Fort Loop east of town: details are available from the park visitor centre.

Out of town, be sure to take a ride on the 🚡 **Jasper Tramway**, a cable car 6.5km (4mi) south of Jasper on Whistler Mountain Road (off the Icefields Parkway). It's busy in summer, so expect to wait unless you arrive early,

INSIDER INFO

- Visit the park **information centre** (➤ 149) for full details of all park activities.
- If you're without transportation, **shuttle buses** run to the Jasper Tramway in summer from Jasper's major hotels.
- Maligne Tours runs a **shuttle bus to Maligne Lake** from Jasper if you don't have a car. The service is coordinated with cruise departures.

In more depth With a car or bike you might visit **Patricia and Pyramid lakes**, around 5km (3mi) northwest of Jasper. Both have picnic areas, easy trails and opportunities for boating, canoeing, riding and water sports. Lakes Edith and Annette (6km/3.7mi northeast) are a little quieter, and offer trails and pleasant grassy and sandy areas on which to stretch out.

but the wait is worth it for the views from the 2,300m (7,546ft) upper station, where there's a restaurant, interpretive centre and a trail that continues up Whistler Mountain (2,495m/ 8,151ft) for even more majestic panoramas.

Maligne Falls and Canyon

Maligne Valley

The Maligne Valley is Jasper's most popular excursion. Maligne Lake Road runs east from Jasper for around 48km (30mi) along virtually its entire length, passing two worthwhile stops en route – Maligne Canyon and Medicine Lake. It then culminates in magnificent style at Maligne Lake, the largest – and by general consent most beautiful – lake in the Rockies (▶ right). Most people drive or take a tour along the road and then join one of the fantastic 90-minute boat trips on the lake. These rides are extremely popular, however, so be sure to reserve in advance through Maligne Tours (▶ 162).

Insider Tip

First stop in the valley is **Maligne Canyon**, 11km (7mi) from Jasper, a gorge carved by the Maligne River. An easy trail loops down part of the canyon from the parking area (allow 25 minutes), with interpretive boards explaining the canyon's origins along the way. The Maligne area takes its name from the French for "wicked," an epithet applied by a Belgian Jesuit missionary, Father de Smet, to a crossing he made of the Maligne River in 1846 – and given that he was a hardened traveller, said to have covered 290,000km (180,000mi) in the course of his journeys, it must have been bad.

After 32km (20mi), Maligne Lake Road reaches **Medicine Lake**, best known for its strange fluctuations in level, the result of water entering and draining from lakebed sink holes – there is no natural surface outlet. The mechanics of the huge underground complex of springs and channels riddling the limestone bedrock are not yet fully understood. Few people linger at Medicine Lake, however, but head for **Maligne Lake**, a sublime ensemble of water, forest and mountain. You'll find parking areas, a warden station, restaurant and a quay, together with the easy **Lake Trail** (3km/2mi) along part of the eastern shore.

Above: A black bear near Patricia Lake

Above right: Couple canoeing on Lake Maligne

✚ 200 A5

Parks Canada Information Centre
✉ 500 Connaught Drive, Jasper
☎ 780/852-6176 or 780/852-6177 for trail office; www.pc.gc.ca/jasper
🕐 Mid-Mar to mid-May and mid-Sep to Oct daily 9–5; mid-May to mid-Jun 9–6; mid-Jun to mid-Sep 8:30–7:30; Nov to mid-Dec Fri–Sun 9–5, closed rest of year
💲 CDN$9.80

Tourism Jasper
✉ 500 Connaught Drive ☎ 780/852-6236 or toll free 1-800/473-8135; www.jasper.travel 🕐 Jul, Aug daily 9–9

Yellowhead Museum and Archives
✉ 400 Bonhomme Street ☎ 780/852-3013; www.jaspermuseum.org
🕐 Jun–Sep 10–5; Oct–Apr Thu–Sun 10–5 💲 CDN$6

Jasper SkyTram
✉ Whistler Mountain Road ☎ 780/852-3093 or 1-866/850-8726; www.jasperskytram.com 🕐 Late Mar to late May and early Sep to Oct 10–5; late May to late Jun 9–8; late Jun to early Sep 8–9 💲 CDN$39.95

③⑧ Yoho National Park

Yoho takes its name from a Cree indigenous word meaning "awe" or "wonder," a fitting memorial to the sheer majesty of the landscapes in a region many consider to be the finest in the Rockies. Glorious trails provide some of the country's best hiking, although roads also afford a spectacular window onto some of the park's most remarkable scenery.

Yoho is neatly bisected by the Trans-Canada Highway, which runs in tandem with the old Canadian Pacific Railway roughly east to west along the valley of the Kicking Horse River. Just off the highway at the heart of the park lies Field, the park's only village and site of the visitor centre. Close by are two side roads that provide access to some of the best trails: one along the Yoho Valley, the other to Emerald Lake.

Shorter trails strike off from points along the Trans-Canada, which is also dotted with limited accommodations options.

Insider Tip
A third region, around **Lake O'Hara**, contains some stupendous paths and a beautiful lodge hotel, but road access and numbers are strictly limited (► 152).

Field

As with Banff, Yoho owes its creation largely to the Canadian Pacific Railway. The company built its first hotel at Field in 1886, prompting the creation of a small reserve a few months later. In 1911 the area was extended and became Canada's second national park. The railway is still one of the park's sights, most notable for its famous ⓘ **Spiral Tunnels**, 7km (4.3mi) east of Field. The figure-of-eight tunnels allow you to watch the front of trains emerging from one part of the mountains before the rear has entered at the tunnel entrance.

Field still looks much as it did in the 19th century: A simple frontier village dwarfed by the looming bulks of Mount Stephen and Mount Dennis. The slopes of the latter contain the celebrated **Burgess Shale**, layers of sedimentary rock that contain the fossils of some 120 different types of soft bodied creatures more than 515 million years old. The site is one of only three that contain such creatures, whose soft-bodies made them ill-suited to the fossilization process. Access to the beds, a UNESCO World Heritage Site, is restricted, but the shales can be seen on guided walks: Contact the visitor centre or book on tel: 1-800/343-3006; www.burgess-shale.bc.ca.

Trans-Canada Highway

Far easier to see are the sights along the two side roads off the Trans-Canada Highway. The first, coming from Lake Louise, is a narrow road with hairpin bends (unsuitable for RVs) that runs north up the **Yoho Valley** about 3km (2mi) east of Field. About 14.5km (9mi) from the Trans-Canada

The clear waters of Emerald Lake

are the **Takakkaw Falls**, whose 256m (840ft) drop makes them some of the highest road-accessible falls in North America. The parking area is the start of many of the trails: The most popular short walks are Point Lace Falls (3km/2mi one way, minimal ascent) and Laughing Falls (3.5km/2.3mi one way, 60m/200ft ascent). The best day walk is the Twin Falls Trail (8km/5mi one way, 300m/1,000ft ascent), which stronger walkers can link with the Whaleback Trail (20km/12.5mi total round trip) for one of the Rockies' most highly rated walks.

Takakkaw Falls

The second road off the Trans-Canada runs 8km (5mi) north from just west of Field to **Emerald Lake**, site of the Emerald Lake Lodge (▶ 162), Yoho's equivalent of the Chateau Lake Louise and Banff Springs. There is a bar and restaurant if you need sustenance for walks such as the easy paths from the parking area to **Hamilton Falls** (1.6km/1mi round trip) and the **nature trail around the lake** (5km/3mi). More demanding walks run to **Emerald Basin** (4.3km/2.7mi one way, 252m/827ft ascent) and **Hamilton Lake** (5.5km/3.4mi one way, 856m/2,808ft ascent).

➕ 200 B4

Park Visitor Centre
✉ Highway 1, 1.6km (1mi) east of Field
☎ 250/343-6783; www.pc.gc.ca/yoho ⏰ Sep to mid-Oct and May to mid-Jun daily 9–5; mid-Jun to Aug 8:30–7; closed rest of year 🎫 CDN$9.80

INSIDER INFO

Yoho can be seen as a day trip by car from Lake Louise (the park is 50km/31mi across). **Accommodations** are costlier and more difficult to find here than in Banff. The fragile ecosystems around **Lake O'Hara**, a scenically stunning area south of the Trans-Canada, mean that all car, bicycle and motorcycle access along the access road is prohibited. The only access to the Lake O'Hara Lodge hotel, the campground and extensive trail network is by a special thrice-daily bus service. Places must be booked (tel: 250/343-6433).

㊴ Kootenay National Park

It's not the scenery's fault that Kootenay is the least visited of the four Rockies national parks – its grandiose mountain landscapes are as mesmerizing as any in Canada. They're also some of the easiest to see, as all you need to do to revel in the park's ranks of snow-dusted peaks and tumbling forests is to follow a single highway.

A trail follows part of the Marble Canyon

The fact that Kootenay is undervisited – the term is relative, as three million people annually come here – is that more visitors prefer to follow the main Trans-Canada Highway through Yoho National Park. In doing so they're missing the Rockies' most easily visited park, a narrow strip of land either side of the Kootenay or Banff– Windermere Parkway (Highway 93).

The park has its origins in a road built in 1910 to link the prairies with the west coast ports. Money ran out with 21.5km (13.5mi) built and British Columbia had to cede 8km (5mi) either side of the road to the Canadian government for cash to complete the project. In 1920, 1,406km² (543mi²) of land were designated a national park.

Take a Hike
Like other parks, you can see Kootenay easily from a car, but you'll be rewarded if you stop at selected spots for a couple of short hikes. The first halt coming from Lake Louise is the **Vermilion Pass**, where the Fireweed Trail (1km/0.5mi) runs through an area destroyed by fire in 1968 but which is already regenerating. About 3km (2mi) south is the **Stanley Glacier Trail** (5km/3mi, 366m/1,200ft ascent), which has good views of the eponymous glacier.

A far easier interpretive trail (1km/0.5mi) follows part of the beautiful **Marble Canyon**, a 40m (122ft) deep gorge, a walk that can be combined with a trail leading south to the **Paint Pots** (also accessible from the highway 2km/1.2mi south). The Paint Pots are a series of pools where waters and mud are stained by iron-laden water bubbling up from mineral springs. Aboriginal peoples from Alberta and British Columbia came to the spot – which they considered sacred – to gather the coloured clays, which they baked and ground to make ochre. This was added to animal fat or fish oil to be used in rock, tepee and body painting.

Insider Tip

The tiny settlement at Vermilion Crossing has a store, fuel, lodgings, summer visitor centre and fine views of Mount Verendrye. One other viewpoint, the **Kootenay Valley Viewpoint**, stands out on the road to the south before it exits the park near Radium Hot Springs. To its south, near the red-rocked Sinclair Pass, you'll see the trail sign for the Kindersley Pass Trail (9.5km/6mi), the best of the longer day hikes.

Vermilion River

🚹 200 C3

Park Visitor Centre
✉ 7556 Main Street East, Radium Hot Springs
☎ 250/347-9505, off season: 250/343-6783; www.pc.gc.ca/kootenay
🕐 Mid-May to mid-Oct daily 9–5; closed rest of year
💵 CDN$9.80

INSIDER INFO

- The best way to see the park is as a **day trip** from Banff, or as part of a loop that takes in Kootenay before heading north from Radium Hot Springs on Highway 95 and picking up the Trans-Canada at Golden to return to Banff or Lake Louise through Yoho National Park.
- Kootenay takes its name from the region's Kootenai or Ktunaxa First Nations peoples, whose name means "people from beyond the hills." It was these peoples who discovered the hot springs at the southern tip of Kootenay Park, now open to 300,000 bathers a year as part of the 🏊 **Hot Springs Pools** (May to mid-Oct daily 9am–11pm; mid-Oct to May Mon–Fri 1pm–9pm, Sat, Sun 10am–9pm; CDN$6.30), 1.5km (1mi) north of Radium Hot Springs village. The springs were bought for CDN$160 in 1890 by Roland Stuart, who sold them to the Canadian government a few years later for inclusion in the park for CDN$40,000. The almost odourless waters emerge from the earth at 44.5°C (112°F) and are mildly radioactive. The radioactivity is harmless – about the same as a luminous watch.
- The Hot Springs Pool is busy, with up to 3,000 bathers daily in high summer, so aim to visit off-peak or late in the evening to **avoid the crowds**.
- Radium Hot Springs has a wide selection of accommodations, but it's not a pretty place, so aim to **stay in Banff** or elsewhere as a base for Kootenay.

At Your Leisure

40 Mount Robson

Mount Robson (3,956m/ 12,979ft) is the highest peak in the Rockies. It's also one of the most impressive, thanks partly to its relative isolation – which emphasizes its height – and to its colossal south face, a sheer rise of some 3,120m (10,236ft). The source of its name is disputed, but to First Nations peoples it was known as the "Mountain of the Spiral Road" after its distinctive rock strata, which resemble a winding path.

The mountain and its surroundings are protected by Mount Robson Provincial Park, an extension of Jasper National Park in all but name. Most visitors content

The south side of Mount Robson

themselves with a view of the mountain from the visitor centre on Highway 16 (88.5km/55mi from Jasper). The alternative is to walk all or part of the Berg Lake Trail (22.4km/14mi one way) to the lake at the foot of the peak. Campgrounds en route make this the Rockies' most popular backpacking trail, but day hikers can simply follow the first third of the trail to Kinney Lake (7km/4mi one way). Note that there are few facilities locally except for the visitor centre.

⊞ 200 off A5
✉ Mount Robson Visitor Centre and Viewing Area, Hwy 16
☎ 250/566-4038; www.env.gov.bc.ca
🕐 May to mid-Jun, Sep 8–5; mid-Jun to Aug 8–7; early-mid Oct 9–4; closed mid-Oct to Apr

Rocky Mountains

A buffalo leading a protected life in a paddock in Waterton Lakes National Park – it won't be forced over the Buffalo Jump

41 Head-Smashed-In Buffalo Jump

Strictly speaking, this extraordinary heritage site is not in the Rockies but where the foothills rise from the prairie. If you're heading to or from Waterton Lakes National Park, then this site definitely warrants a detour. Similar buffalo jumps were common across North America, and were the results of thousands of years' hunting experience on the part of indigenous peoples. Buffalo would be corralled and then stampeded over a cliff, where the dead animals would be stripped for food, hide and bone. The site supposedly takes its evocative name from a young hunter foolish enough to watch the spectacle from below, just as the buffalo were hurtling toward him. Today it is a UNESCO World Heritage Site and consists of an impressive interpretive centre and the protected 10m (33ft) deep bed of ash and bones that accumulated over some

10,000 years of annual jumps.

➕ 201 C1 ✉ Porcupine Hills, Hwy 785, 18km (11mi) from Fort Macleod
☎ 403/553-2731; www.head-smashed-in.com
🕐 15 May to Labour Day 9–5; 10–5 rest of year
🍴 Café ($) 🚍 Regular Greyhound bus connections from Calgary to Fort Macleod
💰 CDN$10

42 Waterton Lakes National Park

Waterton Lakes National Park protects 523km² (202mi²) of the Canadian Rockies in southwest Alberta close to the US border. Its size – less than an eighth the size of Banff National Park – and peripheral position mean that it's usually ignored by most visitors unless they're entering Alberta by road from Montana and other US border states. Other-wise the best approach is to divert here from Calgary, before seeing Banff National Park.

Size apart, the park's scenery is the equal of the more famous national parks to the north, and offers good day and half-day hikes from the only centre, Waterton. One of the most popular excursions is to walk across the US border on the Waterton Lakeshore Trail (13km/8mi) to Goat Haunt in Glacier National Park, the larger US sister park of Waterton Lakes National Park. Together they form the Waterton-Glacier International Peace Park, which joined the UNESCO World Heritage Sites list in 1995. From here you can catch one of the regular pleasure boats on the lake back to Waterton. Consult the park visitor centre for details of trans-border hikes and other walks. Also be sure to drive the park's two scenic roads, both accessed from close to Waterton Townsite.

➕ 201 F1
✉ Entrance Road, Waterton Townsite
☎ 403/859-5133; www.pc.gc.ca/waterton
🕐 Park: year round; visitor centre: May to end Jun and Sep to mid-Oct daily 9–5; end Jun to Aug 8–7; Mon–Fri 8–4 rest of year
💰 CDN$7.80

Where to...
Stay

Prices
Expect to pay per double room per night excluding breakfast and taxes:
$ under CDN$100   **$$** CDN$101–$200   **$$$** CDN$201–$300   **$$$$** over CDN$300

BANFF

Banff Aspen Lodge $$–$$$
Good value and easy access to downtown make this attractive lodge popular. Most rooms have great mountain views, and the hotel has an outdoor hot tub, steam room and sauna, laundry facilities and internet access terminal. A continental breakfast is included.
☎ 200 C4 ✉ 401 Banff Avenue, T1L 1A9
✆ 403/762-4401, reservations: 1-877/886-8857;
www.banffaspenlodge.com

Buffaloberry Bed and Breakfast $$$
This beautiful house blends modern styling with the utmost comfort. The four bedrooms are spacious and come with private bathrooms, under-floor heating, internet access, TV/DVD and an internal sound system. Guests can relax in the Greatroom, with its wood-burning fireplace and patio overlooking Mount Norquay Ski Area. A deliciously satisfying breakfast is included.
☎ 200 C4 ✉ 417 Marten Street, T1L 1G5
☎ 403/762-3750; www.buffaloberry.com

Castle Mountain Chalets $$–$$$
Well placed between Banff and Lake Louise, in a scenic setting in the National Park, these log cabins and chalets, some sleeping four to six people, have impressive features, including kitchenettes; some even have Jacuzzis, dishwashers and fireplaces.
☎ 200 C4 ✉ Bow Valley Parkway, near Castle Junction, T1L 1B5 ☎ 403/762-3868 or toll free 1-877/762-2281; www.castlemountain.com

Fairmont Banff Springs $$$–$$$$
Such is the Fairmont Banff Springs' fame that it is sometimes easy to overlook its size. With 768 rooms, intimate it is not. Also, not all rooms have dramatic mountain views. What you're paying for here is the experience of staying in a slice of history and one of North America's most famous hotels – which is not necessarily the same as saying one of its best hotels. Be sure to find out just where your room is located. Note, too, that the hotel is some way from the centre of town. This said, the hotel's amenities are second to none. All rooms are well appointed – mini bars, ironing board, phone, television and coffee maker – and guests have access to golf, tennis courts, horseback riding, exercise room and facilities in the superlative spa, rated one of the best in North America.
☎ 200 C4
✉ 405 Spray Avenue, T1L 1J4
☎ 403/762-2211; toll free 1-800/257-7544;
www.fairmont.com

RESERVATIONS
For help with accommodations, contact **local visitor centres** in Banff, Lake Louise and Jasper (▶ 138, 143, 149) or try reservation agencies such as www.bannflakelouise.com (an official site) or www.skibanff.com, who will often charge a small fee. For bed-and-breakfast options visit www.cantravel.com; www.canadianbandbguide.ca or www.bbalberta.ca.

Rocky Mountains

Rimrock Resort $$–$$$$

This stunning modern hotel is the best place to stay in Banff if you want to treat yourself. It lies 2.5km (1.5mi) out of town off the road to the Banff Gondola (free shuttle buses run to and from central Banff) and enjoys some sensational views. The main lobby is an architectural tour de force, with huge windows and a colossal chimneypiece, while the 343 spacious rooms are well appointed. Facilities include an indoor swimming pool, 24-hour room service, two restaurants, saunas, masseuse, weight room and squash court.

☎ 200 C4
✉ 300 Mountain Avenue, T1L 1J2
☎ 403/762-3356; toll free 1-889/746-7625; www.rimrockresort.com

LAKE LOUISE

Lake Louise Inn $$–$$$$

This is the most reasonably priced place to stay in the Lake Louise area. In the village, it offers variously priced rooms in a spacious five-building complex, including 27 rooms with air-conditioning and 55 with kitchenettes. Rooms are pleasant and comfortable without being memorable. Facilities include an indoor swimming pool.

☎ 200 C4
✉ 210 Village Road, Lake Louise Village, T0L 1E0
☎ 403/522-3791; toll free 1-800/661-9237; www.lakelouiseinn.com

Post Hotel and Spa $$$–$$$$

The luxurious Post provides an alternative to the celebrated Chateau Lake Louise, with prices that don't cause such a sharp intake of breath. It has a huge range on offer, from spacious rooms and suites to cabins and an eight-bed house. All have a whirlpool tub in the bathroom, and some have fireplaces, seating areas, balcony or patio. The quieter rooms overlook the garden and forest, but everyone gets a view of the mountains. The luxurious spa includes an indoor pool, fitness equipment and treatments, and the restaurant is acclaimed (► 160).

☎ 200 C4
✉ 200 Pipestone Road, T0L 1E0
☎ 403/522-3989 or 1-800/661-1586; www.posthotel.com

JASPER

Alpine Village $$–$$$$

These classic cabins are in a delightful location 2km (1mi) south of Jasper overlooking the Athabasca River, with views of Mount Edith Cavell. Everything is in traditional pinewood and the interiors are stylish. Cabins range from one room to two bedrooms.

✚ 200 off A5
✉ 93A Highway South, Jasper, T0E 1E0
☎ 780/852-3285; www.alpinevillagejasper.com

Fairmont Jasper Park Lodge $$$–$$$$

This Canadian Pacific hotel is Jasper's equivalent of the Banff Springs and Chateau Lake Louise. Five kilometres (3mi) out of town on Lac Beauvert in beautiful countryside, it operates as a virtually self-contained resort village, with 442 rooms (either rustic or modern in style), golf course, tennis courts, boating, horseback riding, six restaurants, heated outdoor swimming pool, fishing and exercise room.

✚ 200 off A5
✉ 1 Old Lodge Road, T0E 1E0
☎ 780/852-3301; or toll free 1-800/540-4454; www.fairmont.com

---

BED-AND-BREAKFAST Insider Tip

Jasper has a large number of **bed-and-breakfast** rooms that make good overnight options given the high prices and unremarkable nature of most of the town's hotels. Try Tourism Jasper for details (► 149).

Jasper House Bungalows $–$$

This complex is in Jasper National Park, with walking trails leading from the cabin door, and great hiking opportunities nearby. There are four types of cabin, spaced out amid trees on the banks of the Athabasca River. Sleeping either two or four people, they all have bathrooms, and some have a separate bedroom and a kitchen-ette in the living area. The Executive Suites also have a fireplace and a balcony overlooking the river. There's also a dining room serving breakfast and dinner – either of which can be delivered to your bungalow.

✚ 200 off A5
✉ On Icefields Parkway 3.5km (2mi) south of Jasper T01 1ED
☎ 780/852-4535; www.jasperhouse.com

Where to...
Eat and Drink

Prices
Expect to pay for a three-course meal for two, excluding drinks and service

$ under CDN$50 $$ CDN$50–$100 $$$ over CDN$100

BANFF

Eden $$$

Eden offers Banff's regional cuisine. Choose, for a complete gourmet experience, the "Grand Degustation" 10-course menu. A multi-award-winning wine list is paired with faultless service and wonderful views.

✚ 200 C4
✉ Rimrock resort, 300 Mountain Avenue, Banff, T1L 1J2
☎ 403/762-1840 or toll free 1-888-746-7625; www.banffeden.com
🕓 Wed–Sun 6pm–9:30pm

Le Beaujolais $$$

Dining rooms in Banff's top hotels are outstanding, but this is one of the best individual restaurants. The elegant interior is wood panelled, the tables covered in crisp white linen, and the food is very French. Eat à la carte, or from one of the set-price menus, and choose wine from a list of 600. Jacket and tie are optional, but this is somewhere to make an effort. You'll need to book.

✚ 200 C4 ✉ 212 Banff Avenue, corner of Buffalo Street, T1L 1B5 ☎ 403/762-2712; www.lebeaujolaisbanff.com 🕓 Mon–Fri from 5pm, Sat, Sun 11:30–3:30 and from 5pm

Juniper Hotel Bistro $$–$$$

Known also as Muk-a-muk (the Chinook word for feast), this bistro is part of the Juniper Hotel. It offers a good selection of West Coast cuisine with lunch specialities such as bison stew and a platter comprising elk pastrami, bison whiskey sausage, candied salmon, artichokes, olives, chutney and pickle. Dinner dishes include tomato soup with organic gin and a tasty seafood hot-pot of sea scallops, wild salmon, halibut, prawns and mussels in a light tomato and fennel broth.

✚ 200 C4 ✉ 1 Juniper Way (Mount Norquay Road), T1L 1E1 ☎ 403/763-6219 or toll free 1-844-370-5619; www.thejuniper.com
🕓 May–Oct 7am–10pm; Nov–Apr 7:30am–9pm

Maple Leaf Grille & Spirits $$–$$$

Canadian cuisine? Yes, there is such a thing, and this is a good place to sample it. Enjoy the best

Insider Tip

Canadian ingredients from a menu that might include dishes such as bison tenderloin with double-smoked bacon, Québec blue cheese and a red wine reduction, or Brome Lake duck with vanilla bean risotto and ginger braised rhubarb sauce. The lunch menu might include a wild game platter (venison, bison, duck), bison stroganoff, or Salt Spring Island mussels steamed in sake, coconut and ginger sauce. Brunches offer some exciting choices too.

⊞ 200 C4 ✉ 137 Banff Avenue, T1L 1C8
☎ 403/760-7680; www.banffmapleleaf.com
🕒 Daily 11–3, 5–late

Saltlik $$–$$$

This striking, modern restaurant serves classic Albertan food – especially steak. Tasty seafood dishes are also available. The adjoining bar is a good place for a drink, light meal or bar snack when the dining room is closed.

⊞ 200 C4 ✉ 221 Bear Street, T1L 1B3
☎ 403/762-2467; www.saltlik.com
🕒 Daily 11:30am–2am

Silver Dragon $–$$

The Silver Dragon, which also has a thriving branch in Calgary's Chinatown, serves great value Cantonese and Peking cuisine. In daylight hours ask for a table by the front window, while you enjoy your Peking duck, hot ginger-fried beef or fresh shellfish from the tank. In summer, you can enjoy patio dining, and there's a take-out service.

⊞ 200 C4 ✉ 109 Spray Avenue, T1L 1C4
☎ 403/762-3939; 🕒 Daily 11:30–10

LAKE LOUISE

Laggan's Mountain Bakery and Deli $

If you just want a quick bite to eat, Laggan's is a friendly place with a great range of soups, sandwiches, bagels and salads, and some

irresistible pastries. They offer a selection of coffees too. For anyone planning a picnic, the deli is the perfect place to pick up a ready-made feast.

⊞ 200 C4
✉ Samson Mall, Lake Louise, T0L 1E0
☎ 403/522-2017 🕒 Daily 6am–7pm

Lake Louise Station $–$$$

This is a novelty, but a successful one: the restaurant occupies the beautifully restored 1909 Lake Louise train station, the village's oldest building, and also has tables in a restored vintage railroad dining carriage, The Delamere. Dining is casual in the station, a little smarter in the carriage. Food is mostly West Coast – herb-crusted salmon, burgers, Caesar salad, steaks and buffalo. There's a lounge bar, and in good weather you can enjoy a barbecue in the station garden.

⊞ 200 C4 ✉ 200 Sentinel Road, T0L 1E0
☎ 403/522-2600; www.lakelouisestation.com
🕒 Station: daily 11:30am–10pm; dining cars: Fri, Sat 6–9

Post Hotel $$$

This is one of the best restaurants in the Rockies, its cuisine a sophisticated fusion of European, Canadian, California and Asian cooking – alongside Albertan beef, foie gras and English pea sauce, you might find fresh scallops on jicama root, and red pepper and mango pineapple salsa with cilantro oil and jasmine rice. Fine food is complemented by 850 wine selections.

⊞ 200 C4 ✉ 200 Pipestone Road, T0L 1E0
☎ 403/522-3989 or toll free 1-800/661-1568; www.posthotel.com 🕒 Daily 11:30–2, 5–9:30

JASPER

Syrahs of Jasper $$–$$$

This a must for gourmets and wine connoisseurs who come here to enjoy sophisticated international dishes with matching wines. The inviting dining area features old wine barrels and subdued lighting, and it comes as no surprise that the restaurant is the recipient of the coveted Wine Spectator Award of Excellence. Be sure to try the Alaska swordfish or one of their delicious vegetarian dishes.

🔲 200 off A5 ☒ 606 Patricia Street, T0E 1E0 ☎ 780/852-4559 or toll free 1-877/232-6397; http://syrahsofjasper.com ⏱ Dinner from 5pm

Bear's Paw Bakery $
This welcoming café and bakery is very popular. The varied home-made food is healthy and well prepared. Also good is the Coco's Café at 608 Patricia Street.

🔲 200 off A5 ☒ 4 Cedar Avenue, T0E 1E0 ☎ 780/852-3233; www.bearspawbakery.com ⏱ Daily 6–6 (later in summer)

Villa Caruso $$–$$$
A long-time carnivores' favourite, Villa Caruso serves beef, seafood and pasta. Pizzas and other dishes are finished in a wood-fired oven, and steaks are cooked in dramatic, sizzling fashion in an open kitchen.

🔲 200 off A5
☒ 2nd Floor, 640 Connaught Drive, T0E 1ED
☎ 780/852-3920; www.villacaruso.com
⏱ Spring–fall 11am–midnight; winter 3–11

YOHO

Truffle Pigs Bistro $$–$$$
Eating-out opportunities in and around Yoho National Park are limited, so it's not competition that has set the standard for this popular place. At Truffle Pigs, part of the Kicking Horse Lodge at the tiny village of Field, you can eat breakfast, lunch and dinner. The Truffle is known for its local and regional sourcing and organic preferences and will cater for special diets where possible. General supplies for self-caterers are also available.

🔲 200 B4 ☒ 100 Centre Street, Trans-Canada Highway, Field, V0A 1G0 ☎ 250/343-6303; www.trufflepigs.com ⏱ 11–9. Breakfast in peak season: 7:30–10:30

Where to...
Go Out

ARTS

The focus of most music, theatre, dance and other cultural activities in Banff is the **Banff Centre**, St Julien Road (tel: 403/762-6100; www.banffcentre.ca). It is also the power behind the prestigious annual summertime **Banff Festival of the Arts**.

NIGHTLIFE

Banff has plenty of restaurants, and bars that stay open late, and in places like the **Elk and Oarsman** (119 Banff Avenue; tel: 403/762-4616; www.elkandoarsman.com) and **Rose and Crown** (202 Banff Avenue; tel: 403/762-2121; www.roseandcrown.ca), there's sometimes **live music** and **dancing** (usually Thu–Sat).

You can also catch a movie at the **Lux Cinema** (229 Bear Street; tel: 403/ 762-8595). Outside Banff, nightlife is scarce.

In **Lake Louise** your best bets are **hotel bars and lounges**, in particular those of the **Post Hotel** (200 Pipestone Road; tel: 403/522-3989) and **Lake Louise Inn** (210 Village Road; tel: 403/522-3791).

The same is true in **Jasper**, although the **Athabasca Hotel** (510 Patricia Street; tel: 780/852-3386) has **dancing and live music** most nights.

SHOPPING

The Rockies are not a natural place to shop, mainly because outside Banff there are very few shops. In Banff, however, you'll find an enormous number of outdoor clothing and equipment stores. Most line

Rocky Mountains

Banff Avenue, or streets nearby: one of the bigger stores is **Mountain Magic Sportswear** (225 Bear Street; tel: 403/762-2664; www.mountain-magic.com).

For books, head to the **Mooseprint Books** (208 Buffalo Street; tel: 403/762-3355; www.mooseprint.com).

Lake Louise village also has several stores, mostly in the small, central **Samson Mall** (a group of shops rather than an indoor mall).

The best outdoor store is **Wilson Mountain Sports** (Samson Mall, 201 Village Road; tel: 1-866/929-3636; www.wmsll.com), which as well as selling clothes and equipment also rents out and repairs bicycles, tents and other mountain equipment.

In Jasper, visit **On-Line Sports & Tackle** (600 Patricia Street; tel: 780/852-3630) for all outdoor equipment sales and rental.

TOURS

One of the largest and longest-established tour operators in **Banff National Park** is **Brewster Transportation** (tel: 1-866/606-6700; www.brewster.ca), which runs buses and excursions to the Columbia Icefields from Banff, Lake Louise and Jasper.

In Jasper the major operator is **Maligne Tours** (tel: 780/852-3370 or toll free 1-866/625-4463; www.malignelake.com), for trips to Maligne Lake, boat rides, white-water rafting, horseback riding, guided walking trips and fishing trips.

In Banff, **Lake Minnewanka Boat Tours** (tel: 403/760-5007; www.banfftours.com) offers trips on Lake Minnewanka.

ACTIVITIES

The Rockies national parks offer numerous outdoor activities, and as many tour operators and outfitters. One of the easiest activities to organize for yourself is **mountain-bicycling** – there are plenty of outlets in Banff and Jasper with hourly, daily and weekly rental rates for a wide variety of bicycles.

Horseback riding is also easy to arrange. Rides can last from an hour to a couple of weeks, and can be set up by companies such as **Banff Trail Riders** in Banff (tel: 403/762-4551 or toll free 1-800/661-8352; http://horseback.com), **Emerald Lake Lodge** in Yoho (tel: 250/343-6321) or **Skyline Trail Rides** in Jasper (tel: 780/852-4215 or toll free 1-888/852-7787; www.skylinetrail.com).

Many companies offer **whitewater rafting** – everything from a gentle glide down the Bow River in Banff to the raging white-knuckle rides in the Kicking Horse Canyon.

Try **Wild Water Adventures** in Lake Louise (tel: 403/522-2211 or toll free 1-888/647-6444; www.wildwater.com), or – in Jasper, which has a good choice of trips for all levels of experience – **Jasper Raft Tours** (tel: 780/852-2665 or toll free 1-888/553-5628; www.jasperrafttours.com) and **Whitewater Rafting** (tel: 78-/852-7238 or toll free 1-800/557-7238; www.whitewater-raftingjasper.com).

You can play **golf** at the Banff Springs Golf Course and the Jasper Park Lodge. Both rent equipment. **Fishing** and equipment rental can be arranged in most parks: in Banff try **Alpine Anglers** (tel: 403/760-1133; www.alpineanglers.com).

Both Jasper and Banff also have municipal **swimming pools**.

INFORMATION

For full and current information on outfitters, tour operators and outdoor activities contact the excellent visitor and park centres in Banff (➤ 136), Lake Louise (➤ 142), Jasper (➤ 146), Field (for Yoho National Park, ➤ 150) and Radium Hot Springs (for Kootenay, ➤ 154).

Calgary

 **Little Treats**

World's Largest Dinosaur

This attraction is a short drive from the **Royal Tyrrell Museum** (► 168), the huge 👥 dinosaur model is 25m/86ft high and has 106 steps inside that lead up to a viewing platform.

Sweat or Swim with a View

The rooftop sauna and indoor swimming pool at the **Westin Calgary** (► 176) has views of the river, market, city, and snowcapped mountain peaks.

People-watching and More

Eau Claire Market (► 173) is a great place to catch a glimpse of everyday life, so find a nice coffee shop and settle in.

Getting Your Bearings

Calgary rises from the rippling grasslands of prime Albertan prairie in a glittering phalanx of towers and skyscrapers, its majestic city centre one of the most modern in North America. Raised from almost nothing at the end of the 19th century, the city has largely prospered since the 1970s on the back of a burgeoning oil and gas industry, proceeds from which helped forge downtown's modern cathedrals of steel and glass.

Before the oil and gas, Calgary was a cattle town – beef is still an important commodity – and before that a hunting ground for the Blackfoot, Sarcee and Stoney peoples. Today the cowboy heritage is celebrated in the famous **Calgary Stampede**, while the art and culture of the Blackfoot and others are honoured in the magnificent **Glenbow Museum** (➤ 170), Calgary's premier attraction.

The Glenbow alone would make Calgary worth a visit, something it's as well to remember when planning a trip, for too many people treat Calgary as simply a convenient entry point for the Rockies – it's just 90 minutes or so by car from the city airport to the mountain-shaded streets of Banff (➤ 136).

Resist the Rockies' siren call – if you can – and give one of Canada's most immediately likeable and laid-back cities the couple of days it richly deserves.

Calgary's high-rise office blocks – Calgary Tower still provides the best views of the city

TELUS Spark 47

ary
Zoo 46

Bow River

TOP 10

Royal Tyrrell
Museum of Palaeontology   • Drumheller

CALGARY

Dinosaur
Provincial Park

Bassano

Brooks

0   50 km
0   30 mi

Perfect Days in...

The Perfect Day

If you're not quite sure where to begin your travels, this itinerary recommends a practical and enjoyable tour of Calgary, taking in some of the best places to see. For more information see the main entries (▶ 167–175).

⏱ 9:00am

Visit the Calgary visitor information centre in the ⭐**Calgary Tower** complex (▶ 167) then ride to the top of the tower for sweeping views of the city.

⏱ 10:00am

Cross 9th Avenue SE to the **43 Glenbow Museum** (▶ 170), where you can easily spend most of the morning – there's a café for refreshments.

⏱ Noon

Walk north through downtown to the **44 Eau Claire Market** (▶ 173), where there's a huge range of food concessions, cafés and restaurants for lunch. Alternatively, buy a picnic from the market stalls and – if the weather's fine – eat it in nearby **Prince's Island** (▶ 173).

⏱ 2:00pm

Wander around Prince's Island Park and then walk back to the centre of downtown and explore the stores and the malls on **8th Avenue SW** (▶ 178). Make a special point of seeing the **Devonian Gardens**, a huge indoor garden on the upper floors of Toronto Dominion Square.

⏱ 3:30pm

Catch the C-Train eastbound on 7th Avenue SW to City Hall. From here walk four blocks east to **45 Fort Calgary Historic Park** (▶ 174). Alternatively, take a taxi or C-Train to **46 Calgary Zoo** (▶ 174) and, from late 2011, the newly located **47 Telus SPARK. The New Science Centre** (▶ 175), just north on St George's Drive SE (also reached by buses 17, 19 and 119).

44 Eau Claire Market

TELUS Spark 47

Glenbow Museum **43**

Fort Calgary Historic Park **45**

46 Calgary Zoo

⭐ **Calgary Tower**

⭐ **5**

Calgary • **Royal Tyrrell Museum of Palaeontology**

⭐4 Calgary Tower

The Calgary Tower is one of the city's most distinctive landmarks, despite the fact that, since it was built, it has been crowded and overshadowed by the construction of newer and taller structures. However, the tower still provides a wonderful view of the city and beyond – on a clear day you can see as far as the Rockies.

When it was completed in 1968, the Calgary Tower was a symbol of the city's new oil-funded dynamism and commercial vigour. At 191m (627ft) it was also one of the city's tallest structures. These days, the downtown focus has shifted slightly, and as a result the area in which the tower stands has been a touch sidelined. Newer skyscrapers, not least the nearby **The Bow** (236m/774ft), completed in 2012, also mean that it now no longer dominates the Calgary skyline quite so magnificently.

Don't be put off: the views from the **observation gallery** are still highly worthwhile, extending beyond the city's broad low-rise suburbs to the rippling prairies and mountain peaks beyond. In 2005, a new view was added, with the construction of a section of 🏵 **glass floor** in the Observation Deck. Now those who have the nerve can feel suspended in mid-air as they look down at the ground 160m (525ft) below.

Insider Tip

TAKING A BREAK

Try the revolving **Sky 360** restaurant (tel: 403/532-7966; www.sky360. ca) at the top of the tower.

🏛 206 B3
✉ 101-9th Avenue SW
☎ 403/266-7171; www.calgarytower.com
🕐 Jul, Aug, daily 9am–10pm, 9–9 rest of year
🍴 Revolving restaurant and grill restaurant atop the tower ($$–$$$)
🚆 C-Train to Centre Street
🚌 433
💰 CDN$18

The Calgary Tower is a major feature of the city's skyline

⭐️**5** Royal Tyrrell Museum of Palaeontology

The Royal Tyrrell Museum – 140km (87mi) east of the city – is an excellent reason to make a trip to the Alberta Badlands: this is one of western Canada's most popular museums.

The Tyrrell is devoted to dinosaurs, but also appeals by virtue of its position in the so-called Alberta Badlands, an otherworldly moonscape of barren, sun-drilled hills, mud gullies and soaring limestone **hoodoos** at the heart of the Prairies.

The **Alberta Badlands** were created by meltwater during the last ice age and, but for the fact that the region is one of the world's most abundant sources of dinosaur fossils, might have remained merely a diverting geological anomaly. Instead they have spawned three of Alberta's most popular sights: the 🦖 **Royal Tyrrell Museum of Palaeontology**, a superb modern museum devoted mainly to dinosaurs; the **Dinosaur Provincial Park** (▶ Insider Info), a UNESCO World Heritage Site and source of many of the museum's dinosaur fossils; and the **Dinosaur Trail**, a 51.5km (32mi) circular drive from Drumheller embracing some of the most interesting parts of the Badlands.

Foremost of the three is the Tyrrell **Museum**, located in sparse, sombre countryside 6.5km (4mi) northwest of Drumheller. It takes its name from Joseph Tyrrell, who in 1884 discovered an Albertosaurus, the first of the hundreds

Dinosaur diorama at the museum

Royal Tyrrell Museum of Palaeontology

The hoodoes, part of the Badlands scenery near the Royal Tyrrell Museum

of complete dinosaur skeletons since removed from the Badlands.

Today the museum has some 35 complete skeletons, more than any other museum in the world. All are strikingly presented, forming the centrepiece of thousands of exhibits that relate to the dinosaurs' evolution and eventual disappearance. Among the skeletons are the original Albertosaurus and predictable crowd pleasers such as Tyrannosaurus rex, as well as more unusual creatures such as the Xiphactinus, striking for the delicate beauty of its skeleton, and the Quetzalcoatlus, believed to be the largest flying creature ever to have existed.

There's far more to the Tyrrell than old bones, however, for the museum plots a chronological course through evolutionary history, making its points with the help of computer stations, audiovisual aids and hands-on displays – or hands-in displays in the case of some simulated dinosaur dung. You can also watch scientists working on fossils in on-site labs, learn more about Yoho's **Burgess Shales** (➤ 150), or browse the remarkable paleoconservatory, a collection of living prehistoric plants, many of which, fossil research suggests, would have been growing at the time of the dinosaurs some 60 million years ago.

✚ 201 F4 ✉ 6.5km (4mi) northwest of Drumheller
☎ 403/823-7707 or toll free 310-0000 in Alberta and 1-888/440-4240 in the rest of North America; www.tyrrellmuseum.com
🕘 Mid-May to Aug daily 9–9; Sep daily 10–5; Oct to mid-May Tue–Sun 10–5
🍴 Museum café ($)
🚌 Greyhound bus service to Drumheller
💲 CDN$15

INSIDER INFO

■ It's possible to reach Drumheller by Greyhound bus and then take a taxi to the museum, but it pays to **rent a car for the day** in Calgary so that you can explore the rest of the Alberta Badlands.

In more depth About 50km (30mi) from the town of Brooks and some 160km (100mi) southeast of Drumheller is the **Dinosaur Provincial Park**. Its focus is the Field Station, a base for scientific research, but also home to one of the richest dinosaur fossil fields in the world. Most people come for guided walks and the Badlands bus tours, which take you to parts of the park otherwise out of bounds to visitors. For latest schedules and to reserve: tel: 403/378-4344; www.albertaparks.ca/dinosaur.aspx.

Insider Tip

㊸ Glenbow Museum

Pass Calgary by in a headlong rush to reach the Rockies and you'll miss one of western Canada's finest museums – the Glenbow – where outstanding art, historical displays and a First Nations section, second only to the Royal British Columbia Museum in Victoria (➤ 96), provide the perfect introduction to the region.

The Glenbow is one of the new breed of museums – bright, modern and well-designed, which makes it easy to negotiate. Built in 1976, it takes its name from the ranch of the oil tycoon who donated large portions of the museum's collection, and it is his largesse and taste that are responsible for the somewhat eclectic nature of several of the exhibits on the upper floors. The museum presents material using different media.

The exterior of the museum...

Asian Art

The museum's second floor houses **Many Faces, Many Paths: Art of Asia**, an exhibition of sacred objects from the Buddhist and Hindu cultures of Asia. Sculptures in stone, wood and metals, as well as reliefs, masks and paintings from the early centuries ad to the 18th century are on display. The second floor is also used for **temporary exhibitions**, which rotate every three or four months.

Albertan History

The museum's third floor has been redeveloped with the dynamic **Mavericks: An Incorrigible History of Alberta** gallery, an exciting portrayal of the history of the region. Based on a 2001 book of the same name by Aritha van Herk, it tells the stories of 48 remarkable characters who sum up the province's psyche. You will learn not just about the political activists, ranchers, railway builders and oil-men, but also about people like Charlotte Small, who in the early years of the 19th century dragged many of her 13 children an incredible 40,200km (25,000mi) in the wake of her surveyor/fur trader husband; Emily Murphy, Nellie McClung, Irene Parlby, Louise McKinney and Henrietta Muir Edwards, known as the "Famous Five," who campaigned "for women to be recognized as persons" (in 1929!); Fred Bagley, who joined the Mounties at age 15; and Tom Three Persons, who tamed the wildest bucking bronco at the 1912 Calgary Stampede. It's a compelling story, well told.

First Nations Art

Equal weight on the third floor is given to the **Niitsitapiisini: Our Way of Life – The Blackfoot Gallery**, whose collection focuses on the artistic and cultural background of the Blackfoot, Sarcee and Stoney peoples, partly nomadic tribes from North America's plains and interior, as opposed to the coastal peoples – notably the Haida – whose sedentary, fishing-based culture is celebrated in Victoria.

Certain themes are common to both groups, however, most notably the exquisite nature and immense diversity of the crafts, costumes and jewellery displayed, as well as the equivocal language and manifest unfairness of the treaty documents signed by tribal chiefs and white politicians. Other areas of the First Nations section deal briefly with the Inuit and Métis, the latter the mixed-race descendants of European and First Nations parents, a heritage that for years made them some of the most marginalized of all Canadian inhabitants.

Upper Floor

The fourth floor of the museum has an outstanding collection of **gems, stones and minerals**, many of them from the mines of western Canada. It also hosts one of the world's most extensive displays of **arms and armour**, and the associated Warriors section, an exploration of combat across a range of cultures. A third exhibition is **Where Symbols Meet**, a celebration of African achievement. The sculpture that rises up through the floors represents the northern lights.

Calgary

...and a display in the museum: First Nations dance regalia

TAKING A BREAK

Manny's Café, just inside the entrance to the museum, is a good refreshment stop.

✚ 206 B3 ✉ 130-9th Avenue SE ☎ 403/268-4100; www.glenbow.org
🕐 Tue–Sat 9–5, Sun noon–5
🚉 C-Train to Centre Street or Olympic Plaza 💲 CDN$16

INSIDER INFO

- Various **guided tours** are available, not just within the museum but also throughout downtown.
- The hard-to-find **entrance** is a little way east down the street by the Marriott Hotel. There's another entrance from the Stephen Avenue Mall.
- If you have children in tow, visit the 👫 **ARC Discovery Room** on the second floor for art-based activities.

⑭ Eau Claire Market

The Eau Claire Market is a vibrant mixture of food stalls, cafés, specialty shops and restaurants that gives much-needed heart and soul to downtown Calgary. Better still, it lies close to Prince's Island, the city's nicest area of green open space, and the ice-clear Bow River.

The oil boom since the 1970s has been good to Calgary, providing the finances to rebuild or refurbish large areas of the city centre with marble, glass and concrete. While few people have lamented the transformation, there's no doubt the glittering new downtown plazas and skyscrapers rather lack the human touch.

The opening of the Eau Claire Market changed all that, its bold, converted warehouse look deliberately designed to bring life, colour and a sense of focus to the city. The multi-level complex consists of bars, cafés, arts-and-crafts shops, food concessions, cinemas and a lively communal eating area where you can sit and people-watch while digging into food and drink bought from the surrounding concession stands.

Alternatively, take your food to Prince's Island, a couple of minutes' walk to the north, a lovely park area with quiet, shady corners. The Bow River here has a fine waterside walkway, part of more than 200km (124mi) of bicycle and walking routes around the city. For a longer walk, maps of the system are available from the visitor centre.

Eau Claire Market is held in a warehouse set over several levels

✚ 206 C1 ✉ Corner of 2nd Avenue and 2nd Street SW
☎ 403/264-6450 or 403/264-6460; www.eauclairemarket.com
🕐 Stores Mon–Wed, Sat 10–6, Thu, Thu 10–8, Sun 11–5
🍴 Many cafés and food stands ($) 🚃 C-Train to 3rd Street SW 🚌 403

At Your Leisure

45 Fort Calgary Historic Park

Fort Calgary was Calgary's birthplace, a wooden stockade built in six weeks by the North West Mounted Police in 1875 to help curb the lawlessness created by whiskey traders spilling over the border from the United States.

Today the original fort is long gone. The first stockade was pulled down as early as 1882, and the entire fort was rebuilt from scratch following a fire in 1887. It remained a police post until 1914, when the area was sold and redeveloped by the Canadian Pacific Railway. By the 1970s the site was all but derelict, buried under rail tracks and semi-industrial wasteland. Calgary reclaimed the area in 1975 as part of the city's centennial celebrations, producing a broad swathe of parkland but revealing only a few stumps of the earlier forts.

Now a replica of the first stockade has been constructed, complemented by a museum filled with evocative photographs and exhibits that recall the fort's origins and the first half-century of Calgary's existence. The surrounding park is pleasant to wander around, nestled

The replica stockade at Fort Calgary

in a bend of the Bow and Elbow rivers, the "clear running water" that inspired the fort's Gaelic name, Calgary.

Close by lie two other historic properties, **Hunt House** (not open to the public), built in 1876, and **Deane House**, built in 1906 by Superintendent Deane, local head of the Mounties.

🔯 206 D2 ✉ 750-9th Avenue SE
☎ 403/290-1875; www.fortcalgary.com
🕐 Daily 9–5
🚇 C-Train to City Hall 🚌 1, 14
🎟 Site: free; museum: CDN$12

46 Calgary Zoo

Canada's second largest zoo has made strenuous efforts to create "natural" habitats for its 1,200 or so creatures and has won conservation awards for its breeding and reintroduction programs. There are special aspen woodlands, rocky mountains and northern plains habitats, among others, together with the flora and fauna appropriate to each.

There are also underwater viewing areas for fish and marine mammals, including polar bears, as well as tropical, arid and butterfly gardens, an Australian section, a prehistoric park (with life-size dinosaurs), **botanical gardens**,

A red panda in Calgary Zoo

and perennial zoo favourites such as gorillas, elephants, giraffes and Siberian tigers. There are also children's activities, including stories and music times (check on the web or at the entrance).

✚ 206 E2 ✉ 1300 Zoo Road NE
☎ 403/232-9300 or 1-800/588-9993;
www.calgaryzoo.org
🕐 Daily 9–6 (last ticket 5)
🍽 Fast-food concessions ($)
🚇 Whitehorn branch C-Train to Zoo Station
💵 CDN$24.95

47 👫 TELUS Spark

If you are traveling with children, this is a major attraction, offering exhibits designed to appeal to young children, teenagers and adults.

In fall 2011/12, the former Telus World moved to a spectacular, futuristic new complex north of Calgary Zoo, Canada's first 21st-century state-of-the-art science centre.

The new centre offers a blend of high-tech and interactive exhibits as well as continuing to host a wide range of science-related temporary exhibitions on scientific themes.

One of the highlights is the 230-seat **Dome Theatre**, with a curved backdrop and stadium seating. The extraordinary domed roof and screen allows visitors to experience high-definition presentations of everything from the summit of Mount Everest to the depths of the ocean.

The centre's main draw is the **Creative Kids Museum**, for children up to the age of eight, which is divided into exhibition areas devoted to art, drama, music, literature and the visual arts. Among other things, there is the chance to paint and draw on walls and floors (or using a computer screen); play and explore music; or to dress up and perform in the "Theatre" experience. The emphasis here, as elsewhere (and in the new centre), is on interaction, fun and participation as a way of learning.

Another tempting area is the **Amazement Park** (elements of which will be included in the new centre), full of fascinating facts and figures and fun things to do, such as becoming a human bobsleigh in two giant tubes; seeing oneself reflected hundreds of times in two giant mirrors; building an arched bridge; or creating a cacophony in the Magical Music Makers section with drums, 'thunder' sheet, rain stick, howler fan and tubular bells.

✚ 206 E1
✉ 220 St George's Drive NE
☎ 403/817-6800; www.sparkscience.ca
🕐 Daily 9–5 (temporary exhibitions may have longer hours)
🚌 17, 19, 119 💵 CDN$19.95

Where to…
Stay

> **Prices**
> Expect to pay per double room per night excluding breakfast and taxes:
> **$** under CDN$100 **$$** CDN$101–$200 **$$$** CDN$201–$300 **$$$$** over CDN$300

Kensington Riverside Inn
$$$–$$$$
This intimate 19-room boutique hotel is on the banks of the Bow River in the trendy Kensington district. Downtown Calgary is easily accessible via a nearby pedestrian bridge and the accommodation is contemporary, urban, and functional in design with warm tones to lend atmosphere. All the rooms have high-speed WiFi, flat screen TVs, sound systems, and spacious bathrooms. The hotel's Chef's Table restaurant offers gourmet regional cuisine made with ingredients sourced from Alberta.

✚ 206 C1
✉ 1126 Memorial Drive NW
☎ 403/228-4442, or toll free 1-877/313-3733; www.kensingtonriversideinn.com

Days Inn-Calgary Airport **$$–$$$**
Most downtown hotels are not cheap – the edge of the city offers better deals. The surroundings of this modern small hotel are hardly scenic but the hotel has very comfortable business-class rooms and light complementary breakfast. There's an airport shuttle, but to get to downtown, other than by a taxi, it's a 10-minute walk to the C-train light rail system.

✚ 206 off E1
✉ 2799 Sunridge Way NE, T1Y 7K7
☎ 403/250-3297 or toll free 1-800/329-7466; www.daysinn.com

Fairmont Palliser **$$–$$$$**
The Palliser is Calgary's most prestigious hotel, thanks to its pedigree – it's part of the old Canadian Pacific hotel chain (bought by Fairmont) that includes Banff Springs (▶ 157) and Chateau Lake Louise. Built in 1914, it has long been the choice of VIPs and visiting royalty. Rooms are spacious, air-conditioned and decorated in traditional style, and there are steam room, health club and exercise facilities. There's no charge for under 18s sharing with their parents.

✚ 206 B3 ✉ 133-9th Avenue SW, T2P 2M3
☎ 403/262-1234; toll free in North America 1-866/540-4477; www.fairmont.com/palliser

Sandman Hotel Downtown City Centre **$$**
This modern, high-rise hotel is well-located on the western edge of downtown, moments from the C-Train light transit. It has an attractive indoor pool complex.

✚ 206 A3 ✉ 888-7th Ave SW, T2P 3J3
☎ 403/237-8626 or toll free 1-800/916-4339; www.sandmanhotels.com

The Westin Calgary **$$$–$$$$**
Beautifully appointed rooms with modern decor and furnishings distinguish this high-rise hotel in a good downtown location. There are also luxury suites available, and facilities include an indoor swimming pool, rooftop sauna and whirlpool, a gym, restaurant and gift shop. There is a kids' club, no fee for under 18s sharing parents' rooms and pets are accepted. *Inside Tip*

✚ 206 A3 ✉ 320-4th Avenue SW, T2P 2S6
☎ 403/266-1611; toll free in North America 1-800/627-8417; www.westincalgary.com

Where to...
Eat and Drink

Prices
Expect to pay for a three-course meal for two, excluding drinks and service
$ under CDN$50 $$ CDN$50–$100 $$$ over CDN$100

RESTAURANTS

Earls Calgary Downtown Tin Palace $$
This mid-market chain rarely disappoints. Long menus often include surprisingly sophisticated dishes from around the world.

🗺 206 A3 ✉ 2401-4th Street SW, T2S 1X5
☎ 403/228-4141; www.earls.ca 🕐 Mon–Thu 11am–midnight, Fri, Sat 11am–1am, Sun 11–11

Joey Eau Clair $–$$
As part of the popular Joeys chain, you can expect a buzzing vibe and an eclectic menu of New World cuisine here. New twists and bold flavours add a real zing to the long menu of appetizers, salads, steaks, chicken, ribs, fish dishes and stir-fries. Great sandwiches, too. This branch is on the edge of Eau Claire Market.

🗺 206 C1 ✉ 208 Barclay Parade SW, T2P 4R5
☎ 403/263-6336; www.joeyrestaurants.com
🕐 Mon–Sat 11am–2am, Sun 11am–midnight

River Café $$–$$$
This relaxed restaurant should be your first choice if you want a treat in Calgary. The River Café stands in a park by the Bow River just a minute or so from the Eau Claire Market. From the first mouthful you know you're in the presence of superlative chefs. Menus change regularly and feature dishes inspired by the ingredients of the Pacific Northwest (including game) and plates featuring Ocean Wise (➤ 29) sustainably caught seafood. Reservations essential.

🗺 206 C1 ✉ 25 Prince's Island Park, T2P 0R1
☎ 403/261-7670; www.river-cafe.com
🕐 Lunch Mon–Fri 11–3, dinner daily 5–10, brunch at weekends 10–3, closed Jan

Teatro $$–$$$
It's a close-run thing between Teatro and the River Café (➤ left) for the title of Calgary's best restaurant – the two have part-owners in common – and if Teatro tends to attract a touch more praise it's only because both the neoclassical setting and food are rather more formal and showy. The restaurant's housed at the heart of downtown in a grandiose former bank building – suits and cocktail dresses won't be out of place here. The inspiration for the food comes from northern Italy, and includes dishes such as lobster ravioli and rigatoni, but the cooking also embraces Far Eastern and West Coast (fish and seafood) influences.

🗺 206 B3 ✉ 200-8th Avenue SE T2G 0K7
☎ 403/290-1012; www.teatro.ca
🕐 Lunch Mon–Fri 11:30–2, dinner daily 5–10

BARS

Brewsters Brewpub $–$$
Part of a Saskatchewan brewpub chain, Brewsters serves up 14 of its own excellent beers, with names like "Flying Frog" and "Rig Pig Pale

---

AFFORDABLE MEALS Insider Tip
For a huge range of inexpensive places for lunch, don't forget the food halls of the **Eau Claire Market** (➤ 173) and downtown shopping malls.

Ale," plus imported beers. It also offers great food. This is one of five in Calgary. It has a patio for summer days.

✚ 206 A3 ✉ 834-11th Avenue
☎ 403/265-2739; www.brewsters.ca
🕐 Mon 11:15am–11:30am, Tue, Wed until 12:30am, Thu until 1am, Fri until 1:30am, Sat 11am–1:30am, Sun 11am–11:30am

The Joyce on 4th $$

This popular pub in the Mission district is a cut above most mock-Irish bars, not least because of its mix of fittings, many of which are sourced from the old country. The entrance alone sports a tin roof embellished with Victorian light fittings. Inside is an impressive long mahogany bar. Draught Guinness keeps the atmosphere going and there's good food such as Irish stew and fish and chips. There's usually live Irish music and dancing on Friday and Saturday evening.

✉ 506-24th Avenue SW, T2S 0K4 ☎ 403/541-9168; www.calgarysbestpubs.com/joyce
🕐 Mon–Fri 11am–2am, Sat 9am–2am, Sun 10am–midnight

Where to...
Shop

Calgary's ferocious winters mean that most shops are in malls and shopping centres. The main **downtown malls** are between 5th Street SW and 1st Street SE along 8th Avenue. Among them are **Hudson's Bay** (8th Avenue SW; tel: 403/262-0345; www.thebay.com); **The Core** (7th Avenue and 2nd Street SW; tel: 403/441-4190; www.coreshopping.ca); and the outdoor **Stephen Avenue** mall. Specialty stores can be found in the **Eau Claire Market** (► 173) and in the **Kensington** neighbourhood (10th Street NW at Kensington Road).

For a list of stores pick up the monthly **Where Calgary** magazine (www.where.ca/calgary), which is available free from hotels and the visitor centre.

Where to...
Go Out

Calgary boasts plenty of outstanding theatres, movie houses and classical music ensembles, as well as good bars, pubs and clubs for dancing and live music. Much of the city's cultural life revolves around the **Epcor Centre for Performing Arts** and its five performance spaces (205-8th Avenue SE; tel: 403/294-9494; www.epcorcentre.org). Inquire at the visitor centre (► 36) for information on cultural events, in particular for details of concerts by the acclaimed **Calgary Philharmonic Orchestra** (tel: 403/571-0270; www.cpo-live.com).

Contact **Ticketmaster** (www.ticketmaster.ca) for details of **sports events** – notably games with the Calgary Flames ice hockey team – and tickets for a range of cultural and sports events.

To hear live blues, visit **The Blues Can** (1429 9th Avenue SE; tel: 403/262-2666; www.thebluescan.com) in Inglewood, and for rock and pop music head to **Broken City** (613 11th Avenue SW; tel: 403/262-9976; www.brokencity.ca).

Country music is popular and **Ranchman's** (9615 Macleod Trail; tel: 403/253-1100; www.ranchmans.com) has won the Canadian Country Music Association's award for best club for the last five years running.

Castle Pub (1217-1st Street SW; tel: 403/264-5759) often has live music, as do numerous places on **17th Avenue**, also known as "Electric Avenue" because of its concentration of bars and clubs.

Walks & Tours

Walks & Tours

1 VANCOUVER
Walk

DISTANCE 3km (2mi) **TIME** 2 hours; allow extra time for window-shopping, refreshment stops and visiting museums **START POINT** Canada Place ✚ 205 E3 **END POINT** Granville Island ✚ 204 C1

This walk takes you across Vancouver's downtown peninsula from north to south, starting on the waterfront at Canada Place and exploring the city's two key streets – Burrard and Robson. It then touches on Library Square before traversing the hip Yaletown district and crossing False Creek to Granville Island.

❶–❷

Walk around the perimeter of **Canada Place** (➤ 60) if you haven't already done so. Then, with your back to the water, cross the plaza area and main road in front of you and bear right a few steps before turning left onto Burrard Street. Almost immediately on your right as you walk up Burrard Street is the 1930 **Marine Building** (No 355), designed to suggest a rocky headland. Note the bas-relief motifs on its facade, which portray Zeppelins,

Vancouver's Marine Building

old planes and a variety of marine environments, then admire the amazing door and walk into the lobby to see the inlaid zodiac in the paving, vaulted ceiling and old lift doors. Two blocks farther along Burrard Street on the left, just beyond a pretty garden and waterfalls, is **Christ Church Cathedral**, a 19th-century neo-Gothic building that survived plans by the church authorities to demolish it and sell the site to developers in 1935. Developers did grab the site behind the cathedral, however, obliterating an art deco building here to build the present postmodern Cathedral Place in 1991.

❷–❸

Across the road from Cathedral Place, where it meets West Georgia Street, is the grand Fairmont **Hotel Vancouver**, another fine period building (completed in 1929), topped with a distinctive green copper roof

0
0   500

❼ 🏛
Granville
Island
Granville
Bridge

Christ Church Cathedral

Vancouver

massive pendulum and art displays. Cross West Georgia, and continue on Hornby to the **Vancouver Art Gallery** (▶63), whose classical outlines – this was once the city's main courthouse – are straight ahead. The Gallery Café is a good place for refreshments, especially in fine weather, when you can sit outside.

Turn left along West Georgia Street to its junction with Hornby Street. Divert left down Hornby Street to the fascinating **Bill Reid Gallery of Northwest Coast Art** (▶65) Return to the junction with West Georgia Street, cross over and visit the HSBC Bank's **Atrium Gallery** reception area with its

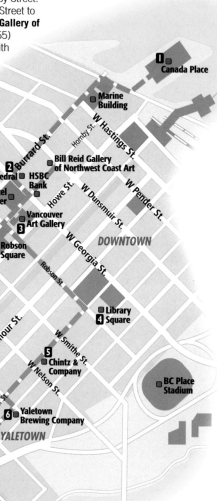

Walks & Tours

Inside Vancouver Art Gallery

3–4

The gallery's main entrance opens onto Robson Street by way of **Robson Square**, a partly sunken city plaza. Turn left on Robson Street and continue through the busy pedestrian flow. Cross Granville Mall, Seymour Street, Richards Street and Homer Street, where the imposing outlines of **Library Square** come into view. This magnificent development contains Vancouver's **main public library** – the striking visual parallels to Rome's Colosseum, say the building's architects, are completely unintentional.

Visiting a library would not normally feature on a sightseeing wish list, but here you should make an exception: the views and interior architecture of the nine-story (seven floors are occupied by the library) structure are magnificent. If you need a break, the postmodern arcade on the building's flanks is full of little cafés.

Insider Tip

4–5

Looking down Robson Street to the east from The Centre in Vancouver for Performing Arts you'll see part of **BC Place Stadium**, a great-domed building in the distance. A survivor of the '86 Expo, it's used as a sports and trade show area: it features one of the world's largest air-inflated domes, its Teflon-fiberglass roof supported by 16 jet-engine fans.

Locals refer to it as the "mushroom" or "marshmallow in bondage" – after its shape – but it's not really worth a diversion. Instead you should turn south and follow Homer Street, passing Chintz & Company on the left, an Aladdin's cave of a shop (➤82).

5–6

There's little of note on Homer Street, but just as you start to get bored, turn left into Helmcken Street and suddenly you enter **Yaletown**, once a semiderelict district but now one of Vancouver's trendiest quarters. You won't be able to miss the area, as the signs of transformation are everywhere: old warehouses and shops have been converted into hip loft apartments and every street is lined with art galleries, bookstores, bars and restaurants.

This is a great place to window-shop or browse, or to sit with a coffee at a sidewalk café and watch the world go by (old warehouse loading bays now make ideal patio areas). One of the area's key buildings is the large **Yaletown Brewing Company** (1111 Mainland, ➤81) a combination of bar, pub, restaurant and working brewery.

6–7

From Yaletown you need to head west through a mainly residential area, turning right off Hamilton Street onto Davie or Drake Street. Cross Granville Street and Howe Street. When you come to Hornby Street, turn left and you eventually come to the waterfront at False Creek. Here there is a small landing stage where you can catch one of the small ferries that run across to **Granville Island** (➤58), a good place to finish your walk.

From the island you can catch a bus back to the centre of downtown or catch another ferry onward to Vanier Park and the Maritime Museum and Museum of Vancouver (➤66).

2 VICTORIA
Walk

DISTANCE 2.5km (1.5mi)   **TIME** 1 hour 30 minutes; allow extra time for window-shopping, refreshment stops and visiting museums
START/END POINT Inner Harbour Visitor Centre ✚ 203 B3

This walk takes you through the lovely old-fashioned heart of old Victoria, touching on the pretty harbour area and most of the sights and colourful flower-decked main streets. It also delves into some of the smaller streets en route, and explores Market Square and Chinatown, two appealing enclaves of specialty stores.

❶–❷
With your back to the Visitor Centre entrance, turn right and walk down the steps and along the waterfront. Walk up the steps at the far end and cross Belleville Street to look at the **Parliament Buildings** (➤ 90). Then walk east along Belleville Street (away from the water and Parliament Buildings), cross Government Street and turn right at the alley by the totems beyond the **Royal British Columbia Museum** (➤ 96). On your left stands **Helmcken House** (➤ 102) with **St Anne's Schoolhouse** just beyond. Exit onto Douglas Street between Helmcken House and the Schoolhouse. Turn left and then turn left along Belleville Street. Cross right and go through the gardens of the **Empress Hotel** (➤ 104). Exit on Government Street and turn right to the Visitor Centre.

❷–❸
From here you're going to head north along Government Street, Victoria's main thoroughfare, and

Old Town 1880, a sculpture by Luis Merino in Market Square

duck into the smaller streets that run across it from east to west. The first of these smaller streets is Courtney Street, but first walk a few steps beyond the intersection to see (and smell) **Rogers' chocolates** on the right (➤ 107). Then backtrack and turn left (east) on Courtney Street. Cross Gordon Street to reach the **Victoria Bug Zoo** at No 631 (➤ 185), a menagerie of live insects and other tiny creatures – the scorpions and tarantulas are favourites.

Insider Tip

❸–❹
Return to Gordon Street and turn right. At the junction with Broughton Street, turn right. Drop into **Artisan Wine Shop** at No 644 (tel: 250/384-9994; www.artisanwineshop.com) just past Broad Street, for top British Columbian and other vintages. Go back and turn right into Broad

Walks & Tours

Bastion Square in Old Town, the original site of Fort Victoria

Street, and then turn left on Fort Street to return to Government Street. Both Broad Street and Fort Street are full of appealing shops and restaurants. One of Victoria's liveliest restaurants, **Pagliacci's** (► 106), is at 1011 Broad Street, while the city's premier native arts gallery, **Alcheringa Gallery** (► 185), which features aboriginal art by talented artists from the Northwest Coast of Canada, is at 665 Fort Street. On the right hand side of Fort Street is a side entrance to the **Hudson's Bay** department store (tel: 250/386-3322; www.thebay.ca).

4–5

At the junction of Fort Street with Government Street, look for No 1022, on the opposite west corner of the junction. This was once the heart of Fort Victoria, built in 1843 by the Hudson's Bay Company. Light-coloured bricks on the sidewalk and a plaque on the wall mark the site of the original walls, but the fort complex extended beyond Fort and Broughton streets, and reached as far as Bastion Square in the west.

Continue north along Government Street, past View Street on your right. Turn right at the next junction, Trounce Alley, a tempting retreat filled with old gaslights, heraldic crests and colourful hanging baskets. The alley's former bars and brothels have been replaced by a medley of specialty shops and boutiques – **All in Bloom**, a garden store at No 616, midway down on the left, is particularly worth a look. (tel: 250/383-1883)

Turn left at Broad Street, cross Yates Street and turn left at the top of Broad Street into Johnson Street. Cross Government Street and a short way down the westerly continuation of Johnson Street on the right is one entrance to the shops, restaurants and bars of **Market Square** (► 94).

Inside Tip

5–6

Explore Market Square's medley of specialist stores (arranged over two levels) and then return to Johnson Street and turn right (west). Turn right on Store Street and then take the second right turn into the un-marked Fisgard Street, focus of Victoria's small **Chinatown** (► 95). Halfway down Fisgard Street on the right is **Fan Tan Alley**, named after a Chinese gambling game and reput-edly the world's narrowest alley. Formerly it was a hotbed of brothels, bars and opium dens; today it's a rather pale shadow of its former self but is given some colour by several Chinese shops, galleries, boutiques and New Age stores.

6–7

Return to Store Street and turn left. At Johnson Street, go onto Store Street's continuation, Wharf Street. After about 175m detour left into picturesque **Bastion Square**, where you can visit the **Maritime Museum** (► 94) or take time out in one of several cafés and pubs. Walk straight on a short distance, to the

CHINATOWN

6

Fisgard St.

Fan Tan Alley

Centennial Square

5 Market Square

Johnson St.

Store St.

Government St.

Broad St.

Douglas St.

Yates St.

Maritime Museum

All in Bloom

Trounce Alley

View St.

Rebar

Hudson's Bay **4**

Alcheringa Gallery

Langley St.

Fort

7

Pagliacci's

Broughton St.

Artisan Wine Shop

Roger's

Courtney St.

3 Victoria Bug Zoo

Wharf St.

1 Visitor Centre

2

Empress Hotel

Belleville St.

Douglas St.

Humboldt St.

Cridge Park

Royal BC Museum

Helmcken House

Government St.

0   200 m
0   200 yd

BC Legislative Buildings

St Ann's Schoolhouse

corner of Langley Street, and you can indulge in one of the healthy concoctions served up at the **ReBar** at 50 Bastion Square (▶107). Retrace your steps and turn left on **Wharf Street**, which will take you back to the **Inner Harbour** past all sorts of funky stores, cafés, galleries and tattoo parlours. Acclaimed as the city's most picturesque street, it's also a departure point for whale-watching trips (▶89).

PLACES TO VISIT

Alcheringa Gallery
✉ 621 Fort Street ☎ 250/383-8224;
www.alcheringa-gallery.com
🕐 Mon–Sat 10–6, Sun noon–5

Victoria Bug Zoo
✉ 631 Courtney Street ☎ 250/384-2847; www.bugzoo.ca 🕐 Mon–Fri 11–4, Sat, Sun 10–5 💲 CDN$10

3 KELOWNA TO NELSON
Drive

DISTANCE 363km (226mi)
TIME Allow 2–3 days, more with longer stays in Kaslo
START POINT Kelowna ✚ 199 E2   **END POINT** Nelson ✚ 200 B1

There are two principal routes across British Columbia: the Trans-Canada Hwy (Hwy 1) or Hwy 3 close to the US border. The most scenic journey, however, follows a more meandering but more rewarding drive, linking two of the province's regional highlights and their respective main centres – the Okanagan and the Kootenays, and the towns of Kelowna and Nelson – while leaving you well placed for onward travel to the Rockies.

1–2

Begin in **Kelowna** (➤ 114). If time is short, take Hwy 97 north along the east shore of Okanagan Lake to Vernon (46km/29mi), but note that in its early reaches this is a busy and unattractive stretch of road, lined with malls, motels and strip development. If you have time, it is better to cross the town's floating bridge and follow the quieter and more attractive **Westside Road** north on the western shore of the lake. Visit the **O'Keefe Ranch** (➤ 115) and then turn south on Hwy 97 to drive the 12km/7.5mi from the ranch to **Vernon** (➤ 115).

2–3

At Vernon, pick up Hwy 6 east for **Coldstream** and Lumby (26km/16mi). Once clear of the town, the road climbs gently along the **Coldstream Valley**, passing through a beautiful pastoral landscape of orchards, verdant meadows, rolling, tree-covered hills, and venerable ranches distinguished by fine old wooden barns. **Lumby** has a small, summer-only visitor centre (www.monasheetourism.com), with information on the region and the wilds of **Monashee Provincial Park** to the north, reached by a rough road from the tiny settlement of Cherryville, 33km (20mi) beyond Lumby. After Lumby, Highway 6 continues to climb through increasingly impressive scenery – forest, craggy, snow-dusted mountains and flower-filled valleys – finally reaching the **Monashee Pass** (1205m/3953ft). Beyond the pass there is virtually nothing by way of habitation until the ferry terminal at **Needles**, a total of 194km (120mi) from Vernon.

3–4

Take the short ferry (roughly every 30 minutes, 5am–10pm; www.th.gov.bc.ca/marine) across **Lower Arrow Lake** to **Fauquier**, which has a store, motel and gas station, and head north along the lake shore on Hwy 6 to Nakusp (58km/36mi) by way of Burton and East Arrow Park. **Nakusp** is a charming small lakeside town (➤ 122), framed by the imposing Selkirk Mountains to the east, and with boating, hot springs, accommodations and a small public beach for swimming. From just outside town, continue 48km (30mi) southeast through wonderful mountain scenery to New Denver by way of **Summit Lake Provincial Park** (16km/10mi from Nakusp), which has trails and access in winter to a small ski resort (www.skisummitlake.com).

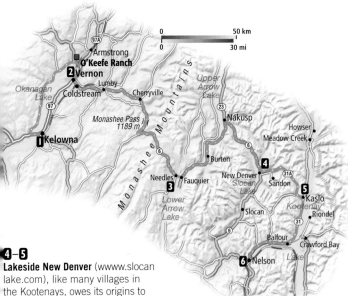

4–5

Lakeside New Denver (www.slocan lake.com), like many villages in the Kootenays, owes its origins to mining, and the silver boom of the 1890s in particular, and retains a pleasing and largely unspoiled pioneer feel. Enjoy its quiet, tree-lined streets and use the village as a base for a detour drive south on Hwy 6 via the **Slocan Lake Viewpoint** (6km/4mi south of New Denver) to Slocan, for more glorious lake and

mountain scenery and the chance to explore **Valhalla Provincial Park**.

You can continue on Hwy 6 to Nelson, but it's worth taking Hwy 31A east to visit the evocative ghost-town at **Sandon** (signed 13km/ 8.5mi east of New Denver). Beyond here, Hwy 31A climbs to Fish and Bear lakes, passing through stupendous scenery before following the Kaslo River to Kaslo (47km/29mi from New Denver, one of BC's most attractive small towns (▶ 121).

5–6

Kaslo makes a good base for a stay of one or two days, with the option of pretty lakeside day-trip drives north to **Lardeau** or **Argenta** before heading south to Nelson (▶ 120) by way of **Balfour**, a distance of 70km (44mi). Beyond Nelson, via Salmo, Hwy 6 and Hwy 3/Crowsnest Hwy offer more majestic scenery en route for **Creston** and Hwy 95 north towards the **Rockies National Parks** (▶ 139–154).

Vineyards in the Okanagan Valley

Walks & Tours

4 LAKE LOUISE
Walk

DISTANCE Chateau Lake Louise to Lake Agnes 3km (2mi) one way,
403m (1,322ft) ascent. Plain of Six Glaciers–Chateau Lake Louise
5.3km (3.3mi) one way, 367m (1,204ft) ascent.
TIME 3–5 hours depending on fitness and additional loops
START/END POINT Chateau Lake Louise ✚ 200 C4

Forests, lakeside views, sweeping valleys, immense mountains, magnificent panoramas and vast glaciers: walks in the sensational scenery around Lake Louise have everything – even a cup of tea at the end. Well-worn paths from the Chateau Lake Louise hotel wind to picture-perfect Lake Agnes, where a wooden "teahouse" offers refreshments, and then continue to a choice of magnificent viewpoints and two straightforward onward options that eventually loop back to the hotel along the shores of Lake Louise. The routes are popular – you won't be on your own here – but the beauty of the scenery easily outweighs the company of others.

1–2

Start on the promenade in front of Chateau Lake Louise. Facing the lake, and with your back to the hotel, follow the path that leads off to your right. Then take the path signed to **Lake Agnes**, which strikes off to the right almost immediately. The trail – which is so well worn it's impossible to lose – climbs steadily through pine forest, with occasional steep zigzags and plenty of breaks to allow superb views across the broad sweep of the Bow Valley. On the valley's eastern flank, beyond Lake Louise village, rises Mount Whitehorn (2,686m/ 8,808ft), focus of the region's skiing. To the south, above Lake Louise, rise Fairview Mountain

(2,744m/ 9,003ft) and, to its right, the redoubtable Mount Aberdeen (3,152m/10,341ft).

2–3

The first major division in the trail comes at tiny **Mirror Lake** (► 189), where you should take the trail to the right signed to Lake Agnes. A short way beyond, the trail steepens and reaches Lake Agnes (2,149m/7,045ft), a lovely upland lake whose abrupt appearance comes as a pleasant surprise – a pleasure surpassed only by the **Lake Agnes Tea House** (open: Jun to early Sep 9–6; early Sep to mid-Oct 10–5:30; www.lakeagnesteahouse.com). The Tea House serves sandwiches, soup, cakes and, of course, tea. You may have to wait a while during frequent busy periods.

The original tea house was built in 1901 as a mountaineering refuge. It was replaced with the present picture-postcard building in 1981.

Many people, having drunk their tea, turn tail for home, but at least two worthwhile onward routes are possible. One is simply to follow the marked trail northeast from the Tea House to **Little Beehive**, a beehive-shaped outcrop and viewpoint. Another is to push on around the lake and complete the longer return route to Lake Louise.

Chateau Lake Louise is the starting point for several good walks

③–④

For the latter option, follow the trail from the Tea House along the rocky northern shore of Lake Agnes. The path crosses the head of the lake and then follows steep zig-zags to a saddle. Go left along a less well-defined trail to reach the top of the **Big Beehive lookout** (2,270m/7,447ft) after 185m or so, a point that offers the most breathtaking

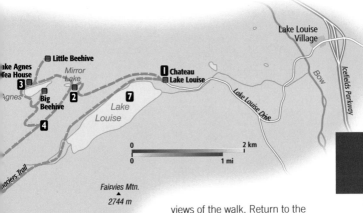

views of the walk. Return to the saddle and pick up the main trail again (turn left), which begins to drop steeply through the trees before meeting another major track.

④–⑤

Turn left here and you come to **Mirror Lake**, where you could retrace the earliest part of the walk in reverse and return to

Lake Louise, with the surrounding scenery reflected in the water

Lake Louise (1–2). For variety, and a longer and more rewarding walk, however, turn right. This takes you along a path that eventually meets the main **Plain of Six Glaciers Trail**, a trail that, to this point, has followed the shore of Lake Louise and traversed the increasingly wilder scenery above it. Following this trail all the way from Chateau Lake Louise is relatively dull, but using it as a route to return to the hotel is far more rewarding. Simply turn left when you meet the Plain of Six Glaciers Trail and walk back down to the lake and hotel.

5–6

For a still longer walk, however, and one that's well worth the extra effort, turn right at the junction and follow the Plain of Six Glaciers Trail as far as it goes – to another tea-house – at the **Plain of Six Glaciers**. This gives you a chance to enjoy a far closer look at the stupendous **Victoria Glacier**, as well as at the vast peaks of **Mount Victoria** (3,564m/11,693ft) and its neighbours that close the valley. The glacier once reached the lip of Lake Louise, but has retreated over a kilometre (0.6mi) in the last 150 years alone. Evidence of this retreat lies in the glacial moraines and stark, rocky scenery in this part of the valley, another good reason for adding this final leg to your walk.

6–7

Take a break at the **Plain of Six Tea House** (open: Jul, Aug 9–6; Sep to mid-Oct 10–5:30) or leave it until later while you continue for another 1.6km (1mi) to reach a narrow stony ridge, known as **The Lookout**, directly above the glacier. Go carefully here as far as you want to go – a high cliff eventually blocks the way. The views are stupendous. Retrace your steps to the tea house and then head all the way back downhill for the long haul along the shores of Lake Louise to the Chateau.

Practicalities

Practicalities

WHAT YOU NEED

	UK	USA	Canada	Australia	Ireland	Netherlands
Passport/National Identity Card	●	●	○	●	●	●
Visa (regulations can change – check before booking)	▲	▲	▲	▲	▲	▲
Onward or Return Ticket	●	▲	▲	●	●	●
Health Inoculations (tetanus and polio)	▲	▲	▲	▲	▲	▲
Health Documentation (► 196, Health)	▲	▲	▲	▲	▲	▲
Travel Insurance	●	●	●	●	●	●
Driving Licence (national) for car hire	●	●	●	●	●	●
Car Insurance Certificate	△	●	●	△	△	△
Car Registration Document	△	●	●	△	△	△

● Required
○ Suggested
▲ Not required
△ Not applicable

Some countries require a passport to remain valid for a minimum period (usually at least six months) beyond the date of entry – check before you travel.

WHEN TO GO

Vancouver

High season   Low season

JAN	FEB	MAR	APR	MAY	JUN	JUL	AUG	SEP	OCT	NOV	DEC
6°C	7°C	11°C	14°C	17°C	21°C	23°C	22°C	19°C	14°C	9°C	6°C
43°F	45°F	52°F	57°F	63°F	70°F	73°F	72°F	66°F	57°F	48°F	43°F

☀ Sun   ☁ Wet   ☁ Cloud

Weather in western Canada is best in July and August, when temperatures can rise to over 26.5°C (80°F), but this is also the busiest time of year to travel. **Summer** is the best time to see the Rockies, though many mountain areas are also busy during the winter skiing season (Dec to Mar). Whistler will normally accumulate some 3m (10ft) of snow over the winter, and Sunshine Village near Banff is another resort with reliable amounts of good snow. **Winter** temperatures can be extremely low up in the mountains. **Early fall** and **late spring** offer the chance to avoid the rains (up to 254cm/100in annually in some areas) in British Columbia, but many sights and smaller museums are open only between Victoria Day (Monday before May 25) and Labour Day (first Mon in Sep).

GETTING ADVANCE INFORMATION

In Canada
■ Travel Alberta 400,
1601-9th Avenue SE, Calgary,
Alberta Canada T2G 0H4
☎ 1-800/252-3782

In the UK
■ Visit Canada
☎ 0870 380 0070
(automated service)

In Australia
■ Canadian Tourism,
Suite 105, Jones Bay Wharf,
26–32 Pirrama Road,
Pyrmont, NSW 2009
☎ 02 9571 1866

GETTING THERE

By Air Both Vancouver and Calgary have busy international airports: Vancouver (tel: 604/207-7077; www.yvr.ca) handles the most flights, but Calgary (tel: 403/735-1200 or 1-877/254-7427; www.calgaryairport.com) is more convenient for the Rockies. Victoria's airport has few direct international flights, but lots of connections to Vancouver and airports in the western United States.

From the US Many airlines fly direct to Vancouver and Calgary from major US airports. From parts of the western United States – notably Seattle – you can travel to Vancouver by bus or train, although the savings over air travel are often minimal.

From the UK British Airways and Air Canada fly directly to Vancouver and Calgary.

From Australia and New Zealand Qantas and Air New Zealand have daily flights to Vancouver.

Ticket prices for flights to western Canada are highest from July to mid-September. Easter and Christmas are also usually expensive, and seats to Calgary may be more difficult to come by during the skiing season. To save money look out for charter deals or special promotions and reserve your tickets as far ahead as possible. Package tours and fly-drive deals arranged before you travel should also offer good value.

TIME

Western Canada is divided between **Mountain Standard Time** (MST) and **Pacific Standard Time** (PST). MST is seven hours behind Greenwich Mean Time (GMT) and two hours behind Eastern Standard Time (EST); PST is eight hours behind GMT and three hours behind EST. **Daylight-Saving Time** (Canadian Summer Time). Since 2007, for daylight-saving time, clocks go forward one hour on the second Sun in March and back on the first Sun in November.

CURRENCY AND FOREIGN EXCHANGE

Currency The units of Canadian currency are the cent (¢) and the dollar: $1 = 100 cents. **Notes** are printed in English and French in the following dollar denominations: 5, 10, 20, 50, 100. **Coins** are issued in denominations of 1¢, 5¢ (nickel), 10¢ (dime) 25¢ (quarter), 50¢, 1$ and 2$. The dollar coin is known as a "loonie" after the bird on one face. Not surprisingly, the two dollar coin is the "toonie." US dollars are often accepted on a "one-for-one" basis, but as the US dollar is usually worth a little more than the Canadian dollar it makes sense to exchange US currency. **Traveler's checks** made out in Canadian dollars. These are widely accepted as cash, and change is given in cash.

Exchange Exchange rates are best in banks, and there is no limit to the amount of Canadian or foreign currency that can be exchanged or brought in or out of the country. You can withdraw money from most Canadian ATMs with a credit or debit card. It is wise to let your credit card company and bank know that you will be traveling in Canada and will be using your credit card. Companies have been known to block cash withdrawals if they are unaware that you are in the country.

WEBSITES

- **Tourism British Columbia:**
  www.hellobc.com
- **Canada Tourism Commission:**
  www.canada.travel
- **Travel Alberta:**
  www. discoveralberta.com

In the US
- www.hellobc.com

In the UK
- http://uk.canada.travel/
  http://uk.britishcolumbia.travel

In Australia
- http://au.britishcolumbia.travel
  http://au.canadatravel

Practicalities

WHEN YOU ARE THERE

NATIONAL HOLIDAYS

January 1: **New Year's Day**; March/April: **Easter: Good Friday** and **Easter Monday**; Monday before May 25: **Victoria Day**; July 1: **Canada Day**; First Monday in September: **Labour Day**; Second Monday in October: **Thanksgiving Day**; November 11: **Remembrance Day**; December 25: **Christmas Day**; December 26: **Boxing Day**

British Columbia also observes **British Columbia Day**, and **Alberta Heritage Day**, both in early August.

ELECTRICITY

 The power supply is 110 volts AC (60 Hz), the same as the US. Most sockets take two-pronged or three-pronged plugs. Visitors from Europe, or anywhere that uses 220/240 volt power, will need to bring a converter and a plug adaptor.

OPENING HOURS

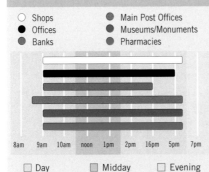

○ Shops
● Offices
● Banks
● Main Post Offices
● Museums/Monuments
● Pharmacies

8am 9am 10am noon 1pm 2pm 16pm 5pm 7pm

☐ Day   ☐ Midday   ☐ Evening

Stores Most open Mon–Sat 9–5:30; some stay open later on Thu and Fri.
Banks Open weekdays 9–4; extended hours on Thu and Fri. Some open on Sat.
Post Offices Open 8:30–5:30 on weekdays, and occasionally Sat 9–noon.
Museums Usually Mon–Sat 9–5:30; limited Sun and seasonal holiday opening.

TIPS/GRATUITIES

Tipping is expected for all services. As a general guide:

Restaurants (service not included)	15–20%
Bar service	15%
Tour guides	optional
Hairdressers	15%
Taxis	15%
Chambermaids	optional
Porters	optional

OUTDOOR ACTIVITIES

Consult visitor centres before hiking in bear country. Beware of the water in the backcountry or in hot springs, which can harbour the giardia parasite. Blackfly and mosquitoes can be a problem in summer. Also check for ticks, which can carry lyme borreliosis.

TIME DIFFERENCES

Vancouver (PST)
12 noon

→

Calgary (MST)
1pm

→

New York (EST)
3pm

→

London (GMT)
8pm

←

Sydney (AEST)
5am

STAYING IN TOUCH

Post Vancouver's main post office is at 349 West Georgia Street; tel: 1-866/607-6301; www.canadapost.ca; open Mon–Fri 9–5:30. Opening times vary in larger city branches. Look out for Canada Post signs inside stores, department stores or train stations.

Telephone Local calls from public pay phones cost ¢50. For long-distance or calls outside an area, you may need to prefix your number with 1. This connects to an operator who will tell you how much your call will cost. Nearly all public pay phones are now operated by credit and/or prepaid phone cards. Reverse charge or "collect" calls are made by dialling O for the operator.

International Dialling Codes
Dial 011 followed by:
US No country code required
UK 44; Ireland 353; Australia 61

Mobile providers and services Canadian providers such as Bell, Telus, and MTS use CDMA technology compatible with US providers, but US visitors should check the charges that apply. Most European phones need triband to secure network access. Rogers Wireless is an exception. It has agreements with some UK and European providers. Check with your provider.

WiFi & Internet Cities such as Vancouver, Victoria and Calgary have numerous cafés, bars and hotels with WiFi or internet connection. Major public libraries usually offer free access. Outside the cities, and across much of rural and mountainous BC and Alberta, mobile and internet coverage will be patchy and non-existent in many remote areas. For a list of free WiFi hotspots visit: www.openwifispots.com/country_free_wifi_wireless_hotspot-Canada_CA.aspx

PERSONAL SAFETY

Western Canada is relatively crime-free, but still take the usual precautions, especially at night in the larger cities.

- Avoid parks, train stations and other non-commercial areas after dark. There have been homophobic attacks in Vancouver's Stanley Park. Vancouver's main bus and rail terminals are in peripheral and relatively poor parts of town, so take extra care if arriving after dark. Also avoid the backstreets of Chinatown after dark and the streets on and around East Hasting, East Cordova, Powell and Main.
- Don't carry around large quantities of cash, and keep passports and credit cards in a pouch or belt.
- Leave jewellery and other valuables in the hotel safe.
- Try not to leave luggage or valuables in cars, including when parking at isolated trailheads in the Rockies parks or other remote countryside.
- Report any crime to the police and note the crime reference number.

Police assistance:
☎ 911 from any phone

POLICE	911
FIRE	911
AMBULANCE	911

Practicalities

HEALTH

 Insurance Foreigners requiring treatment on vacation must pay to use Canada's health service. It is therefore essential to take out travel insurance before your visit. If you become ill you will be treated and charged later.

 Dental services As with all medical services in Canada, dental services are excellent, but you should make sure your travel insurance will cover the cost. If you need dental treatment, your hotel should be able to give you a recommendation; otherwise, consult the Yellow Pages (www.yellowpages.ca).

 Weather Weather can vary even within quite short distances, and can be quite extreme. Vancouver has a temperate climate and can be rainy outside the summer months.

 Medication Medicines can be bought at drugstores. Most towns and cities have at least one 24-hour pharmacy for prescription drugs and other goods.

Safe Water Tap water is safe, except in some campgrounds; spring water in the backcountry should be boiled for 10 minutes.

CONCESSIONS

Students/children Many hotels offer reductions or free accommodations for children sharing their parents' room, and restaurants offer children's menus. Via Rail offers free travel for under-2s, half-price fares for children 2–11, and student rail passes with discounts of 10–50 percent. There are also discounts on entrance charges to museums and other attractions.
Senior Citizens Many museums and attractions offer reductions to senior citizens. There are also concessionary fares on all public transportation, but they may vary depending on the type of ticket bought. Some offer discounts for over-60s, others for over-65s, and you may need to carry proof of age.

TRAVELLING WITH A DISABILITY

All public buildings have wheelchair access. For details on public transportation contact: **Via Rail** (tel: 1-888/842-7245; www.viarail.ca); **BC Transit** (tel: 604/453-4685; www.bctransit.com); **Translink** (tel: 604/953-3333; www.translink.ca); **Calgary Transit** (tel: 403/537-7997; www.access-calgary.ca). **The BC Coalition of People with Disabilities** (tel: 604/875-0188 or toll free 1-800/663-1278; www.bc cpd.bc.ca) can also advise.

CHILDREN

Special attractions for children are marked out in this book with the logo shown above.

RESTROOMS

Restrooms can be found in public buildings, museums, fast food restaurants, shopping centres and transportation terminals.

LOST PROPERTY

Visitor centres have details of lost property offices. Report a loss to the local police, and get a copy of reports to back up travel insurance claims.

CONSULATES & HIGH COMMISSIONS

 UK ☎ 604/683-4421 www.ukincanada. fco.gov.uk

US ☎ 604/685-4311 www.vancouver usconsulate.gov

 Ireland ☎ 604/683-9233 www.dfa.ie

 Australia ☎ 604/684-1177 www.dfest.gov.au

 New Zealand ☎ 604/684-7388 www.nz embassy.com

Road Atlas

For chapters: See inside front cover

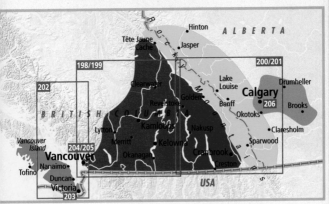

Key to Road Atlas

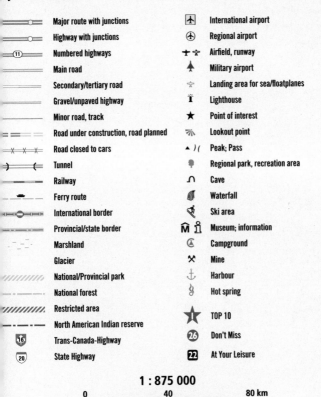

Major route with junctions		✈	International airport
Highway with junctions		⊛	Regional airport
⑪ Numbered highways		✛ ✛	Airfield, runway
Main road		✦	Military airport
Secondary/tertiary road		☆	Landing area for sea/floatplanes
Gravel/unpaved highway		⍭	Lighthouse
Minor road, track		★	Point of interest
Road under construction, road planned		🔭	Lookout point
⤬ ⤬ Road closed to cars		▲)(	Peak; Pass
)﹘(Tunnel		♠	Regional park, recreation area
Railway		∩	Cave
Ferry route		⧊	Waterfall
International border		⛷	Ski area
Provincial/state border		M̂ ⍰	Museum; information
Marshland		Ⓒ	Campground
Glacier		⤬	Mine
National/Provincial park		⚓	Harbour
National forest		⚱	Hot spring
Restricted area			
North American Indian reserve		★	TOP 10
⑯ Trans-Canada-Highway		㉖	Don't Miss
⑳ State Highway		㉒	At Your Leisure

1 : 875 000

0	40	80 km
0	25	50 mi

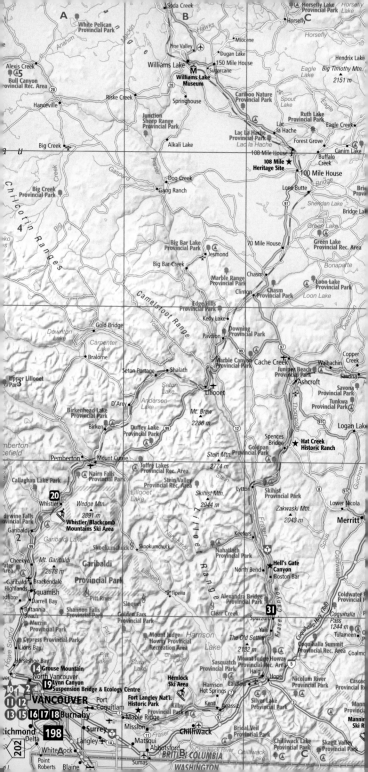

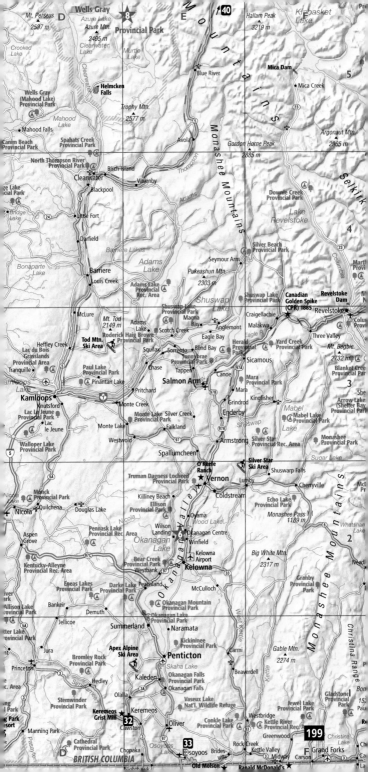

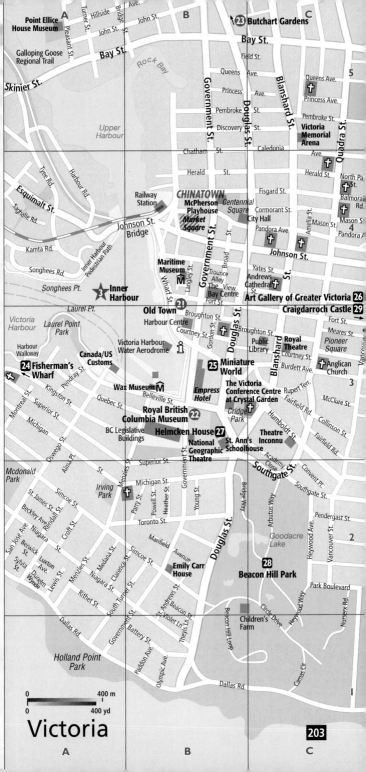

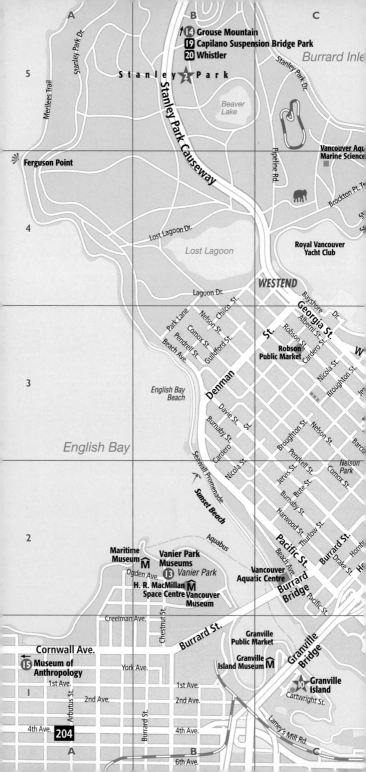

A

- Stanley Park Dr.
- Merrilees Trail
- Ferguson Point

B

↑14 Grouse Mountain
19 Capilano Suspension Bridge Park
20 Whistler

S t a n l e y ★2 P a r k

Beaver Lake

Stanley Park Causeway

Lost Lagoon Dr.

Lost Lagoon

Lagoon Dr.

Park Lane
Nelson St.
Comox St.
Pendrell St.
Guilford St.
Beach Ave.

Chilco St.

Denman

English Bay Beach

Davie St.
Burnaby

Cardero

Nicola St.

Seawall Promenade

Sunset Beach

Aquabus

Maritime Museum Ⓜ
Ogden Ave.
Vanier Park Museums
13 *Vanier Park*
H. R. MacMillan Space Centre
Vancouver Museum Ⓜ

Creelman Ave.

Chestnut St.

Cornwall Ave.
←15 Museum of Anthropology
1st Ave.

York Ave.

2nd Ave.

Arbutus St.

4th Ave. **204**

C

Burrard Inle

Stanley Park Dr.

Pipeline Rd.

Vancouver Aqu Marine Science

Brockton Pt. Tr

Royal Vancouver Yacht Club

WESTEND

Bayshore Dr.

Georgia St.
Alberni St.
Robson St.
Cardero St.
Robson Public Market

Nicola St.
Broughton St.
Jer

W

Broughton St.
Nelson St.
Pendrell St.
Jervis St.
Bute St.
Burnaby St.
Harwood St.
Thurlow St.

Barc

Nelson Park
Comox St.

Pacific St.

Beach Ave.

Burrard St.
Drake St.
Ho

Burrard Bridge

Pacific St.

Vancouver Aquatic Centre

Granville Public Market

Granville Island Museum Ⓜ

Granville Bridge

10 **Granville Island**
Cartwright St.

1st Ave.

2nd Ave.

4th Ave.

Lamey's Mill Rd.

Burrard St.

6th Ave.

English Bay

5

4

3

2

I

Vancouver

0   500 m
0   500 yd

5

Brockton
Point

Vancouver Harbour

Totem Poles ★

Park Dr.

Deadman's
Island

4

SeaBus Route (nach Lonsdale Quay
& North Vancouver)

Coal Harbour

Coal Harbour Rd.

Vancouver
Travel Info Centre

Marine
Building

11 Canada
Place

Fährterminal

Portside Park

3

...der St.

Melville St.

Georgia St.

Alberni St.

Burrard St.

Hornby St.

Howe St.

W. Hastings St.

W. Cordova St.

Gastown

16   Maple
Tree Sq.

Alexander St.

Powell St.

Thurlow St.

Hotel
Vancouver

Vancouver
Art Gallery

Court
House

12

DOWNTOWN

Granville

Seymour St.

Dunsmuir St.

Richards St.

Harbour
Centre

W. Pender
St.

Cambie St.

E. Cordova St.

E. Hastings St.

E. Pender St.

Carrall
St.

Columbia St.

Main St.

Vancouver Centennial
Police Museum

17 Chinatown

Chinese Cultural
Centre

Ten Ren Tea &
Ginseng Co.

2

Ford Centre for
the Performing Arts

Vancouver
Public Library

Smithe St.

Nelson St.

Helmcken St.

Davie St.

Homer St.

Hamilton St.

Mainland St.

Cambie St.

Robson St.

Library
Square

Expo Blvd.

Sam Kee
Building

Dr. Sun Yatsen
Classical Chinese
Garden

Dunsmuir Viaduct

Georgia Viaduct

...bour
St.

Richards St.

YALETOWN

BC Stadium

Pacific Blvd.

**Plaza of
Nations**

BC Place

Main St.

Pacific Central
Station

Pacific Blvd.

Marinaside   Cr.

Cambie
Bridge

**18 TELUS World
of Science**

Industrial Ave.

1

False Creek

W 1st Ave.

W 2nd Ave.

W 2nd Ave.

Charleson
Park

205

Ave.

Main St.

Calgary

PARKDALE
206

47 TELUS Spark

46 Calgary Zoo

45 Fort Calgary Historic Park

44 Eau Claire Market

43 Glenbow Museum

BRIDGELAND

Bridgeland Memorial

Bow River

St. George's Island

Prince's Island Park

Edmonton Trail

Centre St

YMCA

Chinese Cultural Centre

CHINATOWN

CITY CENTRE

C-Train (202)

3rd St E

4th Ave
5th Ave
6th Ave

City Hall

9th Ave

Olympic Way
11th Ave
12th Ave

Victoria Park

Calgary Exhibition and Stampede Park

Victoria Park/Stampede

Erlton/Stampede

RAMSAY

Spiller Rd

Macleod Trail

C-Train (201)

1st St W

Centre St

1st
17th Ave

2nd St W

13th Ave

14th Ave
15th Ave

4th St W

5th St W

6th St W

7th St W

MOUNT ROYAL

Elbow River

25th Ave

Memorial Drive

Crowchild Trail

14th St W

Kensington Rd

Shaganappi Golf Course

Bow Trail S W

Louise Bridge

Sunnyside

Riley Park

Gladstone Rd

2nd Av

3rd Av
1st Av

Memorial Drive

CHINATOWN

3rd Ave
4th Ave
5th Ave
6th Ave

10th St W (201)

8th Ave

9th Ave

11th Ave
12th Ave

1st St E

2nd St E

3rd St E

City Hall

Olympic Plaza

Epcor Centre for Performing Arts

Stephen Avenue Mall

Devonian Gardens

Barclay Mall

Centre St

1st St W

2nd St W

3rd St W

4th St W

5th St W

6th St W

7th St W

9th Ave

Steven Ave

Calgary Tower

500 m
500 yd

3rd Ave
4th Ave
5th Ave

6th W
C-Train

8th Ave

CITY CENTRE

Blackfoot Trail

1 km
0.5 mi

Index

Index

Credits

1st Edition 2017

Worldwide Distribution: Marco Polo Travel Publishing Ltd
Pinewood, Chineham Business Park
Crockford Lane, Chineham
Basingstoke, Hampshire RG24 8AL, United Kingdom.
© MAIRDUMONT GmbH & Co. KG, Ostfildern

Authors: Tim Jepson, Ole Helmhausen
Editor: Baedeker
Revised editing and translation: Margaret Howie, www.fullproof.co.za
Program supervisor: Birgit Borowski
Chief editor: Rainer Eisenschmid

Cartography: © MAIRDUMONT GmbH & Co. KG, Ostfildern
3D-illustrations: jangled nerves, Stuttgart

Printed in China

Despite all of our authors' thorough research, errors can creep in.
The publishers do not accept any liability for this. Whether you
want to praise us, alert us to errors or give us a personal tip –
please don't hesitate to email or post:

MARCO POLO Travel Publishing Ltd
Pinewood, Chineham Business Park
Crockford Lane, Chineham
Basingstoke, Hampshire RG24 8AL
United Kingdom
Email: sales@marcopolouk.com

FSC
www.fsc.org
MIX
Paper from
responsible sources
FSC® C124385

10 REASONS
TO COME BACK AGAIN

1. **Whales, bears, mountains, prairies, cities…** it is not possible to experience it all in one visit.

2. The Canadians are so **kind and helpful** that you will soon find that you sorely miss them.

3. The beauty of the **night sky** will make you want to see the Milky Way more than once.

4. Where else can you be the **only person** for hundreds of miles?

5. Locals believe that Vancouver is **the pearl of the Pacific**, and the world's most beautiful city.

6. No Sunday drivers and no tailgaters: **Canada's roads** are a driver's dream.

7. No matter whether you are in a city or in the middle of nowhere: the **infrastructure** is excellent.

8. Canada changes with the **seasons** and each season is different.

9. You can never tire of the vast, seemingly endless, rippling grasslands of **prairie**.

10. **Mother Nature** is the greatest show on Earth – Canada's scenery is too beautiful not to be experienced a second time.